RAISING EBENEZER
*A Rearview Look At Life's
"Hither By Thy Help I'm Come"*

By
KENDAL R. UTT

With Apologies to Almost Everyone

Southwestern College Academic Press
Winfield, KS 67156
Copyright © 2012 by Kendal R. Utt

ISBN: 978-1-59831-006-1

All Scripture is from the New International Version
unless otherwise noted

*Dedicated to all those, recorded or not, including my two
Musketeers, who have been an Ebenezer for me;
especially my wife, Joyce;
and our four sons, Justin, Adam, Brandon, and Taylor.*

Table of Contents

Introduction i
Raising Ebenezer: It's About a Song 1
It's About a Place; Any Place 7
It's About People; Any People 13
Sometimes a Good Cry Helps 20
Whatever It Takes 29
You Are Not Far From the Kingdom Of God 38
We Let the Holy Spirit Lead Here! 44
It's About Belief 50
Truth and Consequences 55
Worse Sinners 61
You're Really Going to Love the Garage 65
It's All in Who You Know; NOT! 72
Here, Hold This 82
A Prince of a Man 87
The Good Shepherd 92
The Little Tin Cup 102
Caution! Deceptive Curve Ahead 108
Confiscated: Two Cottontails, One Opossum, and One 22 Rifle 115
Our Little Scarecrow 121
Watch Out for That Dog 126
Bridle Your Tongue 130
When God Does a New Thing 136
What is Good 146
There's Nothing Morbid about It 152
FOCUS 156
Burnt Beans 160
Just an Old Steel Chair 165
You Need the Fruit of the Spirit 170
It's About Home 175
It's About Directions 182
The Mystery of Faith 188
It's About Wrestling 192
Changing Boundaries 197
All I'm Asking is for a Little Respect 204
Even God Takes Amtrak 209

Boys Will Be Boys	215
How Shall We Escape	222
'Ya'll Come Back Now, Hear?	228
Breaking Up is Hard to Do	233
It's About Tension and Stress	238
Never Alone	246
The Best Laid Plans; or We Really Shouldn't Be Here	255
Amen!	265
Notes	273

Introduction

"Tell me a story." These have been the last words spoken before sleep by countless generations of children. One of the favorites my grandmother used to tell went something like this: Once upon a time, there were some children who were very poor. One day they went into the woods with their pet dog Shaggy to gather walnuts. Their mother would make breads and cakes out of the meat and then they would burn the hulls in the stove. The children were busy picking the walnuts up off of the ground as they went from tree to tree. Finally they each had their buckets filled when they realized they had wandered further into the woods than they had ever been. They didn't know exactly where they were. The sky grew dark and it began to snow heavily as they realized they were lost. At first, the large snowflakes stuck to the limbs of the trees and bushes making them look like beautiful ice sculptures. Then the wind began to blow, and it became very hard to see where they were going. They walked and walked through the woods looking for a familiar sight. Tired, hungry, and very cold, they came upon an old cabin. It looked deserted, and no one came to the door when they knocked on it; so they went inside to try and get warm. Looking around, they found a little food they could eat; they also found several large bank sacks filled with money. The cabin was a hideout for a gang of robbers who came in, found the children and tied them up. Shaggy the dog managed to run out the door and later that night had found his way home. The parents had already summoned the sheriff and some of the neighbors to go out and look for the children when Shaggy appeared out of the snow and began to bark. They knew that the dog had left with the children so they followed the dog. They made their way through the snow and wind until Shaggy led them to the cabin where the robbers had the children. The sheriff went in first and captured the sleeping robbers. The children were untied, and the bank's money bags were retrieved. The next day the bank gave the children a nice reward for their help in catching the bank robbers, and they all lived happily ever after.

People have been telling stories to each other since the advent of language. Some of these stories are in the form of oral traditions; cultural, ethnic, moral, or spiritual material used to weave and maintain the fabric of a society, and passed on through succeeding generations. Others have used stories to be viewed as an art form for entertainment. The Hebrew and Christian scriptures contain countless stories, passed on orally, written down, and shared across the millennia. The writer of Hebrews 11:32-34, after going through most of world history finally says:

And what more shall I say? I do not have time to tell about Gideon, Barak, Sampson, who through faith conquered kingdoms, administered justice, and gained what was promised; who shut the mouths of lions, quenched the fury of the flames, and escaped the edge of the sword; whose weakness was turned into strength; and who became powerful in battle and routed foreign armies.

Storytelling is not only a form of art which uses language and other human conveyances, but an important component in the way we pass on our faith; of drawing listeners in to participate in the Word, and not simply be passive listeners. The church has some great storytellers in our pulpits today, who take drama, mystery, history, and allegorical truth and make the Scriptures and the Christian message come alive for their listeners. I am not one of them; I wish I were. The stories which I have developed over the years are as factual as they can be to real events as I have either heard and understood them or experienced them for myself. If we are willing to listen closely and reflectively to those around us, we will discover that just about everyone has something valid and interesting to say; and as listeners, may find ourselves actually participating in oral tradition and storytelling.

Reflection is not just a simple mirrored glance at yourself or that which is behind you. More appropriately it is a state of mind in which one gives considerable concentration surrounding a thought, subject, or experience. Reflection is a natural, contemplative human process; we were made this way in the image of our Creator whose first recorded act of reflection was, "God saw that the light was good." (Genesis 1:4a)

Yet how often do we take the time and effort to be in a reflective state of mind regarding the things which are or have been experienced by us. Were I to make an uneducated guess, I would say that many life events go by without any real effort at reflective thought at all. If we were to become more aware of that intrinsic design at work within us, our view could very well expand to the standpoint of recognizing and gratefully acknowledging the presence and activity of God. To think reflectively, both critically and theologically, will assist any person in having a fuller, deeper understanding of events or personal experiences. This can be as simple as just paying attention to what is going on around us, and attempting to discern just what significance there is in any action which is being played out in our midst. The reflective person will be observant enough to see that in the midst of their own experiences there are stories which are worth telling; there are Ebenezers.

In the summer of 2006 just as I was coming on board as the new Dodge City District Superintendent, several of the other superintendents and I were asked to attend a seminar in Chicago to learn about the restructuring of the church's pension plan. This was sponsored by the General Board of Pensions designed primarily for superintendents and conference benefits officers. During a break, I was standing in the corridor in front of the room where some of the conference seminars were being held when a familiar face came by. I started to think to myself, "I know this guy; I went to seminary with him." I began to have brain synapses fire more rapidly than usual as I continued trying to remember. "Oh, what is his name? Van, Van something, Van der IIorn, Van Hooter, Van Helsing, Vaaaannnn Giesen; that's it Richard Van Giesen." About that time he noticed me and walked over to where I was standing and said, "Kendal Utt! It's been a long time since I've seen you; since seminary probably." "I saw you across the hall, and I knew you were a familiar face from Asbury," I said. After exchanging a few typical pleasantries he added, "The one thing I will always remember about you are the stories you used to tell, especially that one about the Alligator Gar in the Ninnescah River."

For a long time various people have suggested to me that I needed to write a book as they listened to some experience or illustration I had shared in either a sermon or just general conversation. For many of those years I absolutely scoffed at any notion of me writing anything other than a sermon or study guide for a Bible study. My response to such comments probably came from a question I have asked myself a lot over the years, "Who am I? Who am I to write a book anyway? What could possibly qualify me to undertake such a project?" I'm not a scholar in the modern sense of the word. I have no claim to either ability or authority. I command no reputation, nor do I hold any position that would cause me to stand out as an authority on anything. In the spring of 1997, my district superintendent, Tom Schneider, called the Mankato parsonage one evening. I knew immediately what this meant; it was a call from the cabinet. A couple of hundred charges began to run through my mind. Then in his typical pastoral manner he told me to expect a call from Reverend Jim Reed, the Hutchinson District Superintendent. Now I had only about twenty-five charges to seriously think about. Reverend Reed called shortly afterward. The vacuum cleaner Joyce was running went silent, and I heard him ask if I would be willing to go to Pratt. That one had not been a serious consideration. What was the cabinet thinking? Did I just die and go to heaven?

Following my appointment as the pastor of First United Methodist Church in Pratt, Kansas, there were many mornings I would walk across the parking lot from the parsonage to the church and gaze up at the great, bronze cross which gracefully adorned the nearly 100-foot spire. With that powerful vista before me I would ask myself, "Who am I of all the clergy in our Annual Conference to be given such an appointment, such a responsibility as this?" That's exactly how I feel about writing a book. Conversely, by the spring of 2009, I was becoming inwardly impressed, not with myself, but what I may have to share and the prospect of actually setting some of my thoughts down on paper. I felt as though I could attempt to write a book, that I might just have something to say and a way to say it. After all, I did pretty well in writing in college and even in seminary, especially if you didn't count spelling and punctuation.

Still, I have wondered if this venture could be little more than a cathartic activity to satisfy my own ego or simply become a therapeutic exercise in the sustaining of my own self image. Perhaps someday it will be just be a pile of yellowed paper whose content is read by a grandchild to understand how it was at one time. Not too long ago, Joyce, Taylor (our youngest son), and I had driven past the east place to see how Mom's soybean crop was looking. We were on our way to Wellington for her folk's wedding anniversary, so I took the road south where we crossed the Ninnescah River over the old Barner Bridge. As we started up the hill to an area where the hedge trees hung close to either side of the road, I said, "Taylor, if you ever hear me tell or should read about me taking some girls to a haunted house, it was right up here. See where all of these trees are? There use to be a large old two story house in there, and we would bring girls out here to scare them." As there was a combine in the road ahead, I couldn't really look, but Taylor was looking as I drove by. He suddenly exclaimed with excitement, "It's still there Dad. I can see an old white house back there in all of those trees." Perhaps someday when his children look through those dusty pages, he will say, "Your Granddad Utt drove by there one time and showed me that old house."

It has to be more than that, however. There needs to be some real substance, something that matters or makes a difference. If a higher and nobler purpose or rationale to stories doesn't exist, then they become little more than the remembrances of the past, of tradition, of childhood, adolescence, or the various stages of adulthood. For quite some time, the phrase from an old hymn, "Here I'll raise mine Ebenezer, hither by Thy help I'm come" has had a profound, even substantial attraction—a spiritual fascination drawing me into its scriptural and theological reality. It seemed as though it was gnawing upon my heart, ever urging me to comprehend and appreciate just how it was that God was helping me through the things I have heard or experienced during the course of my life. Some of these moments have been treasure troves of guidance and instruction, while most have been simple life lessons. Still others have been painful to say the least with difficulties and even hardships. Through them all I began to see where God was present and at work. These and many other diverse occurrences and episodes which remain vividly burned into my memory are stories which can be entertaining and humorous, deeply thoughtful, or even bring a sense of personal or familial vulnerability. Every one of them to some degree have been Ebenezer moments; God helping me right then and there. Being ever mindful of this and nearing two years after undertaking this project, I find myself completing this heretofore unimaginable effort.

I do not mean to be presumptuous. My hope is that others may be able to discover for themselves (by a reflective process within their own life and experience) times and places where God has been present in more perceptible and affirming ways through this book. I have taken the liberty to include one or two very simple but reflective questions at the end of each section. You are welcome to use these in discovering through your own stories some of those Ebenezer moments.

I feel it is important to note that the spiritual and theological truth contained in John and Charles Wesley, their contemporaries of the eighteenth century, and sources from the nineteenth century, both in written word and lyric is still very relevant for Christians of the twenty-first century. Their language however will often sound archaic; therefore, one must take added care to make the mental connection with the present.

Raising Ebenezer: It's about a Song

Then Samuel took a stone, and set it between Mispeh and Shen, and called it Ebenezer, saying, "Hitherto hath the Lord helped us." (I Samuel 7:12)

Over the last few years, I have learned to be more discriminating and inclusive in my radio listening as I travel. I've become more appreciative of Christian radio. Other than a rock-and-roll "golden-oldie" station, and NPR, it is about all I have set into my radio. These three bring a healthy, well-rounded balance of nostalgia, information, and inspiration. Of the two main Christian stations I receive, one plays music which is predominantly traditional in nature while the other is strictly contemporary music. There is a lot of attention given to contemporary praise and worship music today. This genre is bringing the message of Jesus Christ to a whole new generation which may have never darkened the door of a Sunday school class or church service. Given its popularity and the increase in the median age of today's church goers, churches are asking how they might blend the contemporary into their current style, or develop separate worship services to offer only contemporary music, or keep it out of the church altogether. The growing ministries which are resulting from this type of music, as well as the "worship wars" which are being waged because of it, guarantee there will be a healthy conversation regarding it for years to come. In spite of any person's position they need to realize that every Christian hymn, chorus, or gospel song, including those ancient lyrics preserved within the New Testament, were at one time or another 'contemporary'.

Regardless of where one's preferences lie, it is my personal opinion that there will always be times when only a traditional hymn will fit the moment. The truth is many of the "good old hymns" are being re-recorded by some of contemporary Christian music's greatest artists, giving them a little makeover to speak to a generation of persons who probably never held a hymnal. These aging and time-tested hymns have taken on a similar status as "golden oldie" rock and roll songs—those songs we grew up with on radio and vinyl records. Today when you hear them being played they have the ability to instantly transport you to a time, place, person, or event in your life that is meaningful in one way or another. The same is true for hymns. For instance when I hear "Holy, Holy, Holy," I see a choir marching in procession into the loft of our old Methodist Church; and it seemed like it was sung every other Sunday. "Just as I Am," which is usually a Billy Graham type invitational hymn, again takes me to church where I can still see my grandparents; Granddad kneeling and Grandma, who couldn't kneel due to her bad knees, standing at the communion rail. Then there is "Tell Me the Stories of Jesus, I love to Hear" and I am in the upstairs of the old, bee-infested (during the spring and summer) Sunday school building with Nancy Helm leading the first through third graders in opening exercises.

Most of what we refer to as traditional hymns is much more than just repetitious, inspirational music; they are deep, profound repositories of our faith. Within their verses are stories with historical content woven into the lyrics, spiritual journeys of saints and sinners, and include biblical verse, and Christian theology; teaching, encouraging, challenging, and comforting generations of God's people. John Wesley, in his preface to *A Collection of Hymns for the Use of the People Called Methodists in 1779* writes, "…It is large enough to contain all the important truths of our most holy religion, whether speculative or practical; yea, to illustrate them all, and to prove them both by Scripture and reason; and this is done in a regular order. The hymns are not carelessly jumbled together, but carefully arranged under proper heads according to the experience of real Christians so that this book is, in effect, a little body of experimental and practical divinity."[1]

We all have favorites for one reason or another. My favorite rock song is the haunting ballad, "Maggie Mae;" country and western is, "Take This Job and Shove It;" and for classical it has to be Dvorak's, "The New World Symphony." Having said all that, without any doubt or prevarication, my all-time personal favorite song has to be, "Come

Thou Fount of Every Blessing." This was the first hymn I remember being able to sing from memory. It will also be the last congregational hymn to be sung with me present in a church.

There is quite a story behind the life of the author, Robert Robinson, at least as told by Carl F. Price in his book, *One Hundred and One Hymn Stories*. Robert was born in England in 1735 and at a young age, his father died. While running with a wild crowd of boys, one Sunday in 1752, the group brought some liquor to an old woman who was a fortune teller so as to enjoy a good laugh as they listened to her various prophecies. When she came to Robinson, she became more serious and told him that he would live to see his children and grandchildren. The prophecy sobered him up with the thought of the responsibilities of life. Shortly afterward he heard the Reverend George Whitfield preach a sermon on "The Wrath to Come" and fell under a conviction which lasted three years. When he turned twenty, he found himself in a crowd listening to John Wesley preach, and following that he came to the "Fount of Every Blessing", with the prayer, "Here's my heart, O take and seal it," and soon afterward entered the ministry. In 1757, while pastor in Norwich, England, the memory of his conversion brought an appreciation of that experience and he composed that marvelous hymn.

Come, thou Fount of every blessing,
Tune my heart to sing thy grace;
Streams of Mercy, never ceasing,
Call for songs of loudest praise.
Teach me some melodious sonnet,
Sung by flaming tongues above;
Praise the mount! I'm fixed upon it,
Mount of thy redeeming love.

The story continues that in later years he became rather careless in his personal conduct, and one day while riding in a stage coach, he was reproved by a woman for his behavior who then quoted at least a portion of this hymn to him. Upon hearing her recitation of the hymn, he replied: "Madam, I am the poor, unhappy man who composed it; and

I would give a thousand worlds if I had them, to enjoy the feelings I had then."[2] I hope for Mr. Robinson's sake, that encounter was an Ebenezer moment. I suppose it was, for if I understand other sources correctly, he later became associated with the Baptists.

"Here I raise mine Ebenezer." Those first few words to the second verse of the hymn were always a phrase I had a hard time making any sense out of. Just what, or better who is an Ebenezer? I didn't know any Ebenezers so I couldn't put a face to it. It wasn't until I was a student at Southwestern College that I learned the Ebenezer spoken of in the hymn was certainly not any one particular person, but a type of memorial, a visual acknowledgement of the 'Lord our God' at work in the life of Israel following victorious encounters with the Philistine armies. In order to contextualize this, we need to understand that this is only a small part of a larger narrative in the life of Israel prior to the establishment of the monarchy. The story revolves around the rise in influence of Samuel, and a number of catastrophic events such as the capture of the Ark of the Covenant by the Philistines, their misfortune in trying to keep it, the sudden death of Eli, and the birth of his grandson who was named Ichabod, meaning 'the glory has departed from Israel.' Ebenezer was a simple stone, set in an otherwise unremarkable spot, to ensure the remembering that right there, at that very point in time and place, God helped the people of God.
(I Samuel 1:1-7:17)

> *Here I raise mine Ebenezer;*
> *hither by thy help I'm come;*
> *And I hope by thy good pleasure,*
> *safely to arrive at home.*
> *Jesus sought me when a stranger,*
> *wandering from the fold of God;*
> *He, to rescue me from danger,*
> *interposed his precious blood.*

As I mature, let me rephrase that, as I grow older, attain more experience, and develop more fully my Christian faith, this phrase has turned out to be one of my most appreciated notions about God. Raising

Ebenezer is the one acknowledgment a Christian at any point in his or her relationship with God, or at any level of growth can always give with conviction and confidence; "Here I'll raise mine Ebenezer, hither by Thy help I'm come." What an affirmation of faith; what a declaration of forthright trust in God. Wherever we are, it is because of God's help. Wherever we are going, we'll get there because God will lead us. That declaration can only have its source in a mind and heart that truly senses a profound gratitude, for the activity of the Sovereign and Divine Being at work in a solitary life.

> *O to grace how great a debtor*
> *daily I'm constrained to be!*
> *Let thy goodness, like a fetter;*
> *bind my wandering heart to thee:*
> *Prone to wander, Lord I feel it,*
> *prone to leave the God I love;*
> *Here's my heart, O take and seal it,*
> *seal it for thy courts above.*

The opening lines of Mr. Price's preface to the book above mentioned states, "Every real hymn has its story, if only we could discover it. The background of the author's life, his spiritual experiences, his conflicts, his sufferings, his victories, sometimes a startling incident, sometimes a soul crisis, sometimes a season of exaltation, these things are woven into the thought and feeling of a great hymn."[3]

Given this sentiment, we should all be able to write a hymn, as the same sentiment can be true of almost any person in any type of event or situation. This is possible when people reflect thoughtfully and theologically in regard to what is going on around them, to them, or through them. Theological reflection, while not always theological precision, is the author of many hymns, books, sermons and prayers. Through the phrase "Here I'll raise mine Ebenezer," I am discovering there is quite a story reflective of the marvelous and amazing work of God in the midst of our ordinary, everyday lives.

Reflection:

What are the songs, secular or sacred, that have the power to transport you to a particular place in time, or to suddenly be in the presence with certain people?

What do you think there is about them that gives them such power?

How have the songs of the church done this for you?

It's about a Place; Anyplace

When he reached a certain place, he stopped for the night because the sun had set. Taking one of the stones there, he put it under his head and lay down to sleep. He had a dream in which he saw a stairway resting on the earth, with its top reaching to heaven, and the angels of God were ascending and descending on it. Above it stood the Lord, and he said: "I am the Lord, the God of your father Abraham and the God of Isaac. I will give you the land on which you are lying"...Early the next morning, Jacob took the stone he had placed under his head and set it up as a pillar and poured oil on top of it. He called that place Bethel. (Genesis 28:11-18)

When Jacob left his home to escape the anger of his brother and find a wife, he stopped for a simple, uncomplicated nights rest, and wound up having an interesting visitation of God through a dream. To commemorate the event, he set up a stone and called the place Beth-el which means House of God. We still acknowledge that place by naming communities, churches, and schools after it; and of course by singing "We Are Climbing Jacob's Ladder" to commemorate the visionary aspect of the dream that began the whole thing in the first place. If you are familiar with the story of Jacob, the remarkable journey he took, and transformation he underwent as recorded throughout the latter portions of Genesis, you understand the importance of the various places he found himself in; places like Beersheba, where he spent a lot of time growing up as a twin brother; Paddan Aram, where he would first glimpse and kiss Rachel; and Haran, where he worked for his Uncle Laban for the hand of his beloved Rachel. Here he got a little tripped up over some technicalities, and wound up staying on a few more years, and gaining a few more wives than he had originally planned. Anyway, he headed home with a lot of extra people he hadn't counted on. There would also be Peniel, where he wrestled with God, and had his name changed from Jacob to Israel; and Bethel, where he would later return to worship. Some of these places were pleasant, some were difficult or dangerous, others were just frustrating, and a few were life changing. Yet, God was with him in every one of those places.

Does this sound familiar? I am convinced the same is true for any person making their way through life's journey; right, wrong, indifferent, or clueless. We call it Prevenient Grace. For John and Charles Wesley it all begins with God's grace, a grace which precedes our own awareness of God or God's activity in our life or the world around us. It is, in the Wesleyan "Order of Salvation," the 'starting place'.

Bishop Scott Jones writes, "Prevenient grace is the love of God at work in our lives from the very beginning…To affirm prevenient grace is to say that God is actively loving all of humanity…Our Doctrinal Heritage acknowledges prevenient grace as the divine love that surrounds all humanity and precedes any and all of our conscious impulses…"[4]

Following his definition of Mr. Wesley's view of prevenient grace, and from the standpoint of raising Ebenezer, we could add, 'God is actively [helping] all of humanity.'

Since the spring of 1871, when two branches of my family, the North's and the Forney's respectively stood on the high elevations of the east bank of the Arkansas River, paused for a moment, and viewed the vast, treeless ocean of big bluestem grass which lay before them, Belle Plaine, Kansas has been one of those countless places. As I have come to understand this "Stone of Help," you really can't have an Ebenezer without first having a place; like a Southwestern College, an Asbury Theological Seminary, a Bentonville, Geneseo, Wellington, Mankato, or Pratt. After all, you have to be somewhere in order for something to happen, right?

If you have watched many World War II movies from the 1940s, it's interesting that the war-time studios made a concerted effort to be geographically and culturally inclusive for their movies that centered on a group of servicemen engaged in fighting the war. There is always the tough guy from New York City, the rich kid from Boston or Philadelphia, the blue collar worker from Cleveland, an innocent farm boy from

Iowa, a Californian, a Texan, and a southerner from Alabama or Mississippi. When you are fighting a war for the life of your country, place becomes really important; especially if you might lose your life for it. The only negative aspect to this comprehensive practice was that the studios pretty well followed the nations, and US military's then current practice of segregation, so that inclusiveness rarely crossed racial lines.

Each of us has a place or places which keep our history, provide our present, and offer our future. The Hebrew word for place, and this is my own uneducated paraphrase, literally means standing grain, or something (or someone) being where it, or they are supposed to be. The people of God have the awesome privilege of being able to look around them at any given time in their life; in any given place they might find themselves, and in any circumstance or situation they may be facing, and have an Ebenezer moment. They should be able to sense that affirmation of faith welling up within them, "Thus far has the Lord helped us." From the standpoint of the Scriptural witness, it has always been the nature of God to be present in our lives wherever we are, and whatever we are experiencing. It should be our nature to always recognize and aver that about God's presence with us, and raise our Ebenezers.

According to the tradition handed down through the North/Schwyhart side of the family, they came to Kansas with seven covered wagons and three generations of folks from Ohio with a brief stay in Iowa, near a town named Belle Plaine; a French phrase meaning beautiful plain. There would have been one more wagon in the mix, as one of the North sisters; Ann, was married to a young man named Nevin. When Nevin's older brother who was in the Army heard that he was preparing to leave for a farming venture in the West, he made a very hurried trip home from his military assignment to convince him to stay in order that there would be someone around to look after their parents as they aged. Well, Nevin and Ann were convinced to stay. They moved up to Monroe, Michigan where they farmed and took care of his folks. Nevin's brother, George Armstrong Custer, went back to his military post confident he had done the right thing; at least in that particular instance. The rest of the family made their way west and finally arrived at the place that would be home for them and future generations. When the question was asked, "What is the name of this place?" by a young and unmarried Aunt Olive, she was told it didn't have one. She stood up in the wagon and said, "Oh, let's call it Belle Plaine."

One of the ways many folks who settled the country (especially those from a European descended population) experienced Ebenezer was through their participating in building communities. I don't necessarily mean buildings and infrastructure, but the institutions of community; schools, granges, government, and of course, the church. For my great-great-great-Grandparents William L. and Matilda North they planted some of the first apple trees in Sumner County and grafted them to develop apples suited for the climate of south-central Kansas. Their work, along with other early area developers in apple production, would one day result in the Belle Plaine High School sports teams being known by the vicious and intimidating name "Apple Pickers." After the 'great apple blight' and the loss of many of the apple orchards, the name was changed to a more subdued "Dragons."

Great-great-Grandfather William Henry Harrison (Tip) North used his wagons to haul freight from the Santa Fe Railroad at Newton, and later Wichita, to Belle Plaine, and on into Indian Territory for the military at Forts Sill and Reno. He and his wife Kate North participated in the building of the early schools in the area, and his sister Olive, taught the first 'subscription school.' I think one of the most important aspects of community building for them had to involve the church. Going to Sunday services for the North family meant loading up a small melodeon (they had brought from Tontogony, Ohio) and a reed organ (with only a few octaves and a set of pedals) into a wagon on Sunday morning, and hauling it into town to provide music for the hymns the early settlers would sing during worship. This made Grandmother North the first church organist in the area.

When it came time to build a structure, the Methodists in the area went to work raising their new building. The project commenced; everyone was excited, but it was all suddenly placed on hold when somebody in the crowd asked the question, "Are we going to be Methodist Episcopal or Methodist Protestant?" It's funny how a simple little question can have such a profound effect on things. This should have been decided already, or at least been in the process of being seriously discussed; but obviously it hadn't. The building sat unfinished for a while until the question could be settled. I am persuaded in my mind that the North's were on the ME side of things since that was what they had been since the Church of England lost the Revolutionary War, and the Methodist Episcopal Church had newly formed. The Forney's on the other hand, were in Fredrick County Maryland in the 1700s just a few miles from where Robert Strawbridge was preaching, and developing early Methodism in that State. Following their move into the Northwest Territories [Ohio], they had at some very early date become Methodist Protestant, and had given land for a Methodist Protestant Church and cemetery to be built in Wheeling Township, Guernsey County Ohio. I don't know how long it took, but when the group made the decision to be Methodist Episcopal, the question was settled, the issue was placed behind them, and they all went back to work and finished the building that would serve the Methodist Episcopal Church and the community for the next ninety years; where five generations of the family would have their funerals, folks would be married, and we would be baptized, learn to worship, grow up in Sunday school, and be conscripted into attending Bible school. I can remember the dozens of old wooden folding chairs that were still being used when I was a young kid. They had bold, black letters painted on the backs. I always wondered who ME was, and why ME had so many chairs around.

Reflection:

What places: cities, towns, buildings, rooms, or even wilderness vistas, stand out, or have been influential for you in your development as a person?

In what ways would you say God was present there?

It's about People; Any People

This is what the Lord says: "For three sins of Israel, even for four, I will not turn back my wrath. They sell the righteous for silver, and the needy for a pair of sandals. They trample on the heads of the poor as upon the dust of the ground and deny justice to the oppressed." (Amos 2:6-7)

Out on the prairie, the pioneers were pretty much in the same general type of situation; they were all at the starting gate of whatever new enterprise was before them. While there was not a lot of diversity in these communities, they were places where the playing field was pretty level. When it came to government for these early settlers, it was just about as much a part of life as anything. It was important; whether you were in the State Legislature, on the County Commission, a Township Trustee, on the School Board, the Justice of the Peace, or simply a voting member of a political party. My great-great Grandfather Anderson Gilbert Forney was a Kansas State Senator from Sumner County in the 1890s. While taking the family into town for Sunday evening services, they found the road blocked by a Missouri Pacific freight train. The train sat there so long that they were late for church. When they got home that night, he sat down and wrote a bill to present on the floor of the Senate in Topeka regulating the amount of time (ten minutes) a train could block a public road. It doesn't have to take much for that 'level playing field' nature of things to be skewed by the intervention of others, and the early railroads seemed to be the earliest entity to do the skewing by the virtue of their unregulated power. This was to be his discovery; and it would be a lot more serious than just trains blocking a road.

A former Republican, he ran as the candidate for the People's Party known as the Populists and served in the Kansas Senate for most of the politically raucous 1890s much to the chagrin of his brother Josephus Forney, a Republican member of the State House of Representatives. They partnered in farming and business, and attended the same church, but couldn't see eye to eye on at least some aspects of politics. The reputation of the Populists, due in part to some of them tending toward radical thinking and behavior, has labeled them fanatics. Today they would most likely be called Socialists. They weren't Socialist though because they didn't believe in subsidies for anybody. They just believed in the level playing field. In fact, he was a committed Capitalist. If Mr. Webster in part defines a fanatic as a person with an intense, uncritical devotion, he was no fanatic. I believe he, like many, was a Populist because he was being critical; that is, able to exercise careful, evaluative judgment of the current state of affairs, some of the causes behind them, and the strong, social justice issues he believed in, and fought to uphold and defend. A number of the bills he wrote were openly ridiculed by many in Topeka as foolishness, because it struck at the heart of justice and fairness. Paul writes in I Corinthians 1:26-28:

Brothers, think of what you were when you were called. Not many of you were wise by human standards; not many influential; not many were of noble birth. But God chose the foolish things of the world to shame the wise; God chose the weak things of the world to shame the strong. He chose the lowly things of this world and the despised things and the things that are not to nullify the things that are.

He was a farmer, stockman, educator, druggist, flour miller, and Christian. He obviously was motivated by an extremely strong sense of ethics and integrity. His only power was derived from those who trusted him as a representative, a neighbor, or friend; and his personal faith, and passionate sense of justice. This would be born out in his later experience of losing nearly everything of what he had worked so hard for throughout his life when he was taken advantage of by a crooked speculator in a Colorado coal development scam. In some ways this scheme, like many, to swindle honest people out of their money was a forerunner of things to come, like Bernie Madoff's ponzi schemes. This, in and of itself is quite a story. But suffice it to say, through it all he always did the right thing; no matter what it cost him.

A.G. Forney identified strongly with the right of farmers, workers, small businesses, and merchants to have a fair chance at the American Dream. Success was not just the privilege of the robber barons. These robber barons were the industrialists and financiers of the mid and late nineteenth century, principally the railroads, banks, and heavy industry who were driving the industrial revolution and westward expansion in America without any thought except for their own enormous appetites for success and wealth at any cost; and what cost there was, was usually not shouldered by them, but came off the backs, and lives of those workers, immigrants, farmers, and small businesses. The Populists held political ideas and agendas intended to safeguard everyone including the ordinary people, or as some would say, "The Little People" their needs, and aspirations. They supported reform and regulation of industries and banks to create competition and fairness. Like so many political attempts to address the need to bring change, even in the hallowed halls of the federal government today, gridlocked with partisan bias, the populists were never very successful in getting their agenda adopted into law.

While some of their motives could be viewed with skepticism, the heart and soul of these people-minded politicians remains relevant. When you think about what and who they struggled with, it sounds a lot like the captains of finance and industry of the latter twentieth and early twenty-first centuries. These are the men and women of today, who like the unscrupulously greedy few from the preceding generations, are doing their best to uphold the traditions of the gilded age. They also are unwittingly illustrating the indictment of the prophets on a people who have turned their back on justice as viewed by the law and covenant of God.

Woe to those who plan iniquity, to those who plot evil on their beds! At morning light they carry it out because it is in their power to do it. (Micah 2:1)

Woe to those who make unjust laws, who issue oppressive decrees, to deprive the poor of their rights and withhold justice from the oppressed...making, widows their prey and robbing the fatherless. (Isaiah 10:1-2)

What the Populists were struggling to communicate and attain politically, is what Jesus announces, begins to build, and invites us into religiously—the Kingdom of God. It is not corporate empires which will rule God's world but the poor and meek, the ones usually left out of the economic equation. Warren Carter, Professor of New Testament at Brite Divinity School, commenting on Jesus' Sermon on the Mount writes,

> *Having been commissioned by God to manifest God's empire [Kingdom] and saving presence, Jesus begins his mission by announcing the presence of God's empire..., forming a new community...The scenes in (Matthew) 4:17-25 have indicated that God's empire, present in a world dominated by Pax Romana, is disruptive and transformative. The Sermon sketches an alternative world marked not by oppression but by restructured societal relationships...It resocializes disciples into a world of justice which differs from their previous life and which conflicts and contrasts with the values, commitments, and practices of the majority who have not encountered it.*[5]

When I entered Southwestern College as a pre-ministerial student, I came with a simple, preconceived notion that the primary message of the Hebrew Prophets were those prophesies concerning the birth, life, death, resurrection, and second coming of Jesus. So naturally I was surprised to learn that there was a whole lot more to this eclectic group of persons; like the fact that they were very people oriented, and had a lot to say about how things should be among people from God's righteous, just, and covenantal point of view. I still have and treasure, a book from a college class I took titled, A Guide to the Prophets. I still use it frequently in teaching, preaching, and for reference. In his comments about the Prophet Amos, Stephen Winward says:

> *In Palestine the ordinary brook is a raging torrent in the rainy season...a brook fed by a spring is perennial or 'ever flowing.' God requires that justice flow like a swollen torrent and righteousness like an ever flowing stream. The dealings of men with one another in every sphere of life, personal, economic, social, and political, must be just and right. Why? Because the God of Israel, [and humankind,] who is made known in his righteous acts and saving deeds, requires it.*[6]

Amos was a prophet whose ministry was somewhere around 760 B.C. He was from the small town of Tekoa, some ten miles south of Jerusalem. He was a shepherd and a dresser of sycamore trees, the fruit of which was a staple diet of the poor. He is aware of other places too; Damascus, Gaza, Tyre, Ammon, Moab, the nation of Judah and finally, Israel. His opening comments seem like a big geographical game of Spin the Bottle with his indictments of the nations of the earth and their sins; only it's not a game. Place and people are the underlying aspects of the prophetic message and the voices of those still crying out for justice. It is in this context that Ebenezer takes place for them.

The Prophets of God are offensive and troublesome to the *status quo* because they point to a power higher than the powerful. I suppose that's one reason why the Christ they foresaw would be born in a manger. The Populists would be equally as offensive and troublesome today in both the eyes of the right and the left, conservatives and progressives, Pharisees and Zealots, just like Jesus found himself. They would also be quite vocal today if they could see how corporate CEOs and Wall Street bankers are making tens and hundreds of millions in "bonuses" and "stock options" on top of highly inflated compensation packages. All the while their companies are being subsidized by government bailouts, and the general citizenry is being plundered, or as the Psalmist puts it, 'we are like sheep to be slaughtered.' And, in 760 B.C., as well as today, as unbelievable as it is, there are those who reject the reality of the prophets, their message, and anything that smacks of "social justice."

We should be grateful that those "Grangers" were compelled by their faith, and driven by a holistic understanding of community, and justice to at least try to make a difference in society as they worked to build their homes in the places they now found themselves, and provide secure, stable communities for following generations to come along. Many of them lived with the understanding that what they were doing was not being accomplished simply by their own efforts, and struggles. The providence of the Almighty was there. They really were experiencing Ebenezer moments.

To move this a little closer to some pivotal events in our lifetime, that prophetic call for justice and righteousness could include a bus in Montgomery, a bridge in Selma, or the fall of the Berlin Wall and the Iron Curtain. We can remember an individual standing before a tank in Tiananmen Square, China and now in Tahrir Square in Cairo, or upon the shores of Tripoli. As far as today is concerned, the issues which are surrounding the fresh clamor for freedom in repressive societies abroad, immigration and the human stories surrounding our need for reform here in the United States, the environment and our addiction to energy with its massive carbon footprint, and the economy and how to fix it at the same time there is the rapidly growing gap/disparity between the wealthy and the poor in our country which is indicative of our current economic ethics. Add to this the political polarity of twenty-first century government and we should just ask, "Where are the prophets?"

When I was the director of the Jewell County Parish, our pastor at the Jewell Salem, and Ionia United Methodist Church was, for a while, a woman who really fit in with our staff and the congregations. However, she would always make the comment about topics or conversational subjects, "That's a social justice issue." I remember responding to her once, "Ann, you view everything as a social justice issue. You can't do that." She agreed at least halfheartedly, but now I might just agree with her. How can we not look at everything from a standpoint of solidly prophetic social justice, even bringing people to a saving faith in Jesus Christ? When it's about people, and that includes all people, there is going to be a prophetic struggle. In the midst of that struggle however there will always be an Ebenezer.

Reflection:

What issues, situations, or conditions regarding justice, fairness, or covenant have you received as a legacy from others in your family or community?

In what ways have they compelled your faith to take a stand publicly?

What do you see currently taking place in which a prophetic response would be appropriate?

Sometimes a Good Cry Helps

To what then can I compare the people of this generation? They are like children sitting in the marketplace and calling to each other: "We played the flute for you, and you did not dance; we sang a dirge, and you did not weep." (Matthew 11:17)

I don't know how old I was, probably four or so, when Mother enrolled me in tap dancing lessons taught by her cousin Barbara Brummett. She was one of Uncle Henry and Aunt Flossie's daughters. I was the same age as her son Bryan. The Brummett kids, Bruce, Bryan, and Brenna, along with their parents, Bennie and Barbara were all extremely talented in singing, dancing, and the like. I think in her heart, Mom really wanted to believe talent was a genetic trait that transmigrated across family tree branches; therefore I should be able to at least dance and sing. I remember being "asked" to sing Rudolph the Red-nosed Reindeer for the Odd Fellows and Rebecca Lodges Christmas Banquet. This would have been my first public solo appearance; it was very traumatic. When I finished singing, I ran through the side door to the kitchen area where one of the Odd Fellows was standing. He said, "You look like you need a drink kid." To which I answered, "I sure do!"

My grandmother made me a little Indian outfit, and Aunt Flossie made one for Bryan. The two of us did a little "tap-Indian dance routine" which should probably make any Native American recoil at that form of abuse of their ancient heritage and culture. I still have a memory of doing that routine in front of the old soldiers in the auditorium at Veterans Hospital in Wichita. The first real dance I went to was in a barn for an eighth-grade Halloween party. There was a record player that played relevant music, but I just felt like a chicken scratching for worms trying to dance. The truth be told, I just couldn't dance. To this day, about the only dance I can do is the Bunny Hop at wedding receptions; so much for transmigrated talent.

I could sing however. In every church I ever served, I sang in the choir. On several occasions I have been honored to sing the opening tenor recitative "Comfort Ye My People" from the Messiah. At Wellington, we formed a male quartet in which I was the first tenor. I wanted to name the group "The Glory Stompers" but that got overruled by the senior pastor, Alan Lindal, who sang the bass in our group. We were known by the much more Methodist name, The Wesley Airs. I have always loved to sing, including whistling, and live by the saying, "He or she who sings, prays twice."

Now crying was a different matter; I was a professional at that. We used to have to travel to Wichita to the doctor, Dr. Jim, who had married one of mom's cousins, a daughter of Uncle Chet and Aunt Mossie. His office was in an upper floor of the old First National Bank building on Douglas Street. The only good thing about being there was that the window in the waiting room afforded one a view of the old Forum in which I would attend my first circus, and the Missouri Pacific, and Midland Valley Depots. The building had the old fashioned elevators with an operator who sat on a little stool and ran a rheostat looking lever. According to Mom, as soon as the doors were closed, (those clear glass doors with chicken wire in them) and the steel gate slammed shut, I started to cry. I cried all the way to the waiting room, then from the waiting room to the examination room, and all the way through the proverbial shot in the hind end. A good spanking and being sent to my room was always an appropriate time for a good cry as well. Sitting in front of the grade school principal and watching him pull out his paddle while addressing me could cause a few tears to form. The time I tried to ramp my bicycle over the spirea hedge created a great deal of crying. Kids cry—that's what they do.

I later gained an understanding of what persons put up with when a kid cries. When Justin was a little short of being three, he and I went to the Pizza Hut in Ellsworth for supper one night. After we were finished, I laid a dollar bill on the table for a tip. He tried to grab it and I said, "No! That's for our waitress." Well he grabbed for it again and knocked over a glass of pop still sitting there. I grabbed him by the arm and he slipped and accidentally smacked his forehead on the table.

There was this long open mouthed exhale of every molecule of air in his lungs, which any parent knows, precedes that deep inhaling of fresh air in order to properly create one of those very loud, everyone in the place can hear, little kid screams. While he was still in exhale mode, I quickly carried him into the bathroom.

It wasn't until the morning Uncle Howard came over to the house to tell us that Macy had died during the night that I learned how to cry in a non self-centered way, and grieve and shed tears of sorrow and loss. Macy Watson was to the Utt kids a third grandmother. Every child should have a third (unrelated) grandmother. She lived just behind us in a house built by her son Joe, who would one day build a new home for us. She had us over there all the time. We would have "tea parties" which were not political, but just opportunities to have some cocoa and cookies. We would play games like, Hide the Thimble, or card games like Books. She was quite an elderly person for the late 1950s. She was raised up on the Ninnescah southwest of Peck, into one of the early day families, and was the true quintessence of a Victorian Lady. Walking to town, or to the Presbyterian Church, she would use one of her many beautiful parasols. She had a house full of knick knacks and figurines. One day, she had us kids pick out whichever one we wanted to keep. She said we would be able to remember her by looking at it when she was gone. I couldn't however imagine life without Macy.

Once when she was quite ill and pretty much confined to bed, I (being a professional at receiving shots at doctors' offices) decided to help. She didn't lock her doors so going over to see her was not a problem. I got Dad's little tote bag, put some cotton balls and a sharpened pencil in it, and headed over to her house. As I walked up to her bed I said, "Macy, I'm going to make you well!" I opened up the little bag and took out one of the cotton balls. I knew the routine as I had seen this done a million times before. I rubbed the cotton ball on her arm and said, "Now I'm going to have to give you a shot in your arm." I took out the pencil which was my syringe and held it to her arm for a few seconds. I then rubbed the spot with a second cotton ball and said,

"There, that should make you get well." There must have been something in me that said my medical skills and whatever else I had done to that point was not going to be sufficient for healing her, so I bowed my head and prayed, "Dear God, please make Macy well. Amen." Macy did get well, at least for a short while anyway. Her testimony would be that my visit and prayer was what got her out of that sick bed.

Macy had quite an Ebenezer moment herself that she shared with us. Years ago, when people would take turns boarding the school teacher from the country in their homes, (I could never imagine living with any of my teachers) it was their turn to host. During this period of time one of her sons was driving a team of horses pulling a wagon down the road when something spooked the horses and they began to run. The young boy couldn't hold them and was pulled off the wagon and was run over. He suffered a severe concussion. The doctor was summoned to the house and after treating his cuts, told Macy that she needed to sit with him through the rest of the day and night, and keep as cold a compress as she could on his head or he could die. She did just what the doctor told her to do. Everyone else, including the school teacher had gone upstairs to bed for the night, and Macy and her son were alone. A very strong thunderstorm arose during the middle of the night and a tornado had formed. As the cacophony of sounds became louder, the people upstairs began running down the stairway, and heading for the cellar. The roof of the house was lifted off with a horrible cracking of timber. Macy said, "At that moment, I felt Jesus put his hand on my shoulder and he said, 'Macy, do not be afraid.' I knew that he was right there with me and my son. So I never moved, and kept his head covered with that compress." Everybody made it through that storm, and Macy's son recovered just fine.

I remember officiating at a wedding a number of years ago. The groom was a U.S. Marine and while we were getting ready prior to the service he was getting into his dress uniform. He really looked sharp in it too. He and his best man, dressing in a tuxedo, were having casual conversation. The best man asked the groom if he thought he would cry during the service. The groom said, I cried at my grandfather's funeral and my father got mad and said 'men don't cry; only women cry!' So I haven't cried since." Now it seems to me that if you don't have anything that is worthy of crying about, then you probably don't have anything worthy of dancing about. I thought that would have to rank right up there in the top ten of the world's worst advice a parent could give a child. I'm glad I never learned that type of life lesson. Yes, as a woman, my mother would cry just watching episodes of Lassie, as she risked her life to save the baby squirrels from the bulldozer, or little Timmy from the abandoned mine cave in. I also consider myself privileged to have been able to see the men in my family cry at quite appropriate times without the worry of losing their sense of being men. Also, we need to remember that the Biblical verse that ranks as the shortest in scripture is John 11:35, "Jesus Wept."

Many years later, I was asked to officiate at a funeral for a family who had no church home or faith background. I gathered with them in the parlor of the Larrison Funeral Home in Pratt to get acquainted and offer some sense of comfort while we were making preparation for the service the next day. I always enjoy finding out as much as possible about the person whose life we are remembering, so I began to ask some reflective questions about these young adults' father. When I asked the question, "What are some of the significant things about your father, and his life that we really need to lift up; to celebrate and remember about his life?" There was total silence. I sat there for what seemed to be an eternity waiting for a response. "Were they just really contemplating deeply and reflecting about their father's life?" I wondered. Finally, the oldest son spoke up and said, "I really can't think of anything." That comment, and its implications, not the death of this man, was the real tragedy that day; at least from my perspective. I wonder if our contemporary culture is becoming so calloused by our intensely visual and graphic lifestyles, without the sense of any essential involvement, or investment from others around us, that we are losing the ability to authentically celebrate another's living or genuinely mourn their passing. As we to some degree witness the deterioration of human relationships, we seem to be seeing simultaneously the loss of ritual and its importance in helping people move through their grief by publicly mourning. There are times when a pastor has few words to offer, but we have always been able to rely on the place of ritual to help accomplish support. If the role of ritual and the faith it is based upon are becoming less a factor in our society, and you don't even have permission to use the tried and true 'and tired' phrase, "He loved life." then how can you possibly communicate anything which deals with the human longing for purpose and meaning in this world? Is there any significance?

During my first year at Southwestern College, there was an itinerant, self proclaimed, independent, preacher who showed up on campus and caused no little stir. He was going around doing things like helping people learn how to speak in tongues and making sure they had an appropriate baptism in the Holy Spirit. One afternoon, following a particular class, someone encouraged me to stick around. There were several of us who sat in an otherwise empty classroom and listened to this 'evangelist.' He told us to just start making noise and it would turn into tongues. Now I have never been one to doubt or ridicule someone else's experience, especially with the Holy Spirit, and if someone testifies to speaking in an unknown language, I will be the last one to question them. Furthermore, I have said several times that if God should ever choose to give me that particular gift, I will receive it with a grateful heart. But for the life of me I could not understand how gibberish could ever be a means in receiving, or manifesting the power and presence of the Holy Spirit, let alone bring honor to God. I found that I was unable to go through the exercise. The whole thing put me in a position where I began to question my sincerity, my faith, and even whether I had a proper relationship with God or not.

Well, needless to say, there was some differing of opinions about all of this, even between the pre-ministerial students. The Chaplin at the school was John Paulin, who was a very well respected and appreciated person on campus. He was quite understanding and deferential of where persons were at in their faith journey, and very helpful to me in my college experience. He played a large role in arranging a meeting at a neutral location, which happened to be the local Episcopal Church Hall. I decided to go and when I walked in I sat quietly at the end of a long set of tables next to Dr. J. Hamby Barton, Dean of the College. J. Hamby was a Southern gentleman who was always dressed in a nice bow tie and drove Jaguars. He taught several classes which I took, and helped me produce my senior project. I really loved that man and had a profound admiration for him. During the meeting with this itinerate preacher, several students were favorable to his message and leadership, Reverend Paulin tried to maintain a neutral balance, and several voiced concern. I just listened to the differing points of view about what was taking place. I had become aware of, and was struggling with the spiritual dimensions of it all and what it might mean for me and my relationship with God. When the meeting ended, Dr. Barton was asked to dismiss the group with prayer. As he began to pray, I suddenly felt like I was really being taken someplace. I had never heard, or maybe hadn't paid attention to a prayer like this before in my life. It was no platitude riddled, stained glassed, high brow prayer. He prayed with such personal depth and passion that it didn't make any difference where you were at around those tables; you had to have been taken through a portal of heaven. It was a prayer born in the deep recesses of that man's soul; produced by his love of God and the students of the institution he served. In the midst of that, I suddenly began to tear up, and then tears turned to an uncontrolled crying and sobbing. I left the room and went into a kitchen and sat on a stool and continued to cry for quite a number of minutes. I think everyone got tired of hearing me cry and left. When I finally left, I was not sure about what had just happened. I had to think about this for some time. There might have been others who thought they knew, but as I reflected, at least I felt I was okay. The fact is it would take several years for me to really understand just what was significant in that experience.

Twenty-five years or so later during Annual Conference, Reverend Paulin, who by this time had retired, caught me in a lounge area and asked, "Kendal, do you remember that evening at the Episcopal Church in Winfield, and the experience you had there?" "Yes, I remember that meeting," I replied. "I've never asked before, but often wondered just what had transpired that night for you," he said inquiringly. My response was then, and is now, that when the venerable Dr. Barton began to pray as he did that night, God bore witness to my life, my soul, that I was indeed a child of God. And at least during that period of time, I had all the things necessary from God to be in relationship with, and service to God. In John Wesley's Sermon, "The Witness of the Spirit II," he writes:

> *But what is the 'witness of the Spirit'? The original word, marturia, may be rendered either...the witness, or less ambiguously the testimony' or 'the record: 'This is the record' (the testimony, the sum of what God testifies in all the inspired writings), 'that God hath given unto us eternal life, and this life is in his Son.'...What he testifies to us is 'that we are the children of God'...I do not mean hereby that the Spirit of God testifies this by any outward voice; no, nor always by an inward voice, although he may do this sometimes...But he so works upon the soul by his immediate influence, and by a strong though inexplicable operation, that the stormy wind and troubled waves subside, and there is a sweet calm; the heart resting as in the arms of Jesus, and the sinner being clearly satisfied that God is reconciled, that all his 'iniquities are forgiven, and his sins covered.*[7]

If John Wesley could have his heartwarming experience during the reading of "Luther's Preface to the Epistle of the Romans," then I could have mine during a prayer by the Academic Dean of Southwestern College. Sometimes tears are to soothe the sorrowing mind and soul, sometimes to express a great joy in our hearts, and sometimes they are simply mysterious visitors from the very depths of our being, whose presence and purpose may remain unrevealed until a proper time. We should never be afraid to cry nor hold back tears for any reason, as they often are valid means of raising Ebenezer; recognizing God's help in our lives.

Reflection:

What are the things, events, or people that bring real celebration into your life?

In what ways do you observe them?

How have you learned to mourn?

Have sudden or unexpected emotional experiences given witness to your faith and relationship with God?

Whatever it Takes

Therefore, since we are surrounded by such a great cloud of witnesses, let us throw off everything that hinders and the sin that so easily entangles, and let us run with perseverance the race marked out for us. Let us fix our eyes on Jesus, the author and perfecter of our faith, who for the joy set before him endured the cross scorning its shame, and sat down on the right hand of the throne of God. Consider him who endured such opposition from sinful men so that you will not grow weary and lose heart. (Hebrews 12:1-3)

Being a short legged person, I have never been a good runner. However, in grade school, I went out for track in the eighth grade. I couldn't run fast, throw far, jump high, or any of the other things most track and field stars could do. But I was on the team. The only event I remember being asked to participate in at a genuine track meet was the 440 relay at a league meet in Oxford. The coach, put me and three other similar athletes together for what would be the final event of the day. We each took our places around the track. The starting gun was fired and the first runners took off as fast as they could with their batons in hand. While looking at the first group of runners on the far side of the field, I noticed that people were getting up and starting to leave the stands. The baton was passed to the next runner who started off down his portion of the relay. More people were leaving. Nobody seemed to be watching what was going on in this relay; my relay. I got ready, had my hand wide open and back to receive the baton and began to run. The pass was successful, and I hurried on toward the final member of our team, passed off to him, and slowed down, stopped, and while catching my breath, looked over at the nearly empty stands. I don't recall that they even took note of who won. Sure I was disappointed, yet we had the satisfaction of knowing we had given it all we had. No one dropped the baton, and we finished the race. We did what we had to do.

In September 1994, just before our son Brandon's third birthday, Joyce said "Kendal, Brandon's getting sick. I think you need to call the doctor's office and get him in." My response was my typical one,

"It's probably just one of those twenty-four hour bugs. He's just going to have to wear it out. Going to see the doctor never does any good for the flu." The next day, Joyce said he was getting worse and that he should go to the doctor. My response was pretty much the same, thinking time would be the best medicine for him. When I came home later that afternoon from the office, I no more than got inside the house when she met me at the door and said, "Kendal, that boy is sick; get him to the doctor!" I went in to the living room where Joyce had him lying on the divan, and picked him up. As I held him, his body was limp; his eyes were rolled back into his head. I called the doctor. The receptionist at the clinic said to bring him in around 5:00, and the doctor would be able to see him.

We took him into the clinic and didn't have to wait very long. Doctor Kimball was the only doctor in Jewell County. He was a member of the Harmony Church, and the only person to continually verbalize that he noticed seeing the coffee mug I forgot on the pulpit during the previous year's Christmas Eve service. When Doc came into the examination room, he looked at Brandon and almost immediately said, "Do you want to go to Mary Lanning Hospital in Hastings, Nebraska, or St. Joseph in Concordia? This boy needs to be in the hospital." I said, "Well Concordia is closer; we'll go there." Doc said, "Alright! I will call them to let them know you are on your way." "Oh!" he continued, "I think we need to take Brandon by ambulance." In a matter of minutes, the EMTs were there loading my little boy up on a gurney and placing him into the bowels of an ambulance. Well, that certainly got my attention, and gave Joyce her first ambulance ride. I went by the house to tell our oldest son, Justin, who was twelve at the time, what was going on and that he needed to look after his brothers, Adam and Taylor, until I got back. I then headed for Concordia. By the time I got there, Dr. Paul Nelson, a pediatrician, wonderful Christian gentleman, and an active United Methodist layperson was in the emergency room with Brandon and Joyce. After looking Brandon over, he ordered a test for diabetes saying, "We've got us a new diabetic here." The test came back negative, and he ordered it taken a second time. Again, it came back negative. In the meantime, Brandon's breath was growing very short and quick, his heart rate was becoming quite rapid, and he was becoming more listless.

Dr. Nelson called the two of us off to the side and said, "I'm not sure what is going on with Brandon. He is experiencing some type of respiratory difficulty. I believe we need to get him to the pediatric intensive care unit at Wesley Medical Center in Wichita. I just got off the phone with the head of the pediatric department there and they will be expecting you." "Oh!" he continued, "Due to the time and distance I think we will be flying him down in a life-watch aircraft." Again the medical conversation was grabbing my attention, and gave Joyce her first flight off the ground in a crowded helicopter. While we were waiting for the helicopter, the Concordia District Superintendent, the Reverend Elsie Crickard and her husband Burr, also United Methodist clergy, and the pastors from the two United Methodist Churches in Concordia gathered with Joyce and me. We entered into prayer for Brandon's life and healing. Unbeknownst to us, there were already thousands of prayers being raised by Catholics, Baptists, Church of Christ, Presbyterians, Lutherans, Christians, and, well let's just say, the Body of Christ was at work that night interceding on our son's behalf.

By now I had called my parents in Belle Plaine, and Joyce's in Wellington to tell them that things are happening pretty fast and that we are going to be heading to Wichita. Mom and Dad threw some things together and headed for Mankato to take care of the boys at the parsonage. Joyce's folks planned to meet Joyce and Brandon at the hospital in Wichita. It was getting pretty late in the night as my colleague, Bill Eisele, pastor of the smaller of the Concordia Churches, drove me down to Wesley to see how things were going and what Brandon's status was. Then the plan was that he would drive me back to Concordia to get my car so I could return to Mankato and conduct a funeral at the church for a County employee who was killed in a tragic accident a few days before. Following the funeral service, I would then return to Wichita.

I was able to sleep most of the way down to Wichita which was a blessing. Once we arrived at Wesley and found a parking space in the garage (which wasn't too difficult as it was really early in the morning), Bill and I headed into the hospital and grabbed the first elevator for the Pediatric Intensive Care Unit. Immediately as I walked off the elevator, I was met by yet another United Methodist pastor, Alan Lindal, who had been my former senior pastor while we were at Wellington, who looked me in the eye and said, "Kendal, You do not have a funeral tomorrow!" He then continued, "Bill can go back and do it for you. You need to be right here." It was at that very moment that it all sunk into the deepest part of my heart and soul how serious this was; that my son was in critical condition and might not live. Now as I understand it if I would have waited another day, or dallied even another hour, or had Doc Kimball or Dr. Nelson tarried in their wise decisions to send him on, Brandon most likely would not be with us today. Bill graciously went back and did the funeral the next morning. Everyone understood.

My parents had spent the wee hours of that morning searching the house and garage for something Brandon might have gotten into that could've poisoned him. Joyce's folks were in a private family area with us as we waited and took turns going into the pediatric intensive care unit, where Brandon lay in a bed with all kinds of wires, tubes, and IVs plugged into him. The doctor said, "We are running a liquid sodium bicarbonate into him. He has a severe case of respiratory acidosis." "What is that?" I asked. "His PH levels are out of line, and his system is becoming acidic. His rapid breathing is his body's attempt to exhale some of it. The sodium bicarbonate is to try and neutralize the acid as best we can." I asked the doctor, "How long before he gets over this?" His chilling response was, "It will be real touch and go for the next twenty-four hours. Even if he recovers, we do not know what is causing this, or whether there will be any lasting effects including the possibility of some brain damage." I surely at that moment felt the same as Charles Wesley when he wrote a hymn for his sick son Samuel, "For a Child in the Small-Pox:

> *Jesus, with human eyes Regard my misery;*
> *My Isaac on the altar lies, And gasps for life to Thee!*
> *Who didst our nature share, And put our frailties on,*
> *For pity's sake the victim spare,*
> *And give me back my Son.*

While the following is slightly out of context, I think the sentiment is quite appropriate to the subject in that Charles wrote another verse on behalf of his son Samuel that seems to indicate the lengths he was willing to go in order to get resolve:

> *Might I live to see him freed,*
> *Nothing more would I desire,*
> *Glad to bow my hoary head,*
> *Happy on thy cross t'expire,*
> *Life and all my friends resign,*
> *Leave them in the hands Divine.* [8]

Due to some of the tests they were running they soon thought he was suffering from a salicylate poisoning or overdose. "Oh great," I thought. "What did we leave lying around the house that Brandon could have gotten into?" They asked us about having salicylates in the house he might have ingested. I said, "I don't even know what a silicilate is; what would these things be in that we would have around the house?" An intern who had been working with the doctor began reading off a long list of things. When he got to grapes, I said, "Oh, he had some grapes the other day." The intern then said that he would have to have eaten several bushels of grapes to get enough salicilates to cause this severe of a condition.

Fortunately the acid levels started to drop and the heightened level of concern began to decrease. His breathing and heart rate finally began to normalize. The little fellow was exhausted, and so were all of us. Four days later, after three ambulance transfers, a helicopter ride, an uncertain night, two nights in the Ronald McDonald House, much kindness, and thousands of prayers later we were able to take our son home and celebrate his third birthday with his brothers and grandparents.

The diagnosis that was finally determined by a metabolic specialist was a rare disease called Maple Syrup Urine Disease, which didn't have anything to do with maple syrup or urine other than the odor it produced. It also didn't have anything to salicylates or poisoning; blessed be God for the same. Its other name is Branched-chain Ketoaciduria; which is why we just tell folks he had MSUD. When they ask, we just say, "It's complicated." The body cannot break down certain amino acids such as Lucien or lysine, and they produce a toxic by-product in the blood which then leads to the respiratory acidosis. Fortunately, Brandon's disease was labeled "intermittent." The doctor said if he had had a full blown case, he probably would not have lived for more than a few months after birth. There were a number of other hospitalizations for him over the next year or so. They always seemed to occur on the weekends which made for very long Sundays with services and trips to a hospital forty some miles away. All together it really made a serious impact on our financial situation, which in some ways we are still dealing with. Still, Brandon was our son, and Joyce and I were going to do whatever it took to take care of him. It was a miracle of God which was performed by and through some pretty incredible timing. If it wasn't for that timing, found in the providential nature of our caring God, and God's people at various places along the way, we wouldn't have made it this far.

A couple of years after we had moved to Pratt, Adam, Brandon, and a number of neighbor boys had gone over to one of the city parks nearby and were playing. Pretty soon Adam and a couple of the other boys came in with Brandon, who was obviously upset, and said that he had been bitten by a coon. "How in the world do you get bitten by a coon in a city park?" I asked. "Well we saw this animal running across the park and we chased it," one of them said. "Adam said that Brandon had tried to catch it and that it turned and bit him on the knee and the hand. I took him to the emergency room at the hospital, and told them what had happened. They cleaned him up and started to give him a number of anti-biotic shots which I could tell were not the most comfortable things for Brandon. We took him home, and the police came to the parsonage. They had the boys lead them to the park and the last place they saw the coon. The officer looked around the bushes and several old vehicles and decided that coon was nowhere in the vicinity. The police officer said that if the coon wasn't found and checked for rabies, Brandon would need the rabies vaccine shots. We took him back to the doctor the next day, and Doctor Fowler said that the shots would be administered, one every so many days. He also indicated that they were very expensive. I asked, "Can't we just wait and see if he starts avoiding water or froths at the mouth?" The doctor didn't think that that was funny and said, "No!" Still, I couldn't believe the amount of money they wanted for the shots; they're mighty proud of that stuff. Brandon got the last one on Christmas morning as we stopped by the hospital on our way to Grandma's for Christmas day festivities. Merry Christmas!

Brandon's illnesses and coon capers, Adams broken arm, Taylor's bike wreck and stitches, and his foot gash and more stitches, were all emergency room visits. Hospitals are very proud of their ER services and ask a hefty sum for their use. Still, you do what you have to do; every time. Whatever it is, we do whatever it takes. It might be a major or minor medical emergency, a life-threatening disease, a legal problem, game wardens, school issues, or a child that has disappeared by running away from home or being abducted. Parents will risk anything—do everything in their power, with all the energy they can muster and all the resources they have at their disposal, to achieve the best outcome in whatever situation they are facing.

The Apostle Paul must have been a sports fan as he used athletic examples such as, "the race," "I run," "I strain," for "the prize" as a competitive athlete would in the Roman stadium. Today, he would probably say, "No pain, no gain" or "Go for the burn." The goal for which we strive, which we have our eye fixed upon is life; life abundant, life eternal; and life, secure, stable, and healthy for our loved ones. To gain an idea of the extent we should be willing to go In terms of our Christian discipleship, Paul's words in Philippians 3:8 pretty well sum it up.

> *I consider everything a loss compared to the surpassing greatness of knowing Christ Jesus my Lord for whose sake I have lost all things press on to take hold of that for which Christ Jesus took hold of me... One thing I do: Forgetting what is behind and straining toward what is ahead, I press on toward the goal to win the prize for which God has called me heavenward in Christ Jesus.*

We will do whatever it takes when it's a spouse or child, but that should be the same when it comes to our relationship with Christ. This is the nature of commitment and of unconditional love; a characteristic which could cost a person everything. It cost God that much. John 3:16 affirms more clearly than any other verse:

> *For God so loved the world that he gave his only begotten Son, that whosoever believeth in him should not perish, but have everlasting life.*

That's one of those passages of Scripture you just can't quote in anything but King James; even if it's hanging on a bed sheet from a railing in the upper section of a stadium during a professional sporting event.

Mr. Wesley writes in his notes regarding this passage:

> *Yea and this was the very design of God's love in sending him into the world. 'God so loved the world'-That is, all men under heaven; even those that despise his love...For what should they believe? Ought they to believe that Christ was given for them? Then he was given for them. 'He gave his only Son'—truly and seriously. And the 'Son of God gave himself Galatians 1:4; truly and seriously.* [9]

There is perhaps the most poignant, paradoxically glorious Ebenezer for any of us; that most essential moment of divine assistance, the "Mount of Thy redeeming love" 'Calvary' and the cross upon which God did precisely what it took for every person in the death of God's Son, Jesus Christ-truly and seriously!

Reflection:

Where have you found yourself ready to do whatever was necessary for someone you love?

In what ways have you 'strained' to reach a goal, maintain a commitment, or save a life?

How does knowing God's level of commitment to you encourage your faith?

What could it mean from a spiritual nature to "consider everything a loss…?"

You Are Not Far from the Kingdom of God

For it is by Grace you have been saved, through faith, and this not from yourselves, it is the gift of God, not by works, so that no one can boast. For we are God's workmanship, created in Christ Jesus, to good works; which God prepared in advance for us to do. (Ephesians 2:8-10)

Student pastors don't know how good they can have it. People are pretty forgiving and caring of you when they know you are somewhere in the "process." From June 1979 to May 1982, I served The McColm's Chapel–Bentonville charge as a student pastor in the Portsmouth District of the West Ohio Conference, Adams County, rural, Ohio River country. This part of Ohio is actually the western edge of Appalachia. Most of the folks were either small tobacco and cattle farmers or worked at Dayton Power and Light, the largest coal fired generating plant in the world at that time. McColm's Chapel was high up on Ginger Ridge between Roush Hill Road and Lick Skillet. You could look out to the east and see the Ohio River below and the hills of Kentucky across the valley. Especially during the early fall season, few vistas anywhere could rival this little country church for beauty and serenity. The "city" church was in Bentonville, the junction of State Routes 41 and 136, better known as "whiskey road" because while Adam's County was dry, Manchester, an old river town, was wet. They said the reason those two roads got so much maintenance attention, was so folks could always get to Manchester to buy their whiskey. Back in the late '70s and early '80s, Bentonville had over a hundred people living there.

Work has never been a problem for me. People have always known I will work hard for an extra few bucks. When I was in the Agri-Business program at Cowley County Community College, our carpool met at the old Wagon Wheel Restaurant. Often when we would get back into town, there would be someone in a pickup, waiting to ask me if I would help them do something. When I got to Bentonville, I was still always ready to work for any of the folks to earn a few extra dollars, as gas had gotten up to the ridiculous price of $1.30 a gallon. I helped plant tobacco, haul tobacco, hang tobacco in tobacco barns, paint roofs with asbestos paint, mow, and fix fence. You name it, I tried it. I even helped Jim Naylor haul a drunk from the Adams County jail to Paducah, Kentucky once in a station wagon owned by the funeral home he worked for. One of the benefits of that little excursion was that Jim and I learned how to hold onto a drink while driving down the road without spilling a drop. It's all in the wrist.

Two of my favorite parishioners while I was there were Sherman and Ethel Beam. They lived about a mile from Bentonville, out Eagle Creek Road and up a long lane, in a grand two story house which well predated the Civil War and had been in Sherman's family for a number of generations. Ethel was the Sunday school teacher for the young adult class which was anybody under sixty-five. Sherman attended the men's class which was taught by Reverend Gill for men over sixty-five. Sherman and Ethel never missed Sunday school or church, so I thought it strange one day to hear Sherman say that he had never been baptized. Here he was, an eighty-year old man still on the church's cradle roll, or probationary membership we called it then.

Ethel called the parsonage one day to ask if I could come out and help Sherman do some repair work on the roof of their hog shed. I was happy to do so, because I knew that meant a world-class farm dinner, not lunch. I put on a pair of my overalls and headed out to Sherman's. Now he hadn't had a hog on the place for ten or fifteen years, but the wind was taking the metal roof off and instead of just tearing the old shed down, he figured it would be easier to make the repairs. I was up on the roof helping fix each sheet of roofing in its proper place and then drive nails into the rafters underneath. We took a little break and were sitting there on top of the hog shed, so I asked Sherman why he had never been baptized and joined the church. His response was quick. "I'm not good enough!" Now what in the world is he talking about? Where could he ever get an idea like that into his head? As I had come to know him, Sherman Beam was a person of impeccable moral character and integrity; honest, well respected, kind, and generous. "There are just some things in my life that aren't very good," he concluded. "Well, it's not about being good enough Sherman, it's about faith. You have faith don't you?" I asked. "Oh you bet" he responded in a micro second. "There are just some things I have to work on." Then the hammers started to drive nails, and we went on with our work until Ethel came out and called us in for dinner. I never brought the subject up again. It was getting near graduation and time to head back to Kansas and an appointment there.

Sherman passed away a couple of years later. When we were back in Ohio for a visit, we had a nice conversation with Ethel. She said that Sherman had Reverend Gill come out to the house, where he "led him to the Lord" and was baptized shortly before his death. It really made my heart glad to hear that. Still, how often do any of us struggle with the notion that we are not good enough for the mercy and grace of God, or that we have not worked hard enough to earn a place in God's Kingdom? We have left something undone or have sins that can only be forgiven by making up for it by our endless hard labor. For some of us, we trust in our good qualities, our moral standing, our being as good as other people, or at least no worse than other people. Mom used to say to me, "Why can't you be like the Helm boys? They're always polite and nice to their sister."

John Wesley's Sermon entitled, *The Almost Christian says*:
> *...being 'almost a Christian' is the having a form of godliness, of that godliness which is prescribed in the gospel of Christ. He then continues to describe the virtues possessed by the almost Christian; honesty, morality, integrity, sincerity, and a real inward principle of religion from whence these outward actions flow.*[10]

Another way to paraphrase Mr. Wesley's thoughts is "having the form but not the power." This really is labor; labor which pains and enslaves the soul, and makes kingdom work more drudgery than a labor of love. It's like the well known quote of St. Augustine:

"You have made us for yourself, O Lord, and our hearts are restless until they find rest in you."

There is no rest until we come to the awareness that it is not any of the above forms, but the mercy of God and the righteousness of Jesus Christ which gives us any hope of standing before God.

After our new church was built in 1966, the old building was given to the city to be used as a teen center. I went to my first school dance in the very room my parents were married in, my sisters and I were baptized in, and where my Granddad Hunt's service would be the very last funeral conducted before moving everything up to the new structure. Granddad was excited about the new church as we all were. He painted the old John Deere walking plow we used to dig potatoes a bright silver, took it into town one Sunday morning to the barren ground the new church would be built on and tied a long rope on it. When the congregation gathered for the groundbreaking ceremony, everyone grabbed onto the rope and pulled the plow making a furrow where the sidewalk would be placed from the parking to the front door. He watched it being built, but never got to worship in it. Now, that sacred room was a place where the only band we had in town, played the only song (or so it seemed) they knew over and over, and it wasn't "Holy, Holy, Holy;" but Iron Butterfly's "In-A-Gadda-Da-Vida."

I would literally have torturous, bittersweet dreams in the night in which we would be moving some pews and chairs back into the old sanctuary in order that we could have church there one last time. These dreams only dealt with the work part, they never quite made it to the actual worship. The demise of the building disturbed me greatly. When the decision was made to tear it down, I was really troubled.

One evening, while visiting with a neighbor, Danny Smith, a good Baptist and a man with a powerful testimony about the saving power of Jesus Christ, I was sharing my frustration about tearing the old church down. Danny said something to me that night I will never forget. "Kendal" he said, "You are looking for something in your life, and you think it is in that old building with all of its wonderful memories."

Danny paused for a moment and then continued, "It is not about a building. I think that what you are looking for will only be found in your relationship with Jesus Christ." Well, it took me a while to think through that, but when I realized what he was saying, it was the best spiritual advice I had received to that point. As I have reflected upon it, I think this conversation at a neighbor's home, over a cup of coffee, was most likely the first real communication God made to me in reference to my call into ministry. Danny and Carol Ann moved to Winfield, and when I started my first year at Southwestern, I lived with them and their family. I still have two items from that old church, a lamp made by Cline Clewell from one of the old balusters that supported the communion rail, and the lightning rod/weathervane which came off the steeple. Uncle Howard had retrieved it before the building was taken down, and Aunt Dorothy gave it to me after his passing.

Sherman, like so many, was never really very far from the Kingdom of God. He simply needed to quit trying so hard; give up on attempting to achieve his own understanding of goodness, and allow Jesus to be his righteousness. He had his Ebenezer, but it was a long time coming. The good news is we don't have to travel that far down the road of life in order to experience one. Understanding what laboring for the Kingdom really means, is to express one's faith in terms of Christian vocation, a Wesleyan understanding of discipleship. According to Paul Wesley Chilcote,

Christian vocation, then if it is to be true to the Wesleyan spirit, must be rooted in the transforming experience of God's grace manifest in Jesus Christ and realized through the power of the Holy Spirit. This is where our journey must begin. [11]

He then further defines this understanding of Christian vocation as first, a 'Gift', nothing we can hope to earn or create; rather an empowering of God. Secondly it is a 'Calling' not just to assent to a set of beliefs, but to follow Christ; not simply be a believer, but an active disciple. Thirdly, it is 'Community,' where it is all lived out in what I would take to mean, the community of the baptized, the church; the collective body of Christ in its various stages of development, where all are nurtured, and empowered to serve. So it's not about work at all; it's about being. This concept of discipleship should bring us into a deeper awareness of both our dependency upon, and freedom in Christ and humankind's liberation from the tyranny of works righteousness.

Reflection:

Are you working to presuppose faith, or does your faith give you opportunities for work?

Where do you see yourself allowing Christ to work out those things you can do nothing about?

How is the concept of Christian vocation being lived out in your everyday discipleship?

We Let the Holy Spirit Lead Here!

Quench not the Spirit. (1 Thessalonians 5:19)

In May 1979 I was ordained as a Deacon in the church at the Kansas West Annual Conference. Shortly after that, I was ready to move to Bentonville, Ohio and start my new life as a Student Pastor. To celebrate, a couple of friends took me to the old Chisholm Trail Drive-In Theatre at Wellington to see a movie. It just happened to be the original "Halloween" showing on the night before I was leaving. I had never seen anything so scary in my life, and now I was going to go live all by myself for the very first time, and was convinced I would probably get murdered by a knife wielding maniac, in this strange new town in Ohio. It would take me a couple of weeks before I would be comfortable turning the hall light out at night. When it became time for my first Sunday in the two pulpits I was excited, and McColm's Chapel being the outpost, it was first.

I have vivid remembrances of my introductory earlier in the spring with the District Superintendent, Reverend Donald Mumma, and the two Pastor Parish Relations (PPR) Committees. At some point in the introduction, a man from the McColm's Chapel Church looked at me with the straightest face and asked, "What Bible do you preach from?" Fortunately I had just been given a brand new Thompson Chain Reference King James Version Bible on the same night that I was given my first robe. Well I got the first question right. Then I was told that I would not wear a robe because they didn't want any Popery there. There would be Sunday Morning Service, Sunday Night Service, Wednesday Prayer Meeting at Bentonville, and Thursday Prayer Meeting at McColm's Chapel.

On that first Sunday, I was quite appropriately attired in my new three piece polyester suit with my new Thompson Chain Reference King James Version Bible. When I arrived at McColm's Chapel, I asked for a bulletin and was told, "We don't use bulletins. We let the Holy Spirit lead here!" So I figured I'd better try to play it by ear as best

I could. There was a prelude, and then I got up and introduced myself and welcomed everybody to the service. The song leader came up and asked for someone to pick a hymn which we sang and then another hymn which we sang. Then it was prayer time. They all came forward and knelt around the "altar" or communion rail. One of the men said, "Brother Utt, would you please lead us in prayer?" I responded in an authoritative voice, "I'd be very glad to." I bowed my head and said, "Dear Hev" and at that point they all began to pray; out loud, very loudly, all at once, at the same time. I was stunned to the point I'm pretty sure I stopped praying. The prayers increased in volume to a grand crescendo and then rapidly dropped off to some muffled 'amens' and 'thank you Lords.' It was my first experience with what they referred to as united prayer.

Following our prayer time together, it was testimony time. So I asked if anyone had a testimony. A number of folks stood up and shared what God had done for them during the past week. For some of them it was the same thing God had done for them last week and every week for the past forty years. Then it was time for the offering. The two Bailey boys came down and got the offering plates and walked down the aisle passing the plates. When the piano stopped playing the offertory music, I said, "Let us all stand and sing the Doxology." Well they all were standing; and staring at me. I looked at the pianist; she was looking back at me. I finally said, "Don't you sing the Doxology?" The pianist said, "No! We've never sung that one here before."

Well after that eternal moment, I read the Scripture lesson, which was the text for the sermon. Then there was the special music which was anyone who wanted to get up and sing a song either a cappella or to a guitar. Some of those well known songs were "The Gray Speckled Bird," "Dust on the Bible," "Forty Pieces of Silver," and "I Wouldn't Take Nothing for My Journey Now." This led into the sermon which I bravely delivered followed by an invitation for somebody to do something. After the closing prayer, I headed for my second round at Bentonville.

That evening was to be a welcome dinner at the church out on the

Ridge, and they all showed back up to give me proper welcome. Needless to say, we had a great relationship over the three years I was there. I remember helping them paint the church. On the north side, the peak of the roof was at its highest and no one would climb that high on the ladder. Billy, one of the men said, "Preacher, why don't you get up there and paint out that peak? If you were to fall off, you'd be more near ready to go than any of the rest of us." Well, I showed them; I went right up that ladder with a small bucket of paint and a brush and finished the painting.

I wouldn't take "nothing for my journey" there for anything; not a single minute of those years at McColm's Chapel or Bentonville. My last Sunday there I reminded the McColm's Chapel folks that my first Sunday when they told me, "We don't use a bulletin here, we let the Holy Spirit lead." And I said, "You know what? Every Sunday for the last three years, you have had a prelude, two hymns, united prayer around the altar, testimony time (with usually the same testimonies), the offering, scripture lesson, special music, sermon, a hymn of invitation and closing prayer. You could have just as well have had a bulletin!" And then, we sang the Doxology.

The one fact was they did not quench the spirit. Bulletin or no bulletin, country church or city church, piano or organ, they did let the Holy Spirit lead. If someone had something to say, they said it. If somebody got saved, they all knew it; if there was a sorrow or a victory, they all shared in it. If someone got blessed, they were all aware of it. One little old lady by the name of Gladys, would sometimes get "blessed" during a hymn or to someone's special number and all of a sudden you would see her shoes come flying off and out in the aisle she would go and dance in the Spirit and would usually end up with some type of testimony. She and her husband had a little farm down on the creek where we held Sunday afternoon baptism services. I also discovered that if they had a division, it would not last long; or at least not way too long.

At the end of my first summer there, the teachers of the Adams County School District went on strike. I could certainly understand it;

the district was way too big, the buildings were way too old and unmaintained, the textbooks were outdated, and the teachers were overworked and underpaid. The district had been formed when DP&L built the large power plant in the southwest corner of the county. Everyone wanted a piece of the tax revenue, so they just put the whole county into one big unwieldy organization. One of the leading teachers in the strike was a member of the Bentonville Church. They were a good family, in church every Sunday, active in the community, nice people. One of the leading parents opposed to the strike was in the Bentonville Church. They were a good family, in church every Sunday, active in the community, nice people. They were also very close friends; that is until the strike, which shut down the schools for a couple of months. The issue was so divisive, it affected families and friendships. These two friends had for all practical purposes stopped speaking, even at church. I didn't know what to do. I was clueless, as we hadn't studied strike ministry in seminary yet. But the Holy Spirit knew exactly what to do. One Sunday during the heat of the strike we observed World Communion Sunday during the regular worship service. I had them come to the communion rail. I had served a couple of tables and one of the last groups to come up had first, the woman who was part of the strike, she kneeled down and was in an attitude of prayer. The woman who was part of the opposition came up and looked around for an open place and finding only one, she knelt down right beside the other woman. The bread was passed, the cups were passed, the dismissal was given and the folks invited to rise and go in God's peace. The two women stood, looked at each other, and embraced with tears.

Bishop Mack B. Stokes writes in his book on <u>The Holy Spirit in the Wesleyan Heritage</u>:

From the Wesleyan emphasis on the Holy Spirit, we learn that the nature of the Spirit is to act purposively. The Spirit is headed somewhere and wants to take us along. Where? Toward inner holiness that leads to our outer holiness. The Holy Spirit is God's grace acting, moving, and stirring within us as the Will to Love. Hence, the Spirit brings the living Christ into our souls and fills us with his compassion and concern. [12]

There certainly was a 'purpose' of the Spirit moving the moment in God's direction. It was a Spirit led, Ebenezer moment.

Perhaps we would be better off if our church bulletins were of a more informative nature rather than a prescribed order of how things shall be in worship. Louise Turner was the director of music at the Pratt Church. She had held that position for well over twenty years before she retired in 2005. She and her husband Dick were about as faithful a couple as you could find anywhere. Dick had been an educator and later a school administrator. Louise was an excellent musician, and one thing the United Methodists of Pratt never wanted for, was really great music in their worship. There were times when there would be several musical specials and Louise, being a perfectionist, was a stickler for not having two numbers "back to back." "Maybe we could have one of the Scripture lessons here to split up these numbers," she would say. While I would usually accede for the sake of worship flow, my standard reply was always, "The purpose of the Word of God is not to separate two musical numbers!" I do like structure from a certain standpoint, but I also like it when God is spontaneous, and unprompted in worship. I have prayed many times in private as well as during the pastoral prayers before the congregation, "Please Lord, do something this morning that isn't printed in the bulletin!"

Reflection:

What Spirit led moments have you experienced in which you have been moved in a God direction?

Where have you seen or felt the Holy Spirit wanting to lead you?

Have you been reluctant to follow the leading of the Holy Spirit?

What defines or characterizes the leading of the Spirit to you?

In what ways have you seen or felt the Spirit quenched?

It's about Belief

I am the resurrection and the life. He who believes in me will live, even though he dies; and whoever lives and believes in me will never die. Do you believe this? (John 11:26)

During my student pastorate, I had a little neighbor girl who used to come over occasionally if I was out in the yard or walking over to the church. She and her family went to a Jesus Only, or Oneness Church. This particular religious group believes only in Jesus, and denies the doctrine of the Holy Trinity, and they are pretty clear about that. In Bentonville, there is The Burning Heart Campground. It belongs to a local association of Holiness Churches and once a year they hold Camp Meeting. Our Bentonville Church would let out prayer meeting and attend at least one evening service in the Tabernacle. On that particular evening, the singing was going on and on and I noticed a man down in the front center of the room that was really getting into the music, raising his hands high into the air. The evangelist finally took his place in the pulpit and said, "I have been asked to speak to the issue of Baptism prior to my sermon tonight. When we baptize people it is to be according to the teachings of the scriptures in the name of the Father, the Son, and the Holy Ghost." At that, the man sitting in the front stood up and pointed at the evangelist and screamed, "It is only in the name of Jesus that man is to be baptized!" The preacher said, "Sir, you are out of order." With that, the man grabbed his wife and kids and walked out of the tabernacle. Well, needless to say, I had never seen or heard anything like this in my entire life. As I later found out, this man was a Jesus Only preacher and the evangelist obviously knew it, or had been informed of it, so they both provoked each other on doctrine and belief to the discomfort of everyone else present.

Getting back to the little neighbor girl, she just loved to talk. Any conversation with her would eventually end in a dialogue that went pretty close to the following. "Do you believe in dancing?" she asked. "Well I am not a dancer, but I know lots of people who enjoy going dancing, so I guess it's okay if you want to." "We don't believe in dancing," she said. "Do you believe women should wear pants?" "Well, I suppose if that is what a person wants to wear then I guess it is okay." "We don't believe women should wear pants, only dresses or skirts." "Do you believe women should cut their hair?" On and on the questions would go. I remember thinking it odd that most of the questions seemed to deal with what women couldn't do. Didn't they have any prohibitions for the men? By the time they moved away, I knew everything the little girl didn't believe in, but virtually nothing she did believe. The world often has that view of the church in general. They think they know what it is we don't believe in, but really have no clue about what we do believe. For many of us, it is seemingly easier to describe what it is we don't believe as it is the things we do believe. Perhaps it's because most people find it easier to defend disbelief as opposed to witness to the genuine character of the Christian faith. I don't think we all need to be apologists in our expertise, but being able to share what we believe in should come more natural than it often does.

In 1951, Edward R. Murrow, the great radio and early television reporter, introduced a radio program for CBS entitled, "This I Believe" which was to be a forum for persons from every aspect of life in America to share the things they believe in. It ran for several years and is now a project of This I Believe Inc. It still offers people across the broadest spectrum of thought, an opportunity to share just what it is they believe. In that first introduction by Mr. Murrow, he shares the following comment.

> *This reporter's beliefs are in a state of flux. It would be easier to enumerate the items I do not believe in, than the other way around. And yet in talking to people, in listening to them, I have come to realize that I don't have a monopoly on the world's problems. Others have their share, often far bigger than mine. This has helped me to see my own in truer perspective: and in learning how others have faced their problems, this has given me fresh ideas about how to tackle mine.* [13]

In the Lazarus Narrative in John's Gospel, Martha and Mary are confronted with one of life's traumatic experiences; the death, seemingly untimely, of a close loved one. For Martha, the question of faith is quite direct, as it is asked by Jesus himself. It's a question which asks for a direct yes or no. Don't dance around with what you don't believe, but affirm what it is you do believe and then act upon it; as Martha did when she left Jesus to go get her sister and bring her to the grave of Lazarus.

In the fall of 2000, my Father, who while overweight, was in extremely good health and really tried to take good care of himself. Following some tests, the doctor discovered he had a malignancy on one of his kidneys. He was scheduled to have that kidney removed on October 6. While I couldn't make it in time to see him prior to his surgery, I was there for the long wait with mom, my sisters, Uncle Doyle and the preacher. It became obvious later, that something went terribly wrong during that surgery: or as old Doc Freeman from Pratt said, "somebody let a major artery get away from them." as he was given an inordinate number of pints of blood. I went back to the hospital on the following Monday, and was told that Dad was not doing very well, but he was responding to our conversations and knew we were there. He would later lapse into a brain dead state and linger for the rest of the month of October. On a Sunday, the day before he died, my mother, sister and I gathered beside his bed for a little family service. I didn't have a fancy oil pix, so I washed out a small lip balm container and placed some olive oil in it. We were in a hospital room with a dying man so there really wasn't any point in going fancy anyway. I used the oil to anoint my father, prayed for his total and perfect healing, and offered him up to the keeping of the Almighty God. Early the next morning, Mom could hear the fluid building up in his breathing and said, "We should call the nurse to come in and get the fluid off of him." I just happened to be at his side and noticed the he was making what I call 'the death grimace' and I said, "I don't think that will be necessary Mother." She too came along side Dad, put her hand on his, and he died. No! He lived!

Gwendoline Sanders, one of the unique personalities that made Belle Plaine so colorful was a local author of books and poetry. I am fortunate to have an autographed copy of her book of poems, <u>Until the Day Breathes and These Enchanted Ones</u>. Her poem, "The Lord and Will", has comforted me at times and rang certainly true in regards to Dad's passing.

And the Lord walked in the dew-drenched coolness of the early morning and saw a kindly lad wondering beside a brooklet peopled with sun-fish,

The Lord placed his arm around the lad's thin shoulders. 'Walk with me Will, in the gentleness of thy childhood, walk beside me.'

The years blossomed and some fruits borne were sweet beyond telling while others were as bitter as gall.

Some of the loads he found to be light and joyous, others grievous to bear.

Again the Lord laid His hand of Will's shoulder.

'I shall walk with thee, Will, I shall walk with thee.'

The whispered cadence of the marching years mingled with life's lengthening shadows. At the close of a summer's day the Lord saw Will, his white hair damp upon his pillow.

Taking Will's hand into His own, the Lord said, 'See yonder fair land? It is time for us to go. We shall walk together, Will, we shall walk together. [14]

Still we could not believe what transpired over the last few weeks. I realize there are no guarantees when it comes to surgery, BUT! The questions which had been running in our minds became more vocal as we wanted to know what had happened to Dad. What went wrong? Who was the careless hospital employee or doctor who had dropped the ball on my father? I would have liked to have met that person for just a few moments. Who was responsible? How could this have happened? The questions could have gone on forever. For some, those questions can become an entrapment that energizes all of the negativity and supplants any vital, healthful moving on. Fortunately as a family, we decided to not tarry long in the realm of questions and the unknown particulars surrounding Dad's death. After all, we do not "grieve like those who have no hope." (I Thessalonians 4: 13) We were able to place it into a context of what we did know, and that is intrinsically tied closely to what we believe. Our loved one was a good Christian man whose journey of life ended way before any of us thought it should have. Our faith told us where, and with whom he journeyed now, so in answer to the question of Jesus, "Do you believe this?" We could say, "Yes Lord! You are the resurrection and the life." Anyone who finds themselves plagued by such questions needs to set them aside, at least for a season, and dwell upon those things they know, and can affirm.

My only regret in the whole thing is that on that first Monday following Dad's surgery, as I was ready to leave and head home, I walked up to his bedside. His eyes were momentarily focused on me. I reached through all of the tubes and wires as carefully as I could so as to not cause him any further discomfort, took him by the hand and said, "Dad I'm going home now, I'll see you later. Bye bye." He looked at me, and though encumbered by the respirator tube down his throat, he mouthed "Bye bye." I think those might have been his last words. I have scolded myself many times by my thinking that I should have said to him, "Dad, I love you." Why I didn't, I'll never know, but the one thing I do know is that there had never been any question about that fact on either of our parts.

Reflection:

What have been those times where there was no doubt about what you believed?

How did that belief sustain you?

What are the ways you publicly affirm your beliefs?

Truth and Consequences

The Lord detests lying lips, but he delights in men who are truthful. (Proverbs 12:22)

Dad had an old 1949 Dodge pickup. It had a flathead-six-cylinder engine, a four-speed transmission, and could get up to about 60 MPH but Dad never liked it to go over 40. This is what I learned to drive in. Mom would let me drive it to Henry Stunkel's to get milk and to Mrs. Lawless' to get eggs. You had to double clutch it usually to keep the gears from grinding. It also had some stout grain sides around the bed. At fourteen, after driver's education, I was able to drive it to school and home if Mom or Dad didn't need it.

About the middle of October 1970, while sitting in study hall (the school library up on the second floor), several of us started to make our Halloween plans. Now there were several years during the 70s when Halloween was pretty wild and even destructive. Our idea was not so much to be destructive as it was just messy. My great-Uncle Sam and great-Aunt Gertrude Barner had a large farm four miles east of town on the Arkansas River (that's pronounced ArrrKansas). Aunt Gertrude was Granddad Hunt's sister. She and Sam had one son, Max, who was killed on a bombing mission during World War II. Aunt Gertrude always had a distant look in her eyes as if she was still waiting for Max to come home. On many Saturday's in the fall and winter, Uncle Sam would have me come out and help scoop ear corn out of a large crib into a feed grinder. Uncle Sam had two old broken down hired hands, Earl and Barney. Barney and I were scooping corn and took a short break to catch our breath. Barney looked at me and said, "Kendal, do you ever take any of this dope?" referring probably to marijuana or other drugs. I said, "No Barney, I never have." "That's good," he replied and then gave me this advice. "That stuff will kill you, boy. If you want to get high, what you need is a good fifth of whiskey." One November Saturday, shortly after the celebration of my nativity on the tenth, we were in the house eating dinner. Aunt Gertrude handed me a birthday card; the only one I ever received from her. On the inside she wrote, "I'm sorry that I don't remember many birthdays, especially yours, as it's the day after I lost Max." I always thought this was a poignant commentary on the high price this nation's Gold-Star Mothers and Fathers have been asked to pay for our freedom, including the planning of Halloween pranks.

Every year they had a huge watermelon patch somewhere in the middle of one of the corn fields. Many a Saturday, I earned a few bucks helping to pick watermelons. Uncle Sam would sell them for up to $1.50 apiece. By the end of October, frost or hard freeze had taken care of all the watermelons, so they were just sitting out there in the field rotting. Our great Halloween plan was to sneak out to the patch and load up a truckload of old watermelons, and bring them back into town to, shall we say, distribute them in appropriate locations. I would plan on spending the night at Grandma Hunt's in town, that way I would be able to have the pickup. Grandma wouldn't know that I was not supposed to drive it after 7:00 p.m., so we would be clear there. I would tell her I was going to the Halloween movie at the theatre so I would need to drive there. We would then go get the watermelons. Our route was to go one mile south of town then go east and back north to the melon patch. This way we didn't have to go by our house or Uncle Sam's. This plan was absolutely fool proof.

Halloween night finally arrived. I drove into Grandma's. Later I headed for the show. I was waiting for everyone to gather. What I hadn't counted on was so many others wanting to go. There would wind up being nine of us all together. There were four of us in the front and five in the back of the pickup. As we headed south out of town, the boys in the back were all standing up, yelling, laughing and generally having a good time. We turned off the blacktop onto the gravel road that would take us back east. There was a little curve in the road because of a drainage ditch that emptied into the mighty Euphrates Creek. As we began to enter the curve, something unexpected happened. The pickup didn't follow the curve. It went straight, up over the grader ridge and flipped over and slid the twelve feet to the bottom of the ditch. I had never before experienced anything in slow motion. The horror of that pickup turning upside down and sliding down that ditch lasted for an eternity. There was only one window we could get out and trying to get four scared, tangled, and upside down kids out one small side window was interesting. We crawled up the steep side of the ditch along with the guys from the back. One by one we were all accounted for. I asked if everyone was alright, and they all seemed to indicate they were.

"Okay!" I said, "We needed a new plan." Here is what we came up with. The guys who were in the back would walk back into town and pretend that nothing happened. The four of us in the front would walk to my cousin Kerry's (who was part of the front seat crowd) about three miles down the road and get a couple of tractors and drive them back, pull the truck out of the ditch, and drive or tow it into town. Then we would say that members of the SDS, (that's Students for a Democratic Society) from Wichita came down and beat the truck up. We headed down the road and probably walked no more than several hundred yards when I stopped. I said, "We can't do this!" I told the other guys, "We just need to go into town to the police station and tell the truth." Everyone agreed, and that is what we did. After all, how could any of us explain why the SDS would come down to Belle Plaine on a Halloween night, single out a '49 Dodge pickup in front of the theatre at the main intersection of town, and beat it up?

Our police station was a very small set of rooms behind the city building and next to the two-cell jail. The outer room was where the radio was and the inner room was where the hardened criminals would be questioned and the judge would hold court, and where the police would relax. Now the jail hadn't been used for as long as I could remember, but I could see it being put to use that night. I told whoever was in there what had happened and I needed to call my dad. They handed me the phone and I made the call. Mom and Dad had their good friends Benny and Mary Ruth Howe out playing cards. When Mom answered and I asked to speak to Dad, I could hear Benny say in the background, "He's probably at the police station." Well, that certainly didn't give me additional confidence as I said, "Dad, we had an accident in the pickup and you need to come into the police station." While we were waiting for Dad, Morris Cox, (better known as Old Cigar Butt) the local deputy sheriff was called in. He ordered all of the persons who were in the accident to get back to the station. So one of the boys headed over to the show and got the other five. Dad showed up while Morris was taking names. He stood in the corner, leaning against the wall and was sort of whistling. He looked at me and asked calmly, "Whose pickup were you in Kendal?" Oh no! I thought, hadn't I made myself clear on the phone? He didn't understand. This was not good! "Yours," was the only possible answer I could give to that incriminating question except for taking the Fifth. At that point the whistling stopped, posture changed, and any resemblance of calm was gone.

Morris and Dad drove out to the wreck site. We had to stay in the police station. They were back in about a half hour. Morris sat down behind the desk, grabbed a pen and a notebook and said, "Alright, I am ready for the injury report." No one said anything. He then said, "Now Mr. Utt and I have been out there and looked at that pickup. It is sitting at the bottom of the ditch on its top. There has got to be some injuries." Still nobody said anything. Sensing Morris' growing exasperation Thorne, one of the boys, finally spoke up and said, "I think I corked my little finger." Well that was all Morris could take; the yelling started. We were all sent home. Dad got old Wild Bill Oakley to take his WWII winch truck out and drag the pickup out of the ditch, and set it upright. They brought it out to the house. It had a big dent in the roof of the cab, a single crack in one of the windshields, a crack in one of the grain sides, and a little oil here and there. The pickup fared a lot better than I did. It's amazing that I didn't forget how to drive during the weeks that followed.

There is a real interesting thing about that group of boys. Out of the nine, four became preachers of some form or another; one in the

Church of Christ, two Southern Baptists, (one of those being my cousin Kerry) and me, the United Methodist. Several of the guys shared later that while they had all been standing up, when we turned the corner, just yards before the accident, they all suddenly sat down. When the truck rolled over and slid down the bank of the ditch, they said there seemed to be a force, like a hand holding them down (or up in this case). Anyway you look at it, it was an act of God that except for a corked finger, there was no one seriously injured. Had we not had the conviction to go and tell the truth, and receive the consequences for our Halloween Night's plan gone bad, where might any of us be now? Oh! There was one victim in that accident. It seems that when the truck came to rest at the bottom of the ditch, the cab landed on and killed a possum.

For eighth grade graduation, our local dentist, Dr. Helm and his wife Nancy (and yes, they are the parents of the Helm boys mom always wanted me to emulate), gave me a book entitled, "Security from Above" by Charles H. Schmitz. This little book has been a real treasure to me over the years as it contains so much wisdom for living. I use a few passages from it when I address graduating seniors. There is a little section called "Truth" which quotes Pilate's question, "What is truth?" from John 18:38. Mr. Schmitz says,

You do not possess truth. Truth possesses you...Let not truth become a conversation piece. Do not make an ornament of it. Truth is a subject for life rather than talk...Let truth lead you through the wilderness of your confusions to the promised land. [15]

It's not truth or consequences anymore than it is 'trick or treat,' but rather truth and consequences. Telling the truth, you know that which Pilate couldn't understand in his infamous question, is what put Jesus on the Cross. Mr. Wesley comments on this verse by writing,

What signifies truth? Is that a thing worth hazarding your life for? [16]

Speaking the truth does hazard one's life. Truth is what cost people like Bonheoffer, Gandhi, Martin Luther King Jr., Anwar Sadat, and many others their lives. I'm still learning that the truth and the consequences that might result from it are always better than the false and the eventual consequences which will accompany it. Those moments in which even the truth brings consequences, are Ebenezer Moments.

Reflection:

Is honesty always the best policy?

In what ways have you risked consequences for speaking or telling the truth?

What might hinder you?

Worse Sinners

Now there were some present at that time who told Jesus about the Galileans whose blood Pilate had mixed with their sacrifices. Jesus answered; do you think that these Galileans were worse sinners that all the other Galileans because they suffered this way? I tell you, no! But unless you repent, you too will all perish. Or those eighteen who died when the tower in Siloam fell on them, do you think they were guiltier than all the others living in Jerusalem? I tell you, no! But unless you repent, you too will all perish. (Luke 13: 4-5)

For years, while my grandparent's generation was still alive, we used to have huge family reunions. The Utt's were usually held at Island Park in Winfield, where there were ample attractions for kids to play on and thus stay out of trouble. The Hunts always held theirs in Belle Plaine at the city building as it had a large room adequate for such events, but no playground, just the sidewalk and street. There was quite a group of us cousins who after having eaten, needed some place to work off energy. Behind the city building was of course the police station, then the old two-cell jail, then there was a tall tower, like an old windmill tower, that held the fire whistle which blew one long blast for town fires and two for rural fires, plus the noon whistle which blew every day. Just below that, was the old fire bell, a double clapper bell which in earlier times was the signal for responding to a fire. It is now located at the football field and rung when the home team makes a touchdown; I think.

It was always a fun thing to climb up there and give the old bell a ring and then climb down before anyone could catch you. One Halloween night, we tied some fishing line to the clapper and strung it out across the street into Bertie Bradley's yard. We would tug on the line and ring the bell, and then wait for an officer to come out and wonder where the little ringers had gotten off to. My mother's admonition was always to stay off the tower. There were never any police at the station on Sundays, so the coast was clear there. Several of us began the climb up the vine infested tower to reach for the bell. Well one of us got there first and began to ring it. We all started laughing and began the climb back down. Something happened; I think some vines gave way, which caused several of us to fall to the ground. Someone ran in where the adults were sitting around visiting and said some of the kids had fallen off the bell tower. Here came the parade of mothers. Danny's mother picked him up and said, "Danny, are you all right?" Kerry's mother looked at him and asked if he was hurt. Bryan's mom said, "Are you okay Bryan?" My mother grabbed me by the arm with one hand, and with the other hand said loudly, "I told you 'whap' not to climb 'whap' on that tower 'whap'. Where was the sympathy? Where was the concern? Was I somehow guiltier than the rest of them? Was I at least not worthy of mercy? I can't answer for them, all I know is it was one of those repent moments for me.

There was another prohibition. All of the boys in the neighborhood loved to play down at the railroad bridge that crossed the mighty Euphrates creek. Since the train usually only came in at night to switch the alfalfa mill and the elevator, there was never any concern about trains. Another place of interest was the big terminal elevator just east of the bridge. It was a large concrete grain storage facility that had any number of places a kid could get seriously hurt, hence the prohibition on playing around there. The problem was that it was right in the way of the best short cut to several of my friend's homes and needed to be approached regardless.

One really nice fall Friday after school, several of us from the south end of town walked home and somehow wound up at the elevator. We messed around there for a while having a good time. Wheat was still being loaded out in forty-foot boxcars as this was prior to the general use of covered hopper cars. The railroad had set out a string of empties for the elevator to fill at some point in the next few days. The doors to a few of these boxcars were open so we climbed in and played in there for a while. In one corner was a little pile of wheat which hadn't gotten cleaned out. We started to eat it. Now wheat will make a really nice, but totally tasteless chewing gum if you chew on it long enough.

So we did. When I finally got home, Mom asked where I had been. "Oh, just playing" I answered. She asked, "Where?" Oh just around the neighborhood," I replied. "Where around the neighborhood?" She just couldn't leave it alone. "You weren't down at the elevator were you?" "Well just for a little bit," I confessed. "We saw some wheat in a box car and ate some. That's all we did!" I thought I was going to really get it now. To my surprise, she didn't seem to be mad or upset. All she had to say was, "It was probably treated wheat." Oh no! I thought to myself as one of those pit of the stomach feelings started welling up. I was old enough to know that treated wheat, in preparation for sowing, was quite poisonous. I wasn't old enough to know that they would not allow treated wheat anywhere near a grain storage elevator. I now knew that I was probably going to die.

It just so happened that the church youth group was going to Winfield that night for a skating party. Mom helped sponsor the youth group at that time so I was going along. I still wasn't a good skater, but I had been looking forward to this for several weeks. But this skating party would be different. I went, I put on my rented skates, I got out there on the floor holding onto the rail along the side, and wondered to myself how long will it take before I start getting sick? I wonder if it will be painful. I hope I don't flop around on the floor in front of everybody. Well needless to say I didn't die; I didn't get sick or flop around on the floor. However, I did not enjoy myself that night pondering the fact that if I had just been obedient I would not have been in that state of mind. Another repent moment had just occurred for me.

I have learned over the years that I am in pretty good company as "All (emphasis on the all,) have sinned and fallen short of the glory of God." (Romans 3:23) However, it is no one else's responsibility, and we cannot justify ourselves by the actions of anyone else regardless of who started to climb the tower first. Repentance isn't just for special sinners or the worse sinners; and it's not just for getting forgiven for the really bad stuff we do, those great sins that can lead us to the mourner's bench; or even worse, prison, or a stomach pump; but often it is just simple course corrections in the direction our life may be heading. Anyone who rides with me knows I need many course corrections, and they are not speaking in geographical terms. While taking Taylor to school in the mornings I hear him comment, "Dad, put your seat belt on. Dad, turn your turn signal on. Dad, you don't have say that every time you see a police car. Dad, it's just a stoplight. Dad, roll your window up if you're going to say things like that." While he is annoying, being corrected by someone who should be learning from me can be potent points along with other corrective measures which have been most helpful over the years. God brings things to light for us to work on and hopefully we work on them. Repentance for a Christian could really be viewed as a continual power steering mechanism in our daily discipleship.

> John Wesley writes in his sermon, *The Repentance of Believers*: *It is generally supposed that repentance and faith are only the gate of religion; that they are necessary only at the beginning of our Christian course…But notwithstanding this, there is also a repentance and a faith which are requisite after we have 'believed the Gospel', yea, and in every subsequent stage of our Christian course, or we cannot 'run the race which is set before us'. And this repentance and faith are full as necessary, in order to our continuance and growth in grace, as the former faith and repentance were in order to our entering into the kingdom of God.* [17]

Dealing with repentance and faith moments is a lot better than a public flogging or living in fear of imminent death by poisoned wheat; and we will be much farther down the road of our Christian journey because of it.

Reflection:

Where do you see repentance to be a helpful means in steering your life in positive, God centered directions?

In what ways have you known repentance as powerful 180-degree life-changing events?

You're Really Going to Love the Garage

We are hard pressed on every side, but not crushed; perplexed, but not in despair; persecuted, but not abandoned; struck down, but not destroyed. (II Corinthians 4:8-9)

There are very few persons in the country who do not recognize the name of Greensburg, Kansas as the county seat town in Kiowa County, Kansas that was destroyed by an F5 tornado on the evening of May 4, 2007. It has been the subject of several documentaries and is famous for trying to rebuild as a "green" community. But there is one piece of that story which never made it on the Weather Channel or Discovery Channel.

During my first appointive season as Dodge City District Superintendent, our pastor at Greensburg wanted to move to the Kansas East Conference in order to get closer to some family. When the question was asked about who might follow him there, my suggestion was Terry Mayhew, who I had worked with on the Jewell County Parish a number of years ago, and who was already serving a charge in my district. When we had the current pastor "in" at what would be his new appointment beginning July first, I called Terry and asked him about moving to Greensburg. I don't think he was too happy with my call, but he listened closely as I described the church and community. His initial response was, "I don't want to move." He added that "Mary has a broken ankle and packing and moving would not be good for her." Then came the Coup de Gracie, "Besides, our daughter is getting married in late August in the church here, and I am doing the wedding, and we have a lot of family coming in for that." He concluded by saying, "BUUUUT I'll talk it over with Mary and get back to you." Well he called back a day or so later and said they really weren't eager to move but that if they could stay where they were until after the wedding and begin their new appointment September first, two full months past the conference start date, they would move. "Remember, I have a lot of wood working equipment, so I need a big garage," he said conditionally. I was excited and said, "I will go over and visit with the Pastor Parish Relations (PPR) Committee and work it out." I called Dennis McKinney, a local farmer, and at that time Minority Leader of the State House of Representatives, who was the PPR Chair; told him I wanted to visit about the appointment and set up a meeting at his home with a few other committee members.

On Friday, May 4, 2007, I drove into Greensburg Kansas. I was a little early so I drove around for a few minutes and remember admiring the clean, neat streets and homes. At 2:00 p.m. I went to the McKinney home and the few of us discussed their getting a new pastor. I told them I had a person in mind but that he really needed to stay where he was until the end of August. "So what do you think of a September 1 start date for your new pastor?" I asked. As they discussed it, they were mindful of several things. "It will help our financial situation as we won't be paying a full salary and benefits for a few months." We have a couple of lay speakers in the area who would be glad to fill the pulpit." And then there was one more significant comment; "This will give us time to freshen up the parsonage a little; we just took down a large old tree that might have blown over onto the garage." I asked about the garage and they said well it's a detached garage (it and the parsonage were probably at least eighty years old), but it is big enough you can actually have room for three vehicles. There is plenty of room in it, and it has a nice concrete floor." Anyway, they all seemed to welcome the idea of a postponed appointment.

Now just prior to this meeting, I called the person we were thinking about taking Terry's place on the Plains-Kismet Charge. He was a pastor wanting to move to Western Kansas as that was where his wife's family was from. He was currently serving as an associate at the Bixby United Methodist Church in the suburban Tulsa area. I told him about the situation and asked what a September start date would do to him. He was definitely ecstatic. "That would work out just perfect and give me time to sell the house, and finish up some things here in Tulsa," he said in one of those Praise the Lord voices. Again, things are falling into place I thought, congratulating myself. I'm getting this DS thing down pretty good. As I drove out of Greensburg following the meeting, I noticed one of those storm chaser trucks with the Doppler radar thing on top sitting at the convenience store. "Somebody must think it's going to storm somewhere today" I said to myself. I headed for Dodge and home.

Now Joyce was getting ready for work. At that time she was still working at the Daylight Doughnut Shop in Pratt, about seventy five miles east of Dodge. To get there on US 54, you went right through Greensburg. They started to have some weather announcements on the television. Soon there were reports of strong thunderstorms in Comanche County. Then came the T word. She needed to be at work around 10:00 p.m. It usually took her about an hour and fifteen minutes to get there. Today however, she planned to leave a little early and drop off our son Brandon at a friend's house before going to the doughnut shop. She said, "Brandon, hurry up and let's go so we will be ahead of that storm." The reports only got worse and she asked me if I thought she should go. My response, having lived my life in Kansas and being around a couple of tornadoes, was, "Sure. Just watch out for limbs that might have blown onto the highway." They left for Pratt.

I decided to call Terry and Mary about the meeting earlier at Greensburg. He answered the phone and I said, "Terry, I went over to Greensburg this afternoon and met with several members of the PPR Committee about letting you stay at Plains and Kismet until September 1. They didn't think it would be a problem at all. The person who will be following you was really excited about staying where he is currently until a September 1 start date." At that moment I was thinking how wonderfully everything seemed to be falling into place when I remembered the piece about the garage and said, "Oh, and by the way, you'll really love the garage! It will have plenty of room for both your vehicles and all of your equipment and tools." He sounded like he was more comfortable with the whole thing. He would call me back after talking it all over again with Mary. What I didn't realize during that conversation was that it was probably the moment that the garage was being blown into Edwards County along with the parsonage, the church and almost all of Greensburg.

Greensburg UM Parsonage May 7, 2007
taken from the cement slab where the garage once stood

I became fixed to the television and listened to the reports. They just kept becoming direr all the time. Joyce called on her cell phone and said she was in a long line of cars and trucks just east of Mullinville. She could see emergency lights and lots of emergency vehicles were passing them heading for Greensburg. I told her to turn around and come home. She would not get through for quite a while. I was thankful that my ill-conceived advice had not gotten her and Brandon in any more of a situation than just a long wait in traffic. Of course, had Brandon not been dillydallying around like he usually does, they could have gotten a quicker start for Pratt, and probably been right there in the middle of that tragedy.

"What have you gotten me into?" was the first words I heard on the phone early Saturday morning, as Terry called. "I don't know yet, but it's pretty bad," I said. "Well, Mary and I talked last night, and then we talked some more again this morning. I guess the Lord knows what He's doing, we'll go!" Terry said in a cautious voice. Wow, now there's a step of faith I thought. A preacher who is willing to move from a pleasant community and a really great parsonage, to a new appointment without a church, a parsonage, or a town, and a congregation scattered to the..., well around several places. I tried to call Gene McIntosh, the current pastor there to check on him, I got him on his cell phone because he was in Hutchinson with in-laws. They were all okay and made it to the basement in time. The parsonage was pretty much destroyed. I tried to call Mr. McKinney several times and was finally able to get him on his cell phone only because they had gone down south to his parent's home after riding out the storm in their basement. One of the things he said to me was, "You're the last person to be in our home; it's gone." They were safe however.

No one but emergency personnel was allowed into town Saturday or Sunday. They said people with homes or business there could come in on Monday. Well I got Joyce, my Red Cross card, my district superintendent name badge, and my United Methodist Disaster Relief magnetic sign placed on the door of the district car and headed for Greensburg. As we made our way to the church, what I had taken in with appreciation on Friday, made me nauseous, literally sick to my stomach. After slowly meandering around debris we made it to the church. It was destroyed. The roof was gone over the sanctuary, the parlor, and the education wing. Now I had been told by our conference communications director, to "take your district camera with you and get some pictures of the church and stuff." I started taking photos of the damage; a church missing its roof and much of the stone and concrete blocks, and twisted steel I beams. Clutter was everywhere. I slowly and carefully made my way through the ruined building until I arrived at the now roofless parlor; tables, chairs, lamps, and books jumbled into a heap. Then with the full brilliance of the sun shining on the north wall, was hanging unmolested, a picture of Jesus. It had remained unmoved and unscathed during the violent tempest swirling around it.

Three days earlier the hand of God, which was undoubtedly busy protecting so many hundreds of people, held that picture in its place; a sign that our God isn't going anywhere. That is probably the best picture I will ever take.

Jesus Christ, the same yesterday, today and forever; and on the night of May 4, 2007

I ran into Ken Walker, our pastor from the Havilland and Garfield Churches who was there as part of the County Ministerial Alliance with an orange and green vest on. I said, "I can't find the parsonage. There isn't anything familiar to go by." It is strange how familiarity can quickly disappear following an EF 5 tornado or a category 5 Katrina. "I can get you there! I've already been up there once today," he replied. He got into the car and we finally made it through the debris. Gene and his wife and son were there looking through things. Gene grabbed me and we embraced for a long time. He showed me where they rode out the tornado. Its effects were pretty damaging even in the basement where they had gone. On the east side of the house, they had spray painted a verse of Scripture from II Corinthians 4:9 "We are struck down but not destroyed." Through it all, those words seemed to emulate the good people of the Greensburg Churches as well as the community in general. As it turned out, Gene and his family stayed on for several weeks to give some continuity and the folks at his new appointment in the east conference were quite willing and understanding to let him do that. Through it all I got to shake hands and pray with President George W. Bush along with the members of the Kiowa County Ministerial Alliance. Terry and Mary got moved to Greensburg right after the wedding. Their first parsonage was a very small, one bedroom house which was on the extreme eastern side of town where what few structures that survived were located. I'm not sure where Terry stored his woodworking tools, since there was no garage.

As I continue to reflect on those days, the events leading up to, during, and following, one thing I am sure of; whatever was well and good, and working at the Greensburg Church was not because I had this DS thing down, far from it, but rather it was because God was there the whole time. There were a lot of people in Kiowa and Edwards Counties who were able to raise some pretty amazing Ebenezers; like those words of Paul painted on what was left of the side of a parsonage.

Reflection:

When particular events in your life could be described as disruptive?

Where has the 'Hand of God' been seen working on your behalf in such events?

Is there a way in which this could be true in some of the events leading up to them?

It's All in Who You Know, NOT!

Jesus I know, and I know about Paul, but who are you? (Acts 19:15)

Those words of demonic verification are about to bring some unwitting and ill prepared disciples into a unique confrontation with a force they don't understand, and are not equipped to withstand. In those first few, confusing, horrifying moments following the F5 tornado that blew Greensburg off the map, emergency personnel from surrounding counties began arriving to give what aid and comfort they could. This began one of the largest rescue and recovery efforts in the history of the state of Kansas. As I said, I had been in Greensburg earlier in the day on May 4. I would not be allowed back in until Monday, May 7. Even then, it took me having my Red Cross ID, my district superintendent badge, a large magnetic United Methodist Disaster Relief sign on the driver's side of the car, and a lot of luck. Joyce went with me that first day they were allowing any non-emergency persons back into town. We waited in a long line of anxious residents ready or not to get their first daytime look at what was left of their homes. When I got to the first road block, I told them who I was and what my business in going on was. They said they didn't know if they would let us through the second road block but we could try. After another long creeping wait we made it to two Kansas National Guardsmen who were checking each vehicle. He saw the magnetic sign and I showed him my credentials. He said, "Sir, what is your destination in town?" "I'm going to the United Methodist Church" I answered. He took a yellow crayon type marker and wrote on the passenger side of the windshield the words "Methodist Church" and motioned us through.

The next day, I went to Haviland and picked up Bishop Jones, Lisa Diehl the Conference Communications Director, who had her camera to take some video. With all of my ID, and the yellow crayon markings, we got in again and spent time at the church where the Bishop shared some words with the pastor, Reverend McIntosh, for a video to show to the Churches of Kansas in responding with aid for the community.

Bishop Scott Jones in front of the destroyed United Methodist Church

Each day that I went in, the person at the check point was giving out some new type of ID; a red ribbon on the antenna, a piece of yellow tape stuck to the left side of the windshield. They had all become a part of my car in that first month. There were several times people sought me out because I was the District Superintendent and the highest authority (which is scary) for the Methodists in the area. When Alltel needed to set up an antenna for cell phone reception, they asked me if they could use a portion of the church's property, I said "will it help my cell phone bill go down?" A quick laugh and a "No" later, I told them they were welcome to set up the tower. When the Hutchinson District Hot Food Trailer arrived on Wednesday morning, the same day as President Bush, I was there to help get it set up so they could start feeding people by noon. They had only a few tables and chairs for folks to use. Frantically, they wondered how they were going to be able to get more in time for the first meal. One of the men came up to me and said, "Kendal, who can we get to bring us some more tables and chairs. We could have several hundred people here, especially with the President being in town?" "I know where to get some real close," I said. I went over to the rather destroyed church building and made my way into what had been the fellowship hall. There were a number of wet but undamaged banquet tables; and at least a hundred chairs lying around. I started pushing tables and chairs through a window opening and several men came over to go set them up around the trailer. "Are you supposed to be in there?" one of them asked. "It doesn't make any difference, I think everyone is down around the FEMA Headquarter to see the President, and what they don't know won't hurt them," I said. "And if anyone says anything about these tables being out here, just tell them the district superintendent did it."

This Hot Food Trailer, would serve tens of thousands of meals over the next few months

We got it all set up and ready to go when Ken Walker came running around the corner and said, "Kendal, you've got to come and see this." I followed him around to the north side of the church and there was what looked like a Macy's Thanksgiving Day Parade of red and blue lights on every type of vehicle you can imagine. The street was full for several blocks. Ken said, "The President's coming down the street." "I never knew it took so much to get a President down a street" I quipped as I headed back toward the trailer. It wasn't long and here came Ken back, "Kendal, don't you want to see the President; he's just right out there on the street?" Then almost grabbing me, we headed back around front. We were met by a man in an all black outfit and sunglasses; although it was still very cloudy. He had this black stick in his hand said if you let me wand you, you can go over to where HE is. So I submitted to being wanded. Having been deemed clean, Ken and I walked over where several other pastors from the Kiowa County Ministers Association were gathered. The President spoke to us and began to shake hands. When he shook my hand, he noticed my badge and said, "Kendal, you're a United Methodist. So am I." The group had a word of prayer with him as he headed on off down the street along with all forty-eleven-hundred emergency, communication, secret service, FBI, military, hazmat, anti-terrorist, anti- biological, and anti-viral vehicles. That didn't include the snipers who had by then trained their weapons on some other poor soul. I'm just glad nobody realized I was the one who wrote and emailed to the White House the song about President Bush trying to kill Amtrak. Let's see, how did that protest song go?

"They're not singing 'Hail to the Chief' on Train number 3, but God save Amtrak from GWB." Still, it was a high honor to shake the hand of the President of the United States, even though I was wearing my old straw western hat because of the rain earlier.

Those extra tables and chairs made a big difference. Along with several other feeding stations around the city, our United Methodist Hot Food Trailer sitting on the parking lot of a destroyed church was an important social center for local residents to reconnect

President George W. Bush with Pastor Marvin George, May 9, 2007

with each other. It also provided opportunities to meet and interact with volunteers from all over the state like Reverend Cheryl Bell, then Wichita East District Superintendent.

For people of faith, like the Reverend Cheryl Bell, you can find joy in the smallest of things during the worst of times

Then there was the feeding of our wonderful men and women of the Kansas National Guard. I saw a young guardsman loading about twenty take-out-dinner containers into some kind of a military vehicle. I said, "You must have worked pretty hard to be able to eat that much food." "I'm taking it back to the others in my unit so we don't all have to quit work," he responded. "Where are you from?" I asked. "Humboldt" he said. "Well I want you to know how much you are appreciated. The Guard is doing a fantastic job of helping. If you need seconds, just tell them I told you, you could have some." "Thank you sir," he said as he prepared to drive off.

The Kansas National Guard personnel were the real unsung heroes during the early part of the Greensburg recovery. Due to the amount of reinforced concrete, the church would have to be demolished by a professional contractor. This would cost the church a lot more than I thought it should have, well over $100,000. I determined that they were not going to pay anything to have the parsonage demolished. Through the Mayhews, the folks who would be the new parsonage family beginning in September, we had arranged for a farmer from the Kismet Church to bring in some heavy farm equipment that would get most of the house down. The day before, I had gone down to the area where the Guard was quartered, and found the tent where the command center was located. I walked in and stood there until the ranking officer looked at me and said, "Who are you?" with an unspoken sense of, "how did you get in here?" in his voice. I told him that I was the District Superintendent for the Dodge City District of the United Methodist Church and that I was trying to figure out how to dispose of our parsonage refuse. The Guard was scheduling a lot of the hauling away of debris. There were city crews from all over the state loading and hauling the storm damage to the county landfill which from a distance, had a constantly thick, hellish smoke rising up from all the burning. Once he understood my request, he was very happy to ride to the parsonage with me and see the house and get the location. "I'll have you scheduled for late tomorrow and we will get it hauled away for you." My response was simply of profound gratitude for all that the Guard had done and was doing to help the people of Greensburg.

Bob Walker, the Kismet farmer, who with Terry Mayhew and a farm employee with his two daughters, plus a volunteer crew from Dodge City First United Methodist Church showed up early the next morning. They were all very generous with their time and equipment in helping to get that house down and all the trash placed on the curb for the loaders to haul away. As I stood there getting acquainted with Mr. Walker, a member of the Kismet PPR Committee, I felt a little uncomfortable in knowing that I would be surprising him and everyone else the next evening at a PPR meeting and explaining that their pastor would be moving to Greensburg. And boy, were they surprised! Terry was a good pastor and they all loved him and thought he was staying. At that meeting, and after Bob had come to the realization that shooting me would not improve their situation, I began to share about their new pastor and we concluded that it would work out somehow.

Although I think Renae, their daughter that just got married to a local farmer and belonged to the Plains Church, still had me in her crosshairs.

They did all they could in one day to completely raze the house. Anything left of it was now in the basement. It would be a crew of Bobcats from Pratt and a good friend and church member, Dean Fitzsimmons, who would finish the task and get the concrete floor of the parsonage clean. Indeed, it was a nice clean cement hole, where a house had stood full of a family's possessions.

Now there was one particular person for whom the saying, "It's all in who you know" could have been accurate. Not many people saw him to know anything about who he was or what he was up to. In fact, he only made himself known when he understood there to be a need. His expertise in dealing with issues, or finding and securing needed equipment or other assets earned him the nickname, "MacGyver" after the character on the television show. He had been there almost every day and night since the evening of the tornado. He's a friend of mine by the name of Bill Robbins. The Robbins family had been in the area for quite a while. His father owned and operated the Robbins Ranch that, according to legend, stretched from Belvedere, Kansas to Guymon, Oklahoma. Mr. Robbins was at one time on the Board of Directors of the Atchison, Topeka and Santa Fe Railway which would send a fancy, private car down the rattling tracks of the old Englewood Branch to take him to board meetings. Now I don't know if it was because of his father, or just his own natural abilities, but if there was anyone a person needed to know, Bill knew them. I was constantly amazed at the people he knew, and if he didn't, it wasn't long before they knew him.

He called me up one day and said, "Kendal the Union Pacific 844 steam engine will be coming through Pratt tomorrow. I want to go up to Hutchinson and watch it come in there; you want to ride up with me?" "Sure, I'll go with you" I said. He came by and picked me up at the church and off we went. "I sure wish there was a way for us to have gotten tickets to ride on that thing" he said over and over. "It's too bad we can't get on that train" he repeated several times. When we got there, the area was full of people waiting to see one of the last of the great steam locomotives pull a special Union Pacific passenger train into the former Rock Island Depot in a few moments. We didn't have to wait long. Here she came with a great plume of steam and smoke bellowing out of the stack, the whistle blowing, and bell ringing. It stopped right in front of the depot. Bill went inside. Pretty soon he came back out and said the man in there said there wasn't any way we could get on that train. They let passengers disembark and started loading up the next lucky few to make the journey to Pratt. Suddenly I looked and there was Bill talking to the head conductor dressed in a traditional Union Pacific uniform. I don't know what he said, whose name he dropped, but he looked over at me and motioned for me to follow him. Into the passenger car we went and sat down. I didn't ask any questions, but we were going to ride behind this famous old steam engine, UP #844, all the way to Pratt. Only Bill could have pulled something like this off.

What a lot of people will never know, even in the community of Greensburg, is all of the hours of work this man did on their behalf, and the connections he either had, or developed over those few months of recovery to secure the things that seemed unquestionably impossible to acquire, or have things happen that probably wouldn't have otherwise. Here is a great example of a quiet, unassuming person being used by God to be an Ebenezer to many in the harshest of environments. The only thing that I know of him asking anyone for was when he handed me a Bible and asked if I could get the Bishop to autograph it for him. I thought, you know, I can probably make this happen. When I asked the Bishop of Bill's request, he gave me a funny look like, "Even Bishop's can't autograph Bibles." But he did sign it with words of appreciation for the work Bill had done. There will probably never be a statue dedicated in Bill's honor or memory, but I would almost bet money that if you should be standing next to him when the Pope comes by, you will hear the Chief Bishop of the Roman Catholic Church say, "Well hello Bill, it's certainly good to see you again."

It really isn't who you know that matters in this world; rather it is who knows you. The above mentioned passage from Acts 19, in my warped way of thinking, is one of the funniest situations in the New Testament. Paul is doing mighty wonders in the name of the Lord Jesus, and these Seven Sons of Sceva tried to get into the action and exorcize a demon from a person by dropping names like Paul and Jesus, and they wound up in a pretty frightening and embarrassing situation. I have come to believe quite strongly that if you try to get along by just knowing the right people, or dropping the right names, you will not get very far. It's not who you know, it's who knows you. Who knows your heart, your integrity, abilities, strengths, weaknesses, loyalties, and your faith? Who knows you for the character and strength you exhibit, and the level of dependability you have? Who believes in you for who you are? You may know a politician, judge, or banker, or maybe even a movie star or professional athlete, but they probably don't know you; that is the real you, and they probably don't want to. God does! If the Divine Being takes an interest, and makes an investment in humankind, the only name which is needful for us to know is Jesus. He is the one who satisfies our deepest requests and needs and only asks for our hearts in return.

He is "The stone you builders rejected, which has become the capstone." Salvation is found in no one else, for there is no other name under heaven given to men by which we must be saved. (Acts 4:11-12)

Paul makes the point even clearer in his liturgical and lyrical reference to the unique supremacy of our Lord Jesus Christ.

Therefore God exalted him to the highest place and gave him a name that is above every name, that at the name of Jesus every knee should bow, in heaven and on earth and under the earth, and every tongue confess that Jesus Christ is Lord, to the glory of God the Father. (Philippians 2:9-10)

Reflection:

To put it simply, have you met and become acquainted with Jesus Christ?

What do you think of the statement, "God knows you perfectly?"

In what ways are you known by others?

Here, Hold This

Which of you, if his son asks for bread, will give him a stone? Or if he asks for a fish, will give him a snake? (Matthew 7:9-10)

Out on the farm, there is an old granary that is kind of unique. It had two bins for storing grain. I can remember Granddad Hunt keeping seed wheat in one and corn for the hogs in the other. It also had an upper loft that you needed a ladder to access. It was built in February 1903 by my great-Grandfather Charles Whittingham Hunt. It, like many of the older structures on the farm, was framed with cottonwood lumber which was cut right on the place. I thought it would be a good idea to try and keep the old building from further deterioration and even attempt to restore it; that is, in the Hunt tradition of restoring things, which means taking boards off of one area and putting them on anther, or pulling out the used nails and straightening them to be reused again.

During spring break in March of 2007, Adam my then sixteen-year old and Taylor who was thirteen and I went down to Mom's and spent a couple of days working on the granary. Now there had been some people living on the place for a number of years. What we later found out is that they were meth cookers. In fact, they were cooking their meth in one of the bedrooms of the house. There were cardboard strips stapled to the bottoms of the doors, tape over the keyholes, plastic stapled right into the woodwork to cover up the windows. There were some bad stains on the floor in the center of the room. The walls and ceilings were thick with filthy grime, and there was a smell that nearly made you sick. Fortunately, these people had moved out recently. Anyway the plan for the granary was, that since so much of the outer siding had deteriorated badly and it was a type of siding you couldn't get at your run of the mill lumber yard any more, we would remove part of the boxing from the inside as it was the same as what was on the outside and use it there.

We started our restoration project that morning however by getting the ladder and going up into the loft. We thought we would clean it up as it was full of dirt. There were decades of old mud dauber nests some lumber and big pile of just crud. Well we got rid of the lumber and I stuck a shovel into the pile of crud and heard the most awful bunch of squealing. It was a nest of baby squirrels and they were not happy and Momma Squirrel was not happy, and everyone knows that 'if Momma ain't happy, then nobody's happy.' So we left the loft.

We started moving stuff, mostly old lumber, out of the lower portion of the granary and started to remove some boxing. It was cool and damp, and by about 3:30 in the afternoon we were ready to start cleaning up and heading for town, showers, and supper. While we were putting things back inside to keep the moisture off, I noticed the corner of an object sticking up from behind the boxing, beside the north door between a couple of studs. I reached for and pulled it up. It was an old steel army ammunition box. As I sat it on the ground, Adam asked, "What is it?" "It's an old steel army ammunition box" I said. "And I'll bet it is some kind of drug stuff in it." I flipped the lever and opened up the box. There on the inside was a wad of what looked to be pink bubble wrap. "Okay, this is it" I said as I began to slowly unwrap it. What I discovered inside the wrap was a shiny, silvery plastic, so I began to unfold it. Inside, I thought I saw some drug paraphernalia, but on closer examination it was neatly coiled wire. Then I noticed that at the end of the wire was a long cylindrical object about the size of big tootsie roll. "This is some type of explosive device" I said, still trying to make sense of what I was seeing. "IT'S A BOMB!" I told the boys. "We need to get this into the police station" I said.

Well this is where the whole question of intelligence, no I think acumen is a better term, starts to come into play. This is also where our Bishop's wife (who is the only person who can really tell this story with the real passion it deserves) starts to get intense. To be fair to me, you need to know I do not have a working knowledge of explosives. I've never been around them or handled them, except for cherry bombs on the Fourth of July. I wasn't thinking things through about the implication of being in the proximity of an explosive device. I said, "We need to take this into the police station." And we loaded up our tools and the bomb into the pickup and drove into town. We went to the police station and I got out and grabbed the box and started to go in. I stopped and said, "They won't want this thing in there, here hold this Adam." So Adam stood there beside mom's pickup and held this bomb thing. I went in and said to the only person around, "I have an explosive device outside." His first reaction was to say, "Who are you?" I said, "Kendal Utt." "Oh, your Margie's boy" he said in a relieved tone. He followed me out to where Adam was standing, took the box and opened it up, looked at the package inside, and said, "Yep, that sure looks like some explosives to me." We left it with him and as I started to back out, I could see him walking around the front of the station looking for a bush or some other place to set it down.

Well we ate supper, and were watching the Kansas University basketball game during the March Madness finals. Suddenly the phone rang, and I just happened to answer it. The voice on the other end said, "Could I speak with a Mr. Kendal Utt?" I said, "This is Kendal." The voice continued, "This is the Sumner County Sheriff's Office, and I have some gentlemen here from the Bureau of Alcohol, Tobacco and Firearms office in Wichita who would like to ask you some questions and see the place where you found this explosive device." I said, "Sure, just as soon as the KU game is over, I'll head out there and meet you." I didn't realize that even a KU ball game in March didn't take precedence over the ATF. So the boys and I headed out there and we waited. In a couple of minutes, we saw a string of lights; it looked like a night funeral procession coming down the road. They all pulled into the south drive and drove around to where we were standing in front of the granary. The sheriff's deputy introduced himself and the other officers with him and the two men from the ATF.

The head ATF man started asking questions about my dad. I said that he worked for forty years for Boeing, served in the Army in Korea and has been deceased for over five years. They asked about Uncle Howard, I said he served in the Navy in WWII and worked for Boeing and farmed and has been deceased about nine years. Neither of these men would ever have had anything to do with explosives. He asked about the people who had moved off the place. I said "There's the direction you want to go. We are pretty sure they were cooking meth in the house. But I don't think anyone around here knows where they have gone." "That's alright; we'll find them if we want them," he said with a certain confidence. He asked if we had a ladder so he could make a further search and clear the building. I went to get the ladder out and set it up to the door of the loft. "There's nothing up there but a bunch of stirred up squirrels" I said. "Well, I need to check the space out regardless" he concluded. He had his flashlight and headed up the ladder and disappeared into the loft. He came back out in less than a minute and said, "It's all clear. Boy! You were right about the squirrels." He checked out the bottom level and searched between every exposed stud. "Well the bottom is clean also; how about the house?" We explained that since those people had moved out, it had been thoroughly emptied, and cleaned. There had been new wiring put in so every part of the house had been gone over. They decided they didn't need to search the house.

As we stood out there in the dark, the ATF man said that it might be possible to find more explosive material in one of the other sheds. And that if we did, "to leave it alone and call us!" He continued in a lecturing manner, "This is what we do; it's part of our job! In fact, don't even touch it!" He explained, "That shiny silvery plastic that was around it was a static resistant material to help keep the devise from exploding from any static electricity buildup. These people knew what they were doing. This probably could have been a detonation devise for a larger explosive, like a fertilizer bomb." "Well, I'll call if I find any more of this stuff" I assured him. I guess a few days later, they took the bomb out southeast of town and detonated it. Mom said it made a pretty good bang.

I don't like to feel unintelligent, especially in front of other people, but I guess that's better than feeling hurt, or dead, or causing injury or worse to my sons. The words to that old song, "His eye is on the sparrow, and I know he watches me," may not have a lot of theological content, but I would rather affirm this message than hear a quote from Proverbs about folly or fools; or "There is a time for every season under the heaven." I suppose that even a 'duh' moment can become an Ebenezer moment.

Reflection:

What 'duh' moments have you had?

Are you willing to share any of them?

How have they made you more attentive in handling some of the situations you have had or may face?

A Prince of a Man

A good name is more desirable than great riches; to be esteemed is better than silver or gold. (Proverbs 22:1)

One of my very best friends, Joe Hamilton, and I did a lot of hunting, fishing, and trapping together. One of the best places to do that was in a long, narrow lake that a hundred-forty years ago was part of the Ninnescah River until it changed course down south. The lake and the wooded area surrounding it was known by the old Markley's who owned quite a bit of it as 'The Land of Moo.' As the crow flies, it's only about a half a mile from my grandfather's house. There was a lane back into the woods that the alfalfa mill used during the summer to access a field, and that was our usual way to get in there and run our traps. One day we had a pretty big snow, followed by some extremely cold weather. This meant that the road was impassable, and the lake was frozen, so we decided to ice skate up from the highway. Now to do this, we had to cross about forty yards of the lake on property owned by a person I had never met, or seen, but had only heard about. He was simply known as 'The Hermit.' He lived in a small house just off the highway. An enormous pile of beer cans grew beside the house. There were No Trespassing signs all over the place. We figured that as cold as it was, and as much beer as he obviously drank, he wouldn't be watching. We put on our skates and headed off into the deepest reaches of the Land of Moo to check our traps.

As we came back out, heading for the car, there he was. He wasn't a large man at least from a height perspective. He didn't look all that formidable or threatening. Then he started in on us. "What are you doing on my property, you little expletives?" he asked sharply. Joe said, "We've been up the lake, Mrs. Markley gave us permission to go up there." "Well I didn't give you permission to be on my property! You're trespassing! This is posted land." Then he just kept on going. "I'm going to call the Sheriff and have your expletive, expletive, expletive, thrown in jail you expletive, expletive, expletives! What is your name?"

he asked looking right at Joe. Joe told him who he was. Then he looked at me and said, "Who the expletive are you?" I told him my name and then added that I was Art Hunt's grandson. All of a sudden, a sense of calm came over his face and to his voice. "Art Hunt?" he said reflectively. "He was a prince of a man." He then said he didn't want us out there on the ice because of the danger and for us to head on home. Boy, we dodged that bullet I thought. It made me proud that people, even foulmouthed hermits, could have such good thoughts about my grandfather. Indeed he was a prince of a man. I missed him terribly, as he had been gone for about four years by then. Arthur Gilbert Hunt was a Kansas farmer, born in a log cabin, and who lived most of his life on the place where he had been raised. He met my Grandmother, Ida Schwyhart, at church and Epworth League. Typical of his generation, he was quite diversified. He raised wheat, barley, and corn along with alfalfa hay. There were also livestock, cattle, and hogs. I can just barely remember when they had chickens. It seems that one time Granddad and Grandma went into town and when they got home that night, the local raccoons, who had obviously been planning this for some time, led a massive attack on the chicken houses. They ripped off some wooden shakes from the roof to gain access, and proceeded to kill every last chicken. Grandma said that she would never have another chicken on the place again, so Granddad hooked a log chain to the little chicken house and pulled it off to a brush pile and burnt it. The other one would just languish over the next twenty years into a pile of its own.

Granddad, along with his brother, Uncle Henry, who farmed next to him, also did a lot of carpentry work for folks in the area. People had them build or repair barns and sheds, remodel houses; they even built a number of new homes like the parsonage for the Peck United Methodist Church. They were a good team. They worked hard, were honest, and took pride in what they did. People all over the country knew, respected, and appreciated the Hunt boys.

There doesn't seem to be a lot of demand today for princely men (or princessly women) in our world. In the Huffington Post dated September 24, 2008, Rabbi Shmuley Boteach posted an article titled "Where Have All the Gentlemen Gone?" he writes,

> *Nowhere in the Western world are we raising a generation of men who pride themselves on their restraint and respect toward women [or anyone other than themselves]. As I survey the current cultural landscape, I often wonder where have all the gentlemen gone. Do men today only aspire to an internet startup but not refined character? Do they yearn for the Forbes Four-Hundred list but not to set an example for their own sons of how a great man honors his wife and prioritizes his family?* [18]

I realize the focus of his article is limited to men and their attitudes and behaviors surrounding women, but how true it is of the wider view of society, both men and women. How many children and youth have no example of a moral, faithful, honest, respectful, loving person close to them to emulate? Now being a prince of a man and a gentleman are not exactly synonymous, but they at least run parallel to each other. Both would seem to be able to command the respect of others, based not on what they had, but how they lived.

I had earlier mentioned Dick and Louise Turner. Dick played the violin for the Hutchinson Orchestra for a number of years until he needed to give it up. He sang in the church choir at Pratt until the last couple of years before Louise retired from her position. Dick sang tenor, and he would always sit at the end of the men's row, just a few feet away from where Louise sat at the organ. I generally sat next to him during practice and then during the anthem on Sunday mornings. Dick was a World War II veteran; he served in the Air Corps as a navigator on a bomber. He would say, "The war was a terrible thing; but I enjoyed my time in the service; I had a good time, there were a lot of great people." He was an educator and administrator in Kansas schools. Every time he would mention any of the communities he lived in, he would say, "They were wonderful years; great people." Then he would occasionally talk about Louise and say, "She's a professional; a perfectionist! She is a wonderful woman; I'm really lucky." He would also get humorous and talk out loud during rehearsal. Suddenly I would see Louise's head peer around the music rack on the organ with her glasses down on her nose and her eyes giving us 'the look.' I would say, "Dick, you're being looked at;" and he would quiet down. The thing about Dick Turner was his constant use of the words wonderful and good. He was always so positive, so good-humored, so appreciative of others, and generous with compliments and respect toward others. Just his being around people made him happy. Even if no one else in the congregation thought so, Dick would grab my hand after services and say, "That was a really good sermon." I shared earlier about a funeral where there was no mourning because there was no celebration. Dick passed away late in 2008, and I was honored to officiate at his memorial service in the retirement village where he and Louise had moved after leaving Pratt. Now there was mourning to be sure; but it was only an accent to the great celebration of life we witnessed to that day. These are archetypes of princely, or princessly folk our Western (and Eastern) world should be looking to—should be rising up.

Wouldn't it be so much easier for us (at least most of us could surely find one person in our genetic pool for whom we are proud of) if we could live our lives off the character and good reputation of our parents or grandparents, and share in the respect and esteem they received from others. The truth is, while it can be beneficial at times, especially with hermits who are threatening to throw your expletives in jail, it is something we need to develop on our own. Being a prince of a man, like dancing, doesn't genetically transmigrate. I know I had to come to the understanding behind the meaning of the old phrase, "God has no grandchildren." This is the reason why there is that "Born Again" thing in the Bible that Jesus speaks about to Nicodemus in John 3:3.

Here is a person (Nicodemus) who automatically lives within the great heritage of the Pharisees, and membership in the ruling council. Perhaps this is why he has a hard time at first understanding what Jesus means when he says "You must be born again." Nicodemus, along with every other person will have to come onto the property by legitimate means in terms of being in a saving relationship with God. This is precisely what Mr. Wesley says in his Notes on this verse.

In this solemn discourse our Lord shows that no external profession, no ceremonial ordinances, or privileges of birth, could entitle any to the blessings of the Messiah's kingdom; that an entire change of heart, as well as of life, was necessary for that purpose; [19]

You cannot skate quietly through life on the merits of others. There is no standing before God as so and so's child, a relative of a President, or the descendant of someone who got off the Mayflower. We come to God on God's terms. Still, I am very thankful; I praise God for the good examples of wonderful men and women I've been blessed with for an excellent pattern in living.

Reflection:

Are there persons of faith in your background whose reputation may be hard to live up to?

Do you find it tempting to rely upon the merits of another's good life to balance your own?

How have you experienced the command of Jesus to be "Born Again?"

The Good Shepherds

I am the good shepherd, I know my sheep and my sheep know me. (John 10:14)

My Grandfather Hunt also raised sheep, and he would have them sheared for wool. On really cold mornings when a new baby lamb would be born, he would bring it into the house to warm up a little. This gave my sister and me a chance to pet it. It was about the only way we could get close to a sheep, as they were pretty skittish. In fact, we were told to stay away from the sheep so we wouldn't spook them, or get a head butt from an old buck. That's what always scared me about the sheep was getting butted; but I never did.

Arthur Gilbert Hunt with Kendal, Kenna, and a baby lamb; December 1958

One day my mother was helping Granddad with something in the barn, weaning pigs if I remember right, and the sheep were peacefully lying around in their pen. I thought, I can get in there and walk real slow and maybe pet one or two. Now I had been told to stay out of there. I had been told to leave the sheep alone. I thought they're busy; I can do this; they'll never know. I climbed over the fence, took about three steps, and every last one of those sheep got up, jumped over the fence, ran out the driveway, and down the road. All that commotion brought my granddad and mom out of the barn. Granddad calmly opened the gate and headed out the driveway for the road. Mom, not quite as calm, headed for me. Grandma was standing there by that time, so I tried to stay real close to her. "Now Marjorie, the boy didn't mean to spook the sheep. You're dad will get them back in a minute" she said, buying me a little time. Sure enough, it didn't take long. Granddad just walked out to the road, called the sheep, walked them back into the pen, and closed the gate. He really was a good shepherd. He was a good grandfather. I think I only received one swat from him growing up, and that was for doing something to my sister that she probably deserved, but for which I got in trouble. It was more like a pat, but the thought of getting it from him was a pretty strong lesson.

Granddad had a lot of friends. I remember the first time I went on a coon hunt. The hunting party was Dad, Benny Howe, and Walt Le Force along with Walt's coon hounds and me. As we were walking down a lane along the bank of the Ninnescah River waiting for the dogs to get a coon treed, Walt asked me how my granddad was doing. I said, "Oh he's doing fine." Then Walt said, "The next time you see your granddad, ask him if he still sucks eggs." Well we didn't tree any coons that night, but I had something to talk to Granddad about. The very next time we were out at the farm, I asked, "Granddad, do you still suck eggs?" He gave me the funniest look along with about a one-third smile and said, "Who told you to ask me that?" "Mr. Le Force" I answered. "Awww! Walt was just pullin you're leg and playing a joke on me. I've never sucked an egg in my life."

Whenever he did carpentry work, he would take the time and the effort to save all of the pieces of scrap lumber. Those pieces that were too small to be good for anything else, he brought them home for me to play with as blocks. It gave me something to do out there when he wasn't around to keep me out of mischief.

The barns were the special places, and the old horse barn was by far the best. It was built by my great-grandfather with stables for ten teams of horses, three granaries, a huge hay loft above, and a long driveway down the center. At certain times of the year, the barn would be filled with the nests of barn swallows, and when the eggs hatched, they would swoop at you, and the baby birds would rise up and look over the edge of their nest. The evening air would be filled with the swallows out eating insects. Every now and then, Granddad would take us out to the barn, go to one of the mangers that were part of the structure of each stall, and show us brand new baby kittens all snuggled up in the hay. I guess mangers do make good places to be born. They were always wild, so we could never hold them; still there was tenderness in the moment. I remember feeling like a real farmer, (and a man) the first time he asked me to go up into the hay loft by myself and throw down a bale of alfalfa hay for him to take out to feed the calves. He always worried about us playing up there because the floor, while covered in a layer of hay, had a lot of holes in it; some big enough to let a kid fall right through. The year after he died, Grandma and I were out there to search for some baby kitties, and when startled by a swallow, she looked up and saw an old roaster lid nailed to the underside of the hay mow floor. "Well, I'll swan" she said in a surprised tone of voice. "I've been wondering where the lid to my old roaster had gotten off to. I've looked for that thing for twenty years, and your granddad had it out here all the time."

The last time I was in that old barn, it still smelled like Granddad should be there feeding calves or lambs. It was the day I went to tell the folks that Joyce and I were going to get married. I climbed up into the old hayloft, took off the small access door on the west side of the barn that Aunt Dorothy wanted, and retrieved the old fork carrier that ran on the track in the top of the barn back when they still used a hay grappling fork. I got the fork too.

The Hunt Horse Barn, long after horses, hay, and having fun

Riding on the tractor (his old Allis Chalmers WD 45), the hay rack, or the old box wagon, was always a treat. He never let us ride in the manure spreader. He worried whenever any of us rode with him because he only had one eye that was any good. He had a piece of wood hit him in that eye when he was a boy cutting fire wood. He could see light out of it but that was all. But we could sit on the tool box on the fender and ride while he worked ground. Harvest wasn't the grand production for him that a lot of people conjure when they think of wheat. He had an Allis Chalmers All Crop 66 combine, this meant it had a 5'6" cut and was pulled behind his tractor. It took a lot of rounds around the field to harvest. Mom would help by driving the pickup. When the combine bin was filled to capacity (about twenty bushels), he would waive his hat in the air and off we would go, pull up alongside the combine and it would augur it out. I think the pickup held about two dumps and off to the elevator we'd go. The Farmer's Elevator, an old wooden elevator, was approached from the north and the south. So there would be a long line in both directions. You just had to have the patience to wait for a long time. Finally, when it was your turn to go into the elevator, we had to drive up onto a lift, get out of the truck, and stand alongside the wall of the elevator. They would raise the lift and the pickup would raise high into the air until all the wheat had run out the back, it would be lowered, back to the scale for an empty weight, and then off to the field to do it all over again and again.

    I went to Carl Cooper's farm sale with Granddad and Uncle Henry. I didn't care about what was for sale, I was just glad to be with them. I was playing with my friend, Joe. We were in the barn when Uncle Henry came in and said, "Come on Kendal, we have to leave." I followed him out of the barn, got into the truck with him, and Granddad drove home. What I didn't know was that was when Granddad had his heart attack. It wasn't long after that he went into the hospital. Now that Granddad wasn't able to do his own harvesting any longer, he had a neighbor come and cut it with his larger, self propelled Gleaner combine. He also had a much larger truck. I rode into the elevator with Granddad as he hauled the first load of wheat into town. He pulled into the driveway and fiddled around with the levers until the hydraulic hoist started to raise the bed; we didn't even have to get out of the truck. When it was dumped, he fiddled with the levers until the bed started to come down. As we headed down the road, the bed started to rise back up. I said, "Granddad! The back of the truck is going up again." "I know," he said anxiously, "but I don't know how to get it to go back down." So slowly down the road we went with the bed of this truck sticking up in the air. Fortunately, (or not because of the embarrassment Granddad endured) another neighbor, Cline Clewell came down the road and stopped us. "What's the matter Art?" he asked with a grin on his face. "I don't know how to get this bed to stay down" he answered. Cline hopped in the cab of the truck, and got the levers in the right positions and the bed came down, and stayed down.

    Uncle Howard and Aunt Dorothy raised popcorn for a number of years. When they would pick it, they'd bring it out to Granddad's to shell it. He had an ancient corn sheller. It had a big wheel on one side with a handle on it. As someone would scoop the ears into the sheller, my sisters and I got to have the honor and fun, or so we thought, of turning the wheel that turned the wheels, that shelled the corn. The kernels would fall out into a bucket and the cobs would shoot out into the ground. When we were done, the cobs would be picked up and thrown into the hog lot for the pigs to nibble off the few remaining kernels the sheller didn't get.

He went into the elevator one day to get some feed, and I rode along with him. As I stood beside him when Red Blasdell the manager gave him the ticket, I noticed him writing on it and I said, "Boy you sure can't write very good." Holding up the stub where his right hand used to be, Red just laughed and said "I used to be right handed until I got it cut off out there in the elevator. Now I'm trying to learn to write with my left hand." My grandfather did not laugh when Red did. I got a lecture all the way home about being polite and not making comments about other people.

I used to like to sit with them in church because Gus, the man Granddad usually sat next to, always had a stick of Dentine gum for me. Sitting in between them, I could usually stay out of trouble, which was much harder to do when I sat with George, Ed, or Bryan without any adult supervision. It was good to not cause a commotion during church because it kept Mom from having to leave the choir loft. Whenever you saw my mother stand up all by herself with no music playing, and start down from the choir loft, you knew it wasn't going to be good. On those occasions she would take me out on the side steps of the church for an attitude or behavioral correction that everyone inside could hear, and most likely appreciated.

One day while Granddad was working with Uncle Henry, Grandma who was hanging clothes out on the close line hollered at me. "There's some kind of animal out here that the dog is barking at. Come see what it is." I got over there and saw something I had never seen before. Shaggy, the dog, had it cornered up against the old chicken house and whatever it was, it was hissing and fussing back at Shaggy. "I don't know what it is" I said to Grandma. She came over slowly and got a glimpse of it and exclaimed, "Oh my! It's a badger, stay away from it." Well this was a great day indeed. I was going to get me a badger. I went into the house and got my Daisy BB gun, the one I sold greeting cards to get, and went out to shoot it. I pumped that badger with a hundred shots. It didn't faze him; only made him hiss more. I went back into the house and got the bow and some arrows from my "Red Chief" archery set. The arrows just bounced off of him. I tried dirt clods and hedge apples. Finally I went into the garage and got a shovel. A couple of good whacks on the head and it was all over. I had prevailed against the mighty badger. I wonder now what the game wardens would want for a shovel killed badger out of season, $410.00? The preceding figure will become clearer in a later section; along with the anxiety regarding game wardens.

During this time I was into things like the old west and Indians; goodness knows I had fought enough of them out in the barn. When I saw the claws on this badger I thought to myself, "I can make me an Indian necklace out of those claws." So I went into the house and got one of Grandma's butchering knives and took it out and cut off all four paws of the badger. The only thing I could think of to get the claws out of the paws was to take them into the house and boil them in a pan of water to make the paws tender. I got a big pan and filled it with water, lit a burner on the butane stove, put the paws in and brought them to a rolling boil. About the time they got to boiling really good, Grandma came in and said, "What on earth are you doing on the stove; and what is that smell?" I said "I'm boiling these badger paws. That ought to get em good and tender so I can pull the claws out and make me a necklace." "Oh, for pity sakes!" (one of Grandma's favorite sayings for frustrating moments). "I hope you're about done so I can get that pan washed and get this smell out of the house" Grandma responded with a slight hint of aggravation in her voice. I certainly hadn't noticed any smell. When I took the boiled paws out of the pan and cooled them off under running water in the sink, sure enough those claws came out real easy with a pair of pliers, and I put them in a can. Later, after they had dried I took a hammer and small nail, drove a hole through the paw end of each claw and got one of Grandma's good, strong sewing needles and some dark thread, ran it through the claws, and I had me a genuine badger claw Indian necklace. I was sure I was doing it the old Indian way too.

When Granddad got home that evening, Grandma said, "Art, Kendal killed a badger out by the chicken house and it's lying beside the garage. You need to help him get that dead thing hauled down to the slough and get it out of my yard." Granddad and I grabbed onto the now shortened back legs of the badger and off we went down the lane toward the slough. While he could be around sheep having babies and butcher a hog, Granddad had a real weak stomach about such things as bloody and dead wild animals, and several times he had to put his bandana over his mouth and nose to keep from getting nauseous. Finally, we threw the badger into the hedge row and headed back to the house. Granddad gave me one of his little lectures on just leaving things, like animals, alone. "Just because you see a wild animal, doesn't mean you have to kill it or even bother it. If you leave them alone, they will just mind their own business and go on. They're God's creatures too, and they all have a purpose." He knew how to give pretty good advice about things; like the time we were in the cow lot and with all the manure and old feed around there seemed to be a great number of flies and gnats swarming around, and there wasn't any breeze to keep them away. I asked him, "Granddad?" "What?" he asked back. "If God made everything, why did He make flies and gnats; they're trying to fly up my nose and are getting in my eyes?" Granddad's response was pretty simple; "God made those things so you could have something to complain about." Well I guess I really didn't have much to complain about, not then, and not now.

That's how I was shepherded into life when I was young. My mother and father were pretty good too, especially regarding personal responsibility and respect for others. Still there is just something about grandparents. Joyce's Granddad Brownlee was also a shepherding type. He was a prince of a man, and obviously a good judge of character too.

When we started dating, Joyce told her granddad that I was a great-nephew of Harry Hunt. Harry farmed and operated a gas station on the south side of Wellington and was a good friend of Mr. Brownlee. He said to Joyce, "If he's related to Harry Hunt, he must be a good man."

About a year after we were married, Joyce and I were ready for her to get pregnant, and it just didn't seem to be happening. One evening we had a family meal at our home with all of her people over. She had taken one of those little pregnancy tests earlier in the day and it came back negative. I guess her granddad could sense she was being moody. He sat down beside her and leaned over to her and just talked, reassuring her about life, and time, and waiting for the right time.

Granddad Brownlee with Joyce

That's the sort of shepherding we get from the Good Shepherd, Jesus. We've all seen the picture where he is holding the little lamb and the other sheep are looking with sincere trust up at him as he leads them to wherever it is they are going. It is this Jesus who has the ability to move us with a peace and patience from wherever it is we are, to wherever it is we should be heading in life. Clement of Alexandria was a scholar and one time director of the catechetical school in Alexandria. He is the writer of the oldest known Christian hymn of whose authorship we know. Translated by Henry Martyn Dexter, it bears these words: (You will get the rhythm better if you can recall "Come Thou Almighty King;" and the tune, Italian Hymn)

I am confident that our grandparents were an important part of the Lord's shepherding plan for both Joyce and me.

Ever be near our side, Our Shepherd and our guide, Our staff and song;
Jesus, Thou Christ of God, By Thy enduring word,
Lead us where Thou hast trod, Make our faith strong.

Reflection:

Recall times, places, and the people there who shepherded your life. In what ways were they helpful?

What have you retained over the years of their influence?

How were they a part of God's plan for your growing up?

Is shepherding a helpful metaphor for raising children?

The Little Tin Cup

Come, all you who are thirsty, come to the waters; and you who have no money, come buy and eat! Come buy wine and milk without money and without cost. (Isaiah 55:1)

We were around Granddad and Grandma Hunt all the time because we lived just two miles from them. That doesn't mean that Granddad and Grandma Utt weren't important in our lives, because they were. They were a little older; born in 1887 and 1888 respectfully into early-day families in southeastern Cowley County. Granddad came out of a large farm family near Cedarvale, and Grandma grew up in Maple City where her father, James Harp was the blacksmith. Grandma said she learned the Ten Commandments sitting in a tree while miles of cattle were being driven past by cowboys taking them to the railroad. Granddad Utt worked for the Midland Valley Railroad for most of his adult life. He was a section foreman for the MV which was a line that ran from Fort Smith (Arkansas), Muskogee (Oklahoma), through Pawhuska and the Osage Nation (Oklahoma), Belle Plaine (Kansas), and terminated in Wichita (Kansas), where Metropolitan Baptist Church now stands. Dad was number ten of eleven children that made it to adulthood. He was one of the "depression babies" who along with the rest, grew up in railroad section houses from Silverdale, Kansas to Hardy and Foraker Oklahoma (home to Ben Johnson the actor and Patty Page the singer), and to Belle Plaine where he met Mom. We were pretty far down the line as the grandchildren went with me being number 20 and my sisters being numbers 22 and 23; unless I missed someone.

I always hated to hear Dad say on a Saturday morning or Sunday afternoon, "Get in the car, we're going to Silverdale." That's where they retired from the railroad, and lived until moving back to Belle Plaine in the mid sixties for health reasons. They lived in a limestone house with a wire fence and a white picket gate. There were fruit trees and about a million hollyhocks on the south end of their place. The reasons I hated going there was pretty selfish. First, it was an hour drive down there, and I would always get car sick. That's why I hated to go anywhere, especially on vacations to the Ozarks where there were no shoulders on the road for Dad to pull off when I needed to get out. Second, they didn't have a television; just a very large wood encased radio. Granddad was an avid baseball game listener. Once I got there though, I always had a good time. Grandma always had cookies that she baked, and kept a very special cheese that I called Silverdale Cheese. Since Mom never had it at home, at least that I was aware of. I didn't know it was really called Velveeta.

Now on the side of this little stone house, was a stone garage with a pretty green 1953 Chevy that probably hadn't been driven more than a few of thousand miles if that. Behind the garage was a stone shed that Granddad had all his garden tools in plus a lot of old-time railroad stuff that collectors today would really scramble for. Behind the house quite a ways was another little stone house. It was the outhouse where the older issues of the Arkansas City Daily Traveler Newspaper were kept. Now in-between the house and the outhouse was the well. Since there was no running water or even plumbing in the house, this well was the source for all the drinking, cooking, washing, and bathing that was done. The well was a limestone-lined, hand-dug hole several feet across with a stone box several feet high and several feet square with a big wooden lid and a roof over it. There was a porcelain bucket attached to a rope that went through a big iron pulley. When Grandma needed some water, or they wanted to take a bath, Granddad would lower the bucket into the well, let it fill with water and draw it up, unhook it from the rope, and take it into the house. Sometimes he would let us drop the bucket in and try to pull it up. There was always a bucket of water sitting on the counter in Grandma's kitchen.

Two things I remember about the well. First, you're life depended on never, ever putting anything into the well except the bucket—no rocks, no paper, no peaches or apples (from their orchard), no cats, no spit, no nothing! Secondly, there was a little tin cup which hung on a nail. That little tin cup was what we would get a drink from whenever a fresh bucket of water was drawn. Its continuous presence at the well said that there was always an opportunity for me, or my sisters, or cousins, a neighbor or even a complete stranger, to find a refreshing drink of that cold water. It was a common statement of hospitality to have a cup hanging on a well or near a pump handle.

As folks often referred to as tramps, hobos and such traveled through the country, especially up and down the railroad that ran right in front of any of the section houses in which Dad would have grown up in during the depression and war (or past almost anyone's house for that matter) it was an act of kindness and hospitality to offer someone what you could give. Granddad and Grandma Utt never had much. In fact, we never received any Christmas presents from them, and of course we never expected any. With all of us cousins, it would have cost them a fortune to give us all a present for Christmas. However, I imagine that Grandma would always be able to scare up a chicken leg, (Dad used to say that he had no mental picture of his mother without her standing in her full length apron with a chicken in each hand) and maybe a piece of bread, or even a slice of Silverdale Cheese and a cookie. But even if no one was around, a drink of water was always available; and it was good water, filtered through miles of Kansas limestone rock.

I would continue to learn that lesson years later in my student appointment in Adams County Ohio. At McColm's Chapel, there was Charles and Betty Young who owned and operated the Western Auto Store and the Hotel in Manchester. They lived in an apartment on the first floor of the hotel. I probably over extended my welcome with them, but I sure had a lot of cured ham and red eye gravy at their kitchen table. Sometimes it was just a good cup of coffee with Betty. And if it wasn't in their home, it was a trip to Aberdeen and one of Charley's favorite places, Frisch's, for a Sunday night dinner after church. They really parented me while I was their pastor.

Then there were the Naylors. They weren't United Methodists.

They were members of the Eckmansville Church of Christ In Christian Union Church. Mrs. Naylor, Verna, was the Bentonville Postmaster. When she died in July of 2010 at the age of 93, she was the oldest active postal employee and postmaster in the United States. The post office was a small affair with an antique set of dial post boxes and a window with small bars. You could go through a side door into a room with a couple of couches, a big oil fired stove for cold days, and about a hundred clocks which all chimed; if you were there at 11:00 or 12:00, it was quite a noise. It was the upstairs however that was important for me. There was an outside stairway that led to the porch and the door to the main floor. Verna lived there with her two daughters, Sis and Sue, and their brother, Jim, and there were two more sons in Verna's family. But truth be told, Sis, Sue, and Jim had a lot of other brothers and sisters. Verna had a lot of sons and daughters, who she loved like family including whoever was the mail truck driver. They are probably the most inclusive family I have ever known. My first year in Bentonville Sue and Sis made me an eighteenth-century coat, cape, and clergy collar. These along with a Santa Claus wig and a horse, made me look just like John Wesley as I rode through town for the Harvest Festival Parade. If you, even as a complete stranger were to find yourself in Bentonville, Ohio tonight, Sue Naylor would give you the Presidential Suite (where Andrew Jackson supposedly slept) in the Palace Hotel. Our family feels very honored to be part of that inclusivity. When we would visit, any of the boys would be asked what they wanted for supper, they would tell them. They already knew what I liked. At supper time, the table would be filled with baked steak, fried chicken, roast beef, scalloped potatoes, mashed potatoes, chicken gravy, and beef gravy, anything we wanted. Now that wouldn't happen every day, but after we had driven nine-hundred miles to get there, they were just happy to do it. Everyone needs a place in this world where they can go and be treated to that type of 'extravagant hospitality.' The Bentonville and McColm's Chapel people certainly offer us that.

How do we as individuals or the church re-invent the little tin cup for the twenty-first century? Bishop Robert Schnase, in his book, <u>The Five Practices of Fruitful Congregations</u>, uses his first chapter to deal with developing what he calls radical hospitality.

John Wesley and the early Methodists practiced hospitality in ways so radical in their day that many traditional church leaders found their activities offensive. Wesley preached to thousands on roadsides in open fields in order to reach coal miners, field laborers, factory workers, the underclass, and the poorest of the poor. He invited them into community and nurtured in them a strong sense of belonging as he organized societies and classes for mutual accountability, support and care. [20]

In that chapter there is a section he entitled, "Fresh Flowers, Free Lunches, No Offering" in which he describes three churches. There is a growing suburban congregation that always had fresh cut flowers in the restrooms along with the many other insightful details which were signs of welcome and hospitality. A small rural church would pick a different group each month to fix lunch for farmers, firefighters, teachers, etc. Then there was the African American Church that let visitors know they were their guests and were not expected to feel like they had to give, only receive. It sounds like these very real churches the Bishop described had in one way or another learned the lesson of simple yet radical hospitality; like the little tin cup hanging on a nail for anyone who was thirsty and needed a drink.

As of the last time I was there several years ago, the house is gone, the outhouse is gone, the garage and the little shed are piles of rubble, and the well has been filled in. In fact there isn't much of the little town of Silverdale left. Still, whenever I read this offer of Jesus to a thirsty world, or about Jesus and his encounter with the Samaritan woman at the well recorded in John 4:13-14, and his invitation to drink the water that will quench life's thirst and spring up to eternal life, I am taken back to a simple Silverdale well, a little tin cup hanging on a nail, and the lesson of hospitality that it gave me.

Effie and C. A. Utt, Susie, Kendal and Kenna at the front gate
I guess no one ever took a picture of the well out back

Reflection:

How have you been the recipient of another's hospitality?

Did you experience it in the church?

In what ways do you seek to offer hospitality to others?

    at Home or work?

    at church?

Caution! Deceptive Curve Ahead

Therefore do not let anyone judge you by what you eat or drink, or with regard to a religious festival, a New Moon celebration or a Sabbath day. These are a shadow of the things that were to come: the reality however, is found in Christ. (Colossians 2:16-17)

Following Southwestern College, I attended Asbury Theological Seminary in Wilmore Kentucky. While it is not one of the United Methodist seminaries, most of the students, faculty and administration are United Methodists. It was founded by Reverend Henry Clay Morrison, a preacher and evangelist of the Methodist Episcopal Church South. If my knowledge of history serves me correctly, he preached a revival at Southwestern College at one time in the earlier part of the twentieth century.

One of the issues surrounding the development of Asbury Theological Seminary was to maintain a high regard for the Wesleyan Holiness tradition and be a center for training and education within that aspect of Wesleyan theology and heritage. One of the things you did in attending the seminary was pledge not to use any alcohol or tobacco. Now this is right in the heart of Kentucky bluegrass country. Some of the biggest distillers of Kentucky whiskey and bourbon were just down the road and much of the corn raised in the area went to the distilleries to become whisky. Burley Tobacco was one of the chief cash crops in the area and large tobacco auction warehouses existed in Lexington. Some of the most beautiful horse farms in the country, where the horses live better than many of the people in the area, were between Lexington and Wilmore, where the school was, and horse racing was still the sport of kings. Now that doesn't leave much to preach against in the area pulpits. Still, the holiness culture was so pervasive in the area the local grocery store wouldn't sell tobacco products or beer at that time. Mr. Fitch was a strong supporter of the seminary, and truly a Godly man. I was in Mr. Fitch's grocery store one day to get a bottle of shampoo, can of deodorant, and a bottle of Tums: Super Ultra Mega

EX antacid tablets, when a man passing through asked him, "I can't find your cigarettes. Where do you keep them?" Mr. Fitch said back to him, "We don't sell tobacco products in this store!" To which the traveler responded, "I can't believe a grocery store in the state of Kentucky that won't sell cigarettes!" and he walked out.

One day, I was standing in the lower hallway of Morrison Hall visiting with a few friends between the student post office and the book store as it was then located. I had bought a couple of tootsie pops in the book store and had already begun working on one. I noticed the President of the seminary, Dr. Frank Bateman Stanger, an accomplished author and lecturer, and who had quite an interest and ministry in prayer and healing. He got to the bottom of the stairs and began a conversation with someone. I also noticed him looking down the hall toward us. He then motioned the person he was visiting with on and started to walk towards the general direction where we were. It became clear to me that his eyes were fixed on me and they weren't happy eyes. About the time he got right in front of me, I just happened to pull the tootsie pop out of my mouth. He stopped, looked at my tootsie pop and said, "Oh! There for a minute I thought you had a cigarette in your mouth." Then he walked on.

Now I really didn't have a problem with those prohibitions. I grew up in a home that didn't have alcohol in it, we didn't gamble either, but Dad did like his corn cob pipe and his Sir Walter Raleigh tobacco. I have an old Temperance songbook of mom's by Herbert and Lillie Buffum entitled, "Cleansing Songs: for use in Anti-Tobacco and Anti-Idolatry Campaigns." It is full of old prohibition songs such as The Battle Hymn of the Anti Tobaccoists, "Since the Old Pipe is Gone," "Why Did God Make Tobacco?" and (this one could become popular again) "Second Handed Smoke." One of my favorites is, "They're Drinking Extracts Now "with a verse that reads,

Poor red-nosed bums
without a wife, a sister, or a friend
Must now invent some good excuse
if they have dimes to spend.

Vanilla, Lemon, Peppermint can still keep up a row.
Unless we're careful where we sell,
they're drinking extracts now.

These songs came out during the 1920s for use in temperance rallies and revivals. Fortunately, we have come a long way in our understanding, treatment, and dealing with social problems and addictive behaviors; while at the same time knowing the drugs people have access to in this day and age are certainly a lot more destructive and deadly than any extracts. Still, I am thankful there always have been a sense of temperance, or at least strong moderation, as well as a growing appreciation for Wesleyan holiness. That doesn't mean I have ever considered myself perfect in my spiritual walk or guiltless from the above mentioned sins; but when Bishop Oliphint asked our ordination class if we believed we would be made perfect in love in this life, I said yes; and I still believe that.

My very good friend Joe lost his father the summer before our sophomore year in high school, in a one-car accident on US Highway 81, about a mile and a half north of the county line on a very stormy night. He hit some water running across the road and the car veered into a hedge tree and killed him instantly. One Sunday afternoon, we drove through the cemetery past his grave. Lying in the middle of the road was a nearly full package of Lucky Strike cigarettes. So we picked them up, and as we had planned, headed for the Ninnescah River, on the west side of the Old Maids Bridge for a swim. As always, we had a lot of fun just sitting in the cool river, feeling the shifting sand passing by. We decided to light up a cigarette. Petty soon we had four or five cigarettes at one time in our mouths just puffing away like a couple of old Baldwin steam engines. We went through all of those cigarettes that afternoon in the river. We got out, dried off a little and I took Joe to his house about two miles from where we were. We were sitting at the table about to eat a snack when I noticed his Mother lean down and get real close to him. I thought she was going to give him a kiss. Well, what happened next scared the life out of me; she lit into him like Katie bar the door! "You boys have been smoking! I can smell it on your breath!" Joe was screaming by this time, "No we weren't! No we weren't!" His older brother David said, "Come here and let me smell your breath." So Joe went over and had David smell his breath and said, "Smells like Doritos to me." Now while this wasn't exactly true, to keep from furthering any attention to our breath, Joe said, "Yea, that's right, it's Doritos, we stopped at Pennock's Corner, which we had, (earlier) and got a pop and a bag of Doritos." Earl and Crete Pennock ran a small mom and pop gas station at the Belle Plaine Y, where we often stopped for a bottle of pop and a candy bar. Couldn't buy anything else there, because Crete was a member of the Stitch and Chatter Club with my Grandma Hunt, and there certainly were no secrets in that organization. Well, we probably should have felt a little shame for only telling a half-truth there, but it seemed to lower the anxiety surrounding the issue, and got us on to the snacks.

We also tried cigars. On Friday or Saturday nights, we would go in to the pool hall and maybe play a game or two of snooker. Our pool hall was a wonderful place. I could play dominoes with World War I veterans like Uncle George. If I was on his team, he would always say, "Make a nickel every time you can boy." That is a reference to scoring points during a game. If you won, you received a cardboard token worth five cents. When you got two of them, you could get a bottle of pop. A cue for pool or snooker was fifteen cents. If you won, the loser had to pay the whole thirty cents. There was a counter about a third of the way down on the side with the domino and card tables. I would go over to the side of the counter that was farthest from the table where my Uncle Wendell, one of Dad's brothers, was sitting and ask Tab or Odie for a package of Swisher Sweets Cigars. I would always feel inclined to add the personal request, "Please don't say anything to Uncle Wendell" and they would always respond, "Oh, we won't say anything." It seemed difficult to smoke a good cigar in Belle Plaine with so many relatives. Anyway, for thirty-five cents that was pretty cheap entertainment as we would walk down the tracks of the Atchison, Topeka, and Santa Fe Railway smoking these cigars. When they were gone, we would walk back to town chewing several packs of gum.

Then there was Ripple Night; one of the most terrible, horrible, and most certainly shameful nights of my life and probably Joe's and whoever else was around that evening. During our senior year in high school, we had an older friend buy us a case of Ripple Wine; that's twenty-four bottles, of one the absolutely worst of the extremely low-end, fortified wines, also referred to as hooch, street wine, goon, bum wine, and poverty punch. Our case was a mixture of two flavors, Pagan Pink and Ripple Red. This stuff was so bad; they haven't made it for many years. There are a few things about that night that are somewhat vague, but one thing became very clear to me in its aftermath, that there are some very good reasons why Paul says in Ephesians 5:18 "Do not get drunk on wine." On those exceptionally rare occasions when the events of that night are recalled, there is a sense of laughter mixed in with the indignity, and disgrace.

There is however, a real tragedy surrounding the epidemic of underage drinking in this county. The sad fact is that there are those for whom such experiences are much more than a bad night and a good learning experience. I, like most pastors, have discovered the difficulty in being present with a family who has just experienced any number of results of a loved one who has engaged in underage drinking.

There is a fine, often blurred line between some of the older standards of holiness and legalism which Paul grapples with in Colossians 2:20-23:
> *Since you died with Christ to the basic principles of this world, why, as though you still belonged to it, do you submit to its rules: 'Do not handle! Do not taste! Do not touch!'....Such regulations indeed have an appearance of wisdom, with their self-imposed worship, their false humility, and their harsh treatment of the body, but they lack any value in restraining sensual indulgence.*

Mr. Wesley comments on that value:
> *Yet they are not of any real value before God, nor do they, upon the whole, mortify, but satisfy the flesh. They indulge our corrupt nature, our self-will, pride and desire of being distinguished from others.* [21]

While there is great merit in observing a temperate life, it should be an inward holiness that produces the outward appearance, not the other way around. Holiness is who you are in relationship to God as opposed to a visible piety.

I remember an old retired Methodist Preacher, Reverend Ellis Turner, who was in the church at Geneseo, while I was the pastor there. His favorite Scripture was Isaiah 35:8
> *And an highway shall be there and a way, and it shall be called The Way of Holiness.*

Now my highway of life has included several circuitous detours, wrong turns, and moving violations. There have been stumbles, setbacks, and even backslidings. My guess would be this is probably true of all honest people, especially those willing to admit to having had Lucky Strike moments, or Ripple nights. It's like a highway sign I remember seeing in Kentucky. Shortly following the breakup of my relationship with the first great love of my life, my dear seminary friend and fellow Larabite, Tim Morgan, decided to invite me home with him for the long Easter weekend. We were on our way to his home in Buford, Georgia when alongside the road was this sign which read "Caution! Deceptive Curve Ahead." Sure enough, after going over a little rise in the road, it took an immediate turn to the left which you couldn't see until you were practically in it. Only in Kentucky I thought to myself. I had never seen such a sign before and never have since, but I have certainly gone around several of those deceptive curves for sure. Still the convictions of holiness were always there; even through smoke outs on the river, Ripple night, and anything else I would encounter, and they remained Ebenezers for me.

Reflection:

What deceptive curves have you encountered?

How are you allowing God's work within you to be producing the 'outward appearance'?

Where does the concept of holiness fit in our modern, or post modern age?

Confiscated: Two Cottontails, One Opossum, and One .22 Rifle

But the Lord replied, "Have you any right to be angry?" (Jonah 4:9)

Well, there are times that I would like to think so for sure. At least I'm in good company with the prophet Jonah regarding anger. I would probably be in good company with most of America. We are a nation of very angry people these days. We have Tea Party anger, political/partisan anger, economic anger, domestic anger, road-rage anger. There is consumer anger, employee anger, environmental anger, racial anger, and then the just plain old "I'm just mad" anger. Our post-modern society seems to be living with a proclivity to neurotic traits which allow this anger to remain very close to the surface of what we call civilization; a veneer which is growing thinner all the time. It is as if we all have developed our own personal hot button or golden navel that is way too easily touched off, or as Mom used to say, "You've got a short fuse." For those of us who are prone to light and throw as opposed to lay and light, the short fused firecracker will eventually burn us. For Jonah, his hot button issue surrounded the people of Nineveh, their response, at least in this narrative, to God's word, and probably most significantly, God having mercy on them. Jonah's reaction to this outcome led him to throw one of the best pity parties recorded in Scripture.

I've never thought of myself as having an anger management problem, but I do get angry once in a great while; and most likely can't refer to it as righteous anger. Injustice, both socially and on a more personal level is one quick way for me to get angry. Several years ago, I attended a General Church Consultation on Cooperative Ministry in Irving, Texas. On the way home, while traveling up Interstate 35 through southern Oklahoma, my cell phone rang. It was Joyce wondering where I was. Then she made one of those statements that I just hate, "Well, you're not going to be happy!" Why do people start conversations by saying things like that? So I asked, "What happened?"

"Your oldest son got a ticket" she said. "Speeding?" I wondered. "No" she said, "He shot a possum and the game warden gave him a ticket." Then she added, "They took your rifle Justin was using."

She was right. I was not happy, and the more I thought about it, the more unhappy I got. In fact I was getting angry. Now, I've never been a great fan of game wardens but when the State of Kansas let them start running around with guns, and draw their weapons on sixteen-year old boys on private property for shooting a stinking possum, that borders on, well let's just say my uncles and a couple of million other GIs went to war to fight that kind of behavior in the 1940s. As I later found out, the boys were indeed on private property belonging to the grandparents of one of them. They had been reported by a "concerned neighbor" as possibly being the deer poaching ring from Oklahoma. So a small army of heavily armed men including a sheriff's officer, a highway patrol trooper, two game wardens and a couple of members of the Junior Squirrel Patrol converged on the farm where Justin and several other boys had been hunting possums and rabbits for fun. When they had surrounded and captured the boys, only to find out they were not the villainous Oklahoma deer poaching ring they were hoping for, (I think they just felt plain stupid for stumbling upon such a dangerous gang of hoodlums like these sixteen-year-old possum killers) they decided to write them up to the fullest extent of the law anyway. Yea! I think they were just trying to save face myself. Still my biggest fear was what they would do with my .22 Mossberg rifle; the gun had been my dad's. To lose this gun because my kid killed a possum was the most preposterous, ludicrous, and farcical thing I had ever heard. Still, game wardens are some of the most powerful people in the state of Kansas.

Several days later, I went with Justin to the courthouse to see about the ticket and the fine. We walked up the stairs to the Clerk of the Court's office. Justin presented the ticket, and I asked how much it would be. The woman disappeared for a few moments and came back and said, "Well! It looks like that will be $405.00." "FOOOURRRHH-HUUUNNNDREEEDAAANNNDFFFIIIVEEEDOOOLLLAAAR-

RRSSSS!!!!????" "My God lady! The boy would have been better off getting caught smoking marijuana or drinking a jug of Old Crow Whiskey!!!" I said. "We're talking about a cat-food-stealing, flea-riddled, vermin possum here! Why I've shot truckloads of possums in my day! What kind of a bunch of Nazis are these people?" I continued as my neck veins bulged out from around my shirt collar. The clerk said "Well I'm sorry but Wildlife and Parks set their own rules, the court is only a collection agent." As we walked out of the office, I was still talking about Nazis, and jack boots, and the godless heathen game wardens. "What kind of a lesson about respect for the law do game wardens expect sixteen year olds to learn when they treat them like hardened, professional Oklahoma deer poachers?" I wondered. When we finally got outside and headed for the car, Justin, my oldest son looked at me and said, "Dad, I don't care how much trouble I ever get in, just please don't ever go with me to the courthouse again."

Well some how he got his fine paid, and I got my gun back. Still, I couldn't give up the anger I had about game wardens. In nearly every sermon for a long time afterward, when I wanted to describe hell-bent sinners or the forces of evil, and injustice, I usually included the phrase "like game wardens." It was almost liturgical. Church attendance seemed to increase as people came just to try to hear some new tirade on game wardens. Now to be fair, and show my magnanimity about things, I know that the game wardens do run across some pretty dangerous people out there, especially poachers; so I can sort of, kind of understand their suspicions of unusual activity and their need for self protection.

It wasn't long after all of this that the Presbyterian pastor came by to visit with me about a funeral service. "Kendal, you know we've had a death in our congregation, and I know the service will be too large for our church to handle. Would it be possible for us to use your sanctuary for the service?" Well in my heart and mind I knew this person he was talking about was a good Christian man, a highly respected person in the area, well loved by everyone who knew him, AND a retired game warden. I said to Tom, "Will there be any game wardens at the funeral." He seemed a little surprised with the question and said, "Well, I'm sure there will be a lot of game wardens and others from Wildlife and Parks there." I said, "Well, you can have the funeral service here on one condition; that I hang a dead possum on the front of the pulpit." He had a look that seemed odd for a Calvinist. I told him the Reader's Digest version of the possum story and then in an act of great generosity of spirit, reassured him they were welcome to use our church, and that there would be no dead possum anywhere on the property.

That anger thing was getting rather 'convicting' in a spiritual manner. I recalled my very first pastoral crises; or at least that's what I called it back then. A man, who was a member of the Bentonville Church where I served as student pastor, called me one day and asked if I would come out to their house as he needed to talk with me. So I headed out Old Dutch Road to the place where they lived. I had no more than got sat down in a chair when he said, "Kendal, I have stomach cancer and they don't give me very long to live." We talked al little bit about the symptoms he had noticed and his trip to the hospital where they discovered the cancer. He followed that by saying, "Preacher, I'm scared!" He paused for a few seconds and then added, "I'm not afraid of dying but I got to know that I am right with the Lord. Can you help me?" I said, "Bill what makes you think you're not right with the Lord?" He then shared, "I have been angry with a man in Manchester for twenty years and I know that before I die, I have to make it right with him." He then told me the whole story of this person who at one time was a friend and co-worker, what it was that made him angry, and how he had spent years avoiding and hating this man. Since this was my first real pastoral crises, I said, "Let's pray about it." So I led him through a prayer of repentance and asking for the Lord to come into his heart and life in a saving and healing way; then added, "And make a way for Bill to reconcile his anger with this man."

Well this was obviously an Ebenezer moment for me, because Bill really showed a peace in his spirit and a sense of relief in his personality. He thanked me and I headed back to town. He actually started coming back to church on Sunday mornings. It wasn't but a few days following our first conversation that he went down to Manchester where this other person worked in his business. Bill, as he related the incident to me, walked into the store and headed straight for the man. He noticed Bill and moved toward him. There they stood together for the first time in twenty years. Bill's first words were "I'm sorry!" and he acknowledged that the whole affair that started their estrangement was his fault in the first place. The two embraced, and Bill, though dying of a cancer that could very well have been started by the long term gnawing anger in his spirit, was truly healed.

When we were getting ready to move from Pratt, the church gave us a farewell dinner. Actually it was a roast which was emceed by one of the great pros at puns and putdowns, Gary Schmidt, a strong leader in the church and in the Conference. During the proceedings, Ruth Ann Barker, a member of the Seekers Sunday School Class I had taught, got up and read a poem she had written entitled "The Possum Patrol" a clever piece of prose immortalizing the whole possum, game warden affair.

THE POSSUM PATROL

One of God's beloved creatures is a furry gray animal with odd features.
Part rat with a long tail and a pouch they're often seen flat along the road—Ouch!
Known for their bad habits and messy nests,
some local teens thought they'd rid the area of these pests.
Armed with great-grandpa's shotgun, Justin and friends were out to have some fun!
Due to the glow of the flashlight beam, concerned neighbors called in the S.W.A.T. team.
There was some confusion if they were patrolling possum or poachers of deer,
But, the "Junior Squirrel Patrol" was on the job-so have no fear!
When all the chaos settled down, the gun was confiscated and the youth driven to town.
Four-hundred and five dollars later, Pastor Utt had the gun back and
was a true possum hater.
Kendal has been known to say, "The only good possum is a dead possum."
And much more,
Like: "You can shoot a possum only if it's carrying a knife and barging in your door!"
The possum is one way we know God has a sense of humor, this I know is true.
What other animal looks like that, can play dead, and be of such high 'value?'
Now as we bid farewell to Pastor Utt, our good friend,
We send with him our well wishes without possums around the bend.

Now, many years removed from the original incident, it is more a humorous yet straightforward reminder of how God calls us to avoid, or at best confront our anger in thoughtful, faithful ways. Scripture is full of anger management verses, especially in Ephesians 4:26, "In your anger, do not sin. Do not let the sun go down while you are still angry." I have come to the point where I don't see any difference between Jonah's harboring of his anger about Nineveh and God's acceptance of their repentance and my own feelings about the possum incident. I don't know if Justin or any of his friends really learned any lesson about obeying hunting laws, or if the Fish and Game boys learned anything about appropriate measures in dealing with younger offenders of possum regulations. But I know that when God asks me, as He did Jonah, "Have you any right to be angry?" my answer will always be, "No Sir! That is as long as it doesn't have anything to do with game wardens." Still, when it all boils down, anger is not a right, it's a trait that should probably be kept in check, or we may find ourselves becoming frustrated with the message of God to the Ninevehs of our day.

Reflection:

What are the attitudes, grudges, feelings, which would be good for you to let go of?

How can an emotion such as anger be detrimental to your relationships, your health?

Is there a way that a person's anger can hinder God's working through you?

Our Little Scarecrow

To keep me from becoming conceited because of these surpassingly great revelations, there was given me a thorn in my flesh.
(I Corinthians 12:7)

Our family, I mean the folks, Mom and Dad, Uncle Howard and Aunt Dorothy, and Grandma and Grandpa, had a really big garden for a number of years. There was one part of the garden behind the old chicken house. Then out by the road was where the sweet corn and the potatoes were grown. Roasting ears drenched in butter, and new potatoes fried in their jackets in butter, is some of the best eating a person could ever experience. When the potatoes were ready, Granddad would hook an ancient walking plow to the tractor, and Uncle Howard or Dad would drive the tractor and Granddad would walk behind the plow. When all of the rows were plowed up, the rest of us would start gathering the potatoes into baskets and putting them in the back of the pickup and haul them to the house.

Once when the corn was still short and the potatoes just getting started, it rained. Later that morning, it was still sort of misty, but I needed to get outside for awhile. I put on a jacket of Grandma's that was way too big. I got one of Granddad's old felt hats and put that on, trying to keep it from covering my whole head, and I stepped into his rubber boots that on him would come up just below his knees. On me they were well above the knees, making walking a rather stiff effort. But I wanted to walk through some puddles and mud, so with these uncomfortable boots, draping jacket and overwhelming hat, I headed out toward the garden area by the road. I was just walking and minding my own business, aware of how silly I probably looked, when wouldn't you know it, a car came down the road, sloshing back and forth through the ruts. I recognized it. It was that old 1955 light tan Ford driven by the Rutherford sisters, Nada and Maxine; probably out looking for fishing worms after the rain. Well I didn't want them to see me dressed up the way I was, I knew I looked ridiculously silly, but there I was out in the open, exposed with nowhere to hide. Suddenly I got a great idea; I would freeze into a position with my arms held straight out, and pretend to be a scarecrow. They would drive by and think Granddad had put a scarecrow out there in the garden. The car slowly drove by and disappeared across the mighty Euphrates. I headed back to the house as walking in those tall boot was wearing me out.

Now Maxine ran a small variety store in Belle Plaine that I loved to go in because of the toy corner. It was about the only place in town you could get toys except for the Western Auto. But on this first trip there with Mom after the rainy day experience, I realized I would be tagged for the rest of my life; or at least as long as Nada and Maxine had any memory at all. We walked into the store and the first thing I heard was, "Well there's our little scarecrow!" Maxine exclaimed. "Marjorie," she continued, "Nada and I saw him out in the garden at your folks the other day and it was just so cute how he pretended to be a scarecrow when we drove by." Why couldn't it have been the mailman, or the REA truck, or Cline Clewell, or a complete stranger," I thought to myself. No! It had to be the Rutherford sisters. It seemed like from then on, anywhere they saw me, it was, "How's our little scarecrow today?" Oh, I know they weren't being cruel or anything, but it was embarrassing for a kid, or as I would say now, a humbling experience.

I remember very early on in my ministry serving a parish where we had funds to help people out with a variety of things including utilities, medicine, and help with a first rent payment to help someone get established. As I was the person who normally made the decisions about the use of those funds, a young man who was a senior in high school, and would be graduating in several weeks, came into my office and said he was wanting to go ahead and move out of his parents home and needed help getting into an apartment. I said, "Well, I think we can help you if you think you can sustain yourself from here on." "I have a job" he said. I called the owner of the rental property and visited with him about this young man and that we would be able to get his first month's rent paid. That was easy I thought. That is until that evening when the phone rang and it was this young man's mother on the other end. She was about as mad as Bandit's mother was when I took him from his home. Bandit was my little pet raccoon I had trapped out of a hole in an old cottonwood tree along the banks of the mighty Euphrates Creek which flowed through the farm; and when I tried to pull him out of the den tree, his mother threw quite a fit with gnashing teeth and spit and hissing and claws. It wasn't pretty then or now.

It seems that there had been no conversation between the other members of the family, and I had unwittingly become party to a plan which was not fully endorsed by everyone. In today's language, I had become triangulated. As she spoke in a very loud and high pitched tone, I could occasionally get in a response in like, "You are so right." and "I should have checked these things out." At the end of the conversation, I reassured her that I would do what I could to amend this situation and my mistake. The next day, I went to the school and asked the principal to see the young man. We went into the school counselor's office, closed the door, and began to talk. I said, "You know the rest of your family is pretty upset with this whole notion of you going out on your own right now. I would suggest you back away from this plan to get out on your own, and stay at home for now." Well miracles still happen! He agreed and said, "I guess I can do that." I called the property owner and told him we wouldn't need the apartment. Then I went over to his parent's home, knocked on the door, hoping no one was home. They were. Anyway, we had a very good visit. I think they appreciated the fact I went to the school and talked with him and that I was very understanding and apologetic of the failure on my part. That was just about the largest piece of crow I had ever eaten.

Garry Winget, a well respected, retired pastor in our Annual Conference, and a person who directed our United Methodist Urban Ministries in Wichita so ably for eleven or twelve years, was such a powerful advocate for the poor. He wrote a book several years ago entitled, The Key Ingredient–Humility. When I first looked at this book,

I questioned, this is by the man who should be given his own personal microphone at Annual Conference? Then even he admits in Chapter 1 that as he told a friend that he was doing some work on humility, his friend responded by saying "How can you do that? You are not at all modest." Well Garry probably doesn't know me from Adam, but I certainly know him as being one of the leaders of the Annual Conference when I was in my younger years of service. I remember watching him head to the microphone time after time. I remember poor Bishop Hicks always recognizing him at a microphone as "Jerry" to which Garry would always correct him.

In his chapter, "Humility"–that's a laugh, he writes, "You cannot be humble without a sense of humor...Pride is a barrier to becoming a real person...even being cheap can be an object of pride." [22]

I certainly agree with his first two statements; especially the one about humor. Like Garry, the last one is rather convicting for me. I tend to take great pride in just how cheaply I can get something done. Still, if people can't laugh at themselves, that is to not take them self too seriously (rule #6), they will have a pride problem, and it will be a barrier. It is very helpful to not take yourself too seriously, to not wear your emotions on your shirt sleeve, and certainly not to be thin skinned about everything someone says to or about you.

Now I've never had anywhere near the experiences of a person of Paul's stature; being imprisoned, flogged, beaten, stoned, or shipwrecked, as recorded in II Corinthians 11:23-25. Still, like many, I'm prone to pride and conceit from time to time. I know I would have a far more inflated sense of myself if God, in his infinite wisdom, hadn't given me any number of thorns in the flesh to keep me humble, and any number of continuing humbling experiences. We will probably never know this side of heaven what exactly Paul's thorn in the flesh was, but he understood its purpose for his life and ministry. I've been a scarecrow and I have eaten a lot of crow, and as uncomfortable or distasteful as it may be, I have to take it all positively as God's means in reminding me of my weakness and God's power.

Reflection:

In what ways have you allowed humility to become a part of your personal identity?

Is being humble a point of pride?

What humbling moments have been pivotal to you in positive ways?

Watch Out For That Dog

But the Lord stood by my side and gave me strength......And I was delivered out of the lion's mouth. (II Timothy 4:17)

I was heading to Portsmouth, Ohio about forty miles from Bentonville, and I decided to take US Highway 52, a pretty drive along the Ohio River. The 1973 Chevy Impala I had could launch aircraft off the hood by today's standards. It was a pretty car too and comfortable to drive. But it only got around fifteen miles per gallon and that was going downhill. Tires have always been my nemesis. I've rarely had a vehicle that had good tires on it for very long. On this particular day, about fifteen miles out of Manchester, I had a flat tire. I pulled off the highway and opened up the trunk. The spare was as flat as the tire on the car, so there would be no quick change today. I was just about a hundred yards from a house so I headed for it. It was an old two-story frame house set in a small open area with a barn and a couple of sheds. There were quite a lot of trees as you looked back toward the hill.

I walked up to the back door of the house, as that seemed to be the only one used. There by the back step was an old dog lying down. As I approached him, I said, "Hello pup." He looked up at me, wagged his tail, and went back to sleep. I knocked on the door; no one answered. The screen was shut but the door was open, so I knocked again. Again, no one answered. Finally I decided I would need to go elsewhere for help. As I turned to head back for the highway, I suddenly noticed someone looking at me from behind a tree. I hollered, "Hello! I need to see about using a phone." The man who had been watching me from the trees stepped away and walked toward me. As he got closer, I would have sworn it was none other than Earnest T. Bass, the rock throwing man from the hills on the old Andy Griffith show. He was a dead ringer for him. I identified myself and my need by saying, "I'm Reverend Utt from the Methodist Church at Bentonville. I've got a flat tire on my car and there's no air in my spare. Could I use your telephone?" Now he looked to be quite old enough to be the master of this domicile for sure, so I was surprised when he said, "Well Mom and Dad have gone into town so I'm the only one here." He was silent for few seconds and then continued, "But I guess it's alright if you just want to use the telephone." So we headed back toward the house. As we got close to the back door, he said, "Now watch out for that dog; he bites." Well, sure enough, as we got there, the dog, now aroused from his sleep, jumped up and bit him on the leg. I think he just had him by his pant leg as he was dancing a jig trying to shake the dog loose. He finally got the dog off and said, "See what I mean?" When we got into the house, the kitchen was quite a mess with the cabinets and dinner table full of clutter and I couldn't help but notice the linoleum on the floor, one of those old purple and grey, flowery patterns popular when Hoover was President of the United States. We followed a little path back to the front room of the house where the phone was. I made my call and felt secure in the knowledge that someone was now coming to get me. I thanked the man for allowing me to use the phone and exited the house, walked past the sleeping dog, and headed for my car on the other side of the road and waited for my ride.

    I have always been mindful of God's providential and watchful presence in my life. A lot of people don't believe my mountain lion experience, especially game wardens who deny the existence of big cats in Kansas, (unless you shoot one then would probably want a thousand dollars for it) but it is as true as a plumb line. My dad's brother, Uncle Glenn and Aunt Janice along with my two cousins Bobby and Randy, lived for a while on a farm straight east of Arkansas City on old US 166. The place was where the highway curved to the north and the Silverdale road turned to the south. It was a fun place. It had big barns and sheds, and a pond we could fish in, but "Don't ever get in the water!" was the strong admonition from Aunt Janice. One Saturday morning, after staying all night with my cousins, we went up to the pond. We decided to build a raft and float out onto the water; that way we wouldn't get wet and we wouldn't get in trouble. We got a couple of empty oil drums, some boards, some rope, and wire and started to construct our raft. When we had it to where we thought she was sea worthy, we set it out in the water and climbed on board. We used a long board to push off and as it headed for the center of the pond the rope started to loosen, the barrels started to fill with water, the boards we were sitting on were separating, and we wound up in the pond. Wet and muddy, we headed back to the house. When we walked up onto the porch, Aunt Janice saw us and immediately knew where we had been. Now I didn't realize that she was so religious the way she started talking about God and Jesus in her loud and excited voice. Fortunately we lived through the raft experience.

On one occasion while I was visiting them, I decided to take a walk by myself up to the pasture which was on top of a rock rimmed bluff. From up there you could look down on the barns and the broad expanse of the Arkansas River valley. I stopped by the barn and picked an old wooden handle, probably once holding a pitchfork; I thought I would use it as a walking stick. I followed the cow path as I made my way. I was several hundred yards from the house when something caught my eye. I stopped and turned to the right. What I was seeing there before me, not twenty yards away, was a mountain lion, or cougar, or whatever, just looking at me. Now it took a moment for me to realize this was not a big kitty, or a bob cat, or swamp gas. I was literally standing eyeball to eyeball with a real live mountain lion. After a long few seconds, the mountain lion turned and ran off. I did the only thing I could do. I stood there and watched him run across the pasture and then jump effortlessly through the hedge row. I don't know if it was the stick I had in my hand, or the fact that he wasn't hungry right then, or what. All I know is it decided to run away without making so much as a sound. Whether it's strange dogs, angry aunts, or surprised lions, as I consider it, God has always been my deliverer. It's like a verse from an old song that says:

I saw him in the furnace, he doubted not nor feared;
For in the flames beside him, the Son of God appeared.
Though seven times t'was heated with all the Tempter's might,
He said the yoke is easy, the burden it is light.

Reflection:

Have you experienced any situations where you just felt like your deliverance was a God thing?

What level of confidence have you gained over the years in facing unknown situations?

What lions have you stood eyeball to eyeball with?

Bridle Your Tongue

If anyone considers himself religious and yet does not keep a tight rein on his tongue, he deceives himself and his religion is worthless. (James 1:26)

I really love to watch the re-runs of The Honeymooner's with Jackie Gleason. His character, Ralph Cramden, was usually letting his tongue get him into trouble. Occasionally he would be forced to say, "Me and my big mouth!" We had an old neighbor lady, Mrs. Bowlby. She was a widowed farm wife who had moved into town and lived across the street from us. When I got old enough, I mowed her lawn and around her 126,000 Iris plants. Mom used to pick her up and take her to Sunday school and church with us. Her face was care worn and weathered; leathery from years of working outside in the Kansas climates. One Sunday morning, I turned around (pre-child restraint days) and asked her, "Miss Bowlby, how come your face is so cracked?" She let out big laugh. Mom wasn't laughing. I knew if I didn't do something quick I was going to get one of those oriental death pinches under the thigh that could literally immobilize a child. I had received a number of those over the years. That's why I always hated to sit next to Mom at family dinners. Anyway, being as quick thinking as I could be, I said, "But you sure do have pretty legs Miss Bowlby." I think it was her continued laughter that spared me from Mom's desire to discipline me except for her stern command "Turn around, sit down, and be quiet!"

I know there were times in which I was cheated out of opportunities to speak. In the 1963 Belle Plaine Grade School Operetta, myself and two other third graders were rabbits. My only speaking part was that I would walk out onto the middle of the stage and say, "Hark my Queen, the frogs are coming!" When it came time for my part, my moment of glory before the entire town, I walked out onto center stage with my long, straight rabbit ears, stopped at the appropriate spot and, without waiting for my royal announcement, head frog, Billy Barngrover, and the rest of the frogs came croaking onto the stage anyway, so I slunk back to where the rabbit section was and sat down. Now that was extremely traumatic. That could be one reason I have had a hard time not saying something at any opportunity to this very day.

Just keeping your mouth shut, or at least being careful about what you are going to say is often a tricky feat. There was a sign over the counter at the old Lumber Yard that read, "Make sure your brain is in gear before engaging your mouth!" It hung right next to the sign that read, "FOR SALE ONE HENWAY." to which you were supposed to ask, "What's a Henway?" and Charlie Woll, the man who owned the lumber yard, would light up and say "About five pounds." And then roar with his unique laugh. Still, the first sign was pretty good advice even if it was pretty hard to follow.

When the folks decided to build their new house out on the east side of town, Mr. Watson, a son of Macy Watson, was the builder and realtor who came by to visit with Dad about buying the old house. Dad had bought the house from Uncle Howard before I was born. It was an old two story house built in the late 1870s. In one of the closets upstairs there were a few loose floorboards, and if you took them out, there was a tin lined box where old man Darby, the original builder of the house, kept his money. I guess people didn't trust banks back then either. It had a big front porch with a balcony that we used to like to go out on and play. Dad didn't like for us to be out there however. I don't think it was so much about us falling off and getting hurt as it was his fear of us making the porch roof leak. Anyway, I tagged along as they walked around looking over the outside of the house. Dad made the comment as they looked at a bad place in the foundation on the north side of the house under the bathroom. Dad pointed it out and said, "This is a sore spot on the house." For some reason, I felt a need to say something, so what came out of my mouth was, "If you ask me, the whole house is a sore spot." Well I immediately knew that Dad was not happy. The good news was he couldn't do anything about it with Mr. Watson standing there, but I knew I was in trouble. They must have had a good conversation after I headed into the house, because he had cooled down a little. When Mom asked him how it went, he said, "It went alright; except that little Mr. Utt here needs to learn to keep his big mouth shut." Whenever the word Mister was used in addressing or speaking about me, I knew it wasn't good.

Mouth problems are hard to outgrow. In our freshman year, spring of 1969, our school sponsored a day in which there were no classes, but a set of discussion sessions called a "GAP RAP" to talk about the issues present in the so called generation gap of the late sixties. There were several of the pastors from the community who were part of the adults leading group discussions. The first group I was in just happened to be led by our pastor from the United Methodist Church. He handed out a sheet of paper with various questions on it. One of the questions asked was, "Do you feel that heavy petting is alright?" Well I had the answer for that question, and I was the first to raise my hand. Reverend Dalke said, "Okay Kendal, what do you think?" "Well" I said hesitantly, "I don't think it is right because it is a terrible waste of money!" The room was silent, perhaps even stunned, as all eyes were fixed on me. Following the eternity of the next few awkward seconds, the laughter began when they, and I, realized the question was not "Do you believe heavy betting is alright?" Even if I had understood the appropriate word in the question, my answer would have probably centered on being nice to animals.

At the Geneseo Church, we had a person who had been a member all his life. He usually never missed worship, and sat in the same place every Sunday. His wife was very active in United Methodist Women and other committees around the church. He was a great guy; always friendly and jovial. He would do anything for anybody. His one fault was profanity. His everyday language contained several words and phrases that would cause a sailor to blush. I don't think he realized it anymore; it had become so natural to his conversation. One Sunday morning, the Gospel text was about the Gadarene Demoniac. Somewhere I briefly got off the subject, and made one of those comments that an intelligent preacher would have avoided. I said, "I read somewhere that one sure way to determine possible demon possession is if a person uses a lot of profanity." Suddenly, as with the direction of a great conductor, every head in the room turned to look this particular person. He was suddenly busy looking for a crack in the floor to crawl into. Fortunately, I was able to get back on task and retrieve everyone's attention again toward the pulpit. I had to apologize after service, as he came through the front door. "Oh don't think anything about" he said.

As the associate pastor at Wellington, I was scheduled to preach one Sunday in Advent. I had discussed how bells were used to call people to worship, and then made the following comment; "When it comes to bells, nobody can ring them like English Anglicans." Then I happened to look into the faces of the church's bell choir sitting in the front two pews before me, who had just finished ringing an anthem. In order to redeem myself I added the caveat, "That is the large steeple bells." I also remembered the Sunday I would make public the engagement of Joyce and me to be married. She was going to join the church that day, as she had been a member of Church of Christ along with many generations of her family. So I worded my announcement carefully about the fact that we would be getting married. When I had concluded, there was no response at all. You could hear the crickets down in the boiler room chirping away, but not a peep out of the congregation. I finally broke the silence and said, "People, I think I just announced our engagement." at which point everyone joined in one of those relief laughs and began to applaud which certainly made me feel better. Joyce was scheduled to come forward at the end of the service to join, and my mother was going to walk down with her for support, as Joyce suffered from severe shyness. We had finished singing the last hymn and I invited those wishing to join to come forward. Joyce and Mom made their way to the front of the sanctuary, where I received her into the membership of First Church, Wellington. Everything was going along great; had I stopped right there, I would have had a great day. However, I added the following comment; "You know folks, this is a hard way to do evangelism!" Well the congregation laughed, but poor Joyce turned about fifteen shades of red, and gave me a look that fortunately only myself, the Lord Jesus, and saints Matthew, Mark, Luke, and John in the lancet windows behind me could see.

When Adam and Brandon were still pretty young and Taylor was a baby, we were coming back from Superior, Nebraska one early December afternoon. We had left the highway at Lovewell Lake and headed west to turn on the white rock road for Mankato. Now at that time, there were more deer in Jewell County than people, so it wasn't surprising to see two dead deer next to each other along the road several miles north of town. I know I should have, but I couldn't resist it; as we approached the dead deer I said, "Oh look boys, somebody ran over a couple of Santa's reindeer." Dear God in heaven, when they saw those two deer, they began to cry and squall like a couple of crazed banshees signaling the impending death of a member of the household, which I was gathering was probably going to be me. The boy's cries suddenly paled in comparison to the sounds coming out of Joyce as she chewed on me for saying such stuff to the boys. I should have known better; I did know better. I just blew it. I can only hope that any difficulties any of them might have down the road will not be a result of the trauma I caused them on that day. Then again I wonder.

For preachers, the admonition to bridle your tongue should help her or him to stay on the subject, but it doesn't. During worship in Mankato's Harmony United Methodist Church, I was in the middle of a sermon, doing what I felt at least was a fair job. Suddenly, I was off subject. I said, "And if we don't take care of the environment as good stewards of God's creation, the polar icecaps will melt, the coast will flood, and all the sewer rats from New York City will come here." Well, I got myself back on the message and didn't think any more about it until I was standing at the back of the church greeting people afterward. I saw a woman I had never seen in church before making her way up the isle toward me. When she got to the point of shaking my hand, she introduced herself as Beulah Balch's daughter and said, "I have lived in New York City for over twenty-five years, and I have never seen a sewer rat. I'm the secretary at the Park Avenue Christian Church; they'll really get a kick out of hearing this one." Now I don't think she was upset, as she was laughing about it, but I'll avoid Park Avenue if I ever make it to New York City.

One particular Sunday at Pratt, I was standing in front of the sacristy in the hall behind the sanctuary with my robe on. One of the little Fitzsimmons kids, James, walked up to me and said, "What is that thing around your neck?" They usually attended first service where I didn't wear any vestments. I answered back, "It's a stole." "What's it for?" he asked, continuing the conversation. Just trying to tease the little fellow, I responded by saying, "Well I use it to swat little kids in church when they don't behave." Now about this time, a number of women came running out of every door of the Sanctuary with a deeply concerned look on their face and drawing their hands across their throats saying, "Your mic is on! Your mic is on!" About that time, the prelude began and the lay reader for the day and I walked into the sanctuary to what I remember as being a muffled laughter rippling throughout the congregation. So far, God has allowed me to experience brief bouts of humiliation and correction for a mouth that has been untimely placed in gear; usually with laughter, but always with reconciliation. The Psalmist's request for mouth control is about as good a prayer as one can utter: "Set a guard over my mouth, O Lord; keep watch over the door of my lips." (Psalm 141:3)

Reflection:

What disciplines, exercises or other forms of restraint keep you from saying things that might become regretful?

How have you handled misspoken words either by you, or directed toward you or others by someone else?

When God Does a New Thing

Forget the former things; do not dwell on the past. See, I am doing a new thing! Now it springs up; do you not perceive it? I am making a way in the desert and streams in the wasteland. (Isaiah 43:18-19)

Following the demise of the old 1949 Dodge pickup, which meant my sister got to drive it; Dad bought a 1956 Ford two-door hard-top. It was pretty rusted out around the wheel wells and fenders. The only way you could get it to "lay rubber" was to back up and then drop it into drive and stomp on the accelerator. Still, it was a means of transportation. It would get you home, if you knew all the tricks of starting it. One day after school, I stopped by Granddad and Grandma Utt's. When I got ready to leave, the car wouldn't start, so I went back into the house. "Grandma, could you come outside and help me get my car started?" I asked. "Well I suppose if you think I can help." She answered. When we got out to the car I said, "Now you sit here, and when I holler at you, push the foot feed all the way to the floor, and turn the key until you hear the motor running." I already had the hood up and the air breather off, so all I needed to do was hold down the choke. "OKAY GRANDMA!" I yelled. Grandma floored the accelerator pedal and turned the ignition key, the motor turned over several times and whump, it started. I put the air breather back on, closed the hood, and helped Grandma out of the car. She was so excited. She said "I started a car! I have to go in and tell your Granddad, that I started a car!" With all that excitement, I had to follow her back into the house and listen to her tell Granddad that she had started a car. "I have never started a car before." she said with a sense of accomplishment. I could not believe what I was hearing. Here is my eighty-four-year-old grandmother and she had never started a car in her life, let alone drove one. I guess it's never too late for something new to happen in a person's life.

Starting a car for the first time is one thing, but what is it when your whole world seems to be turned upside down? When everything is suddenly unfamiliar, and what was once believed to be secure assumptions about life have unexpectedly become vulnerable or threatened, the question often asked is, "What happened to the way things used to be?" When the people of God were taken into captivity from Judah and its Capitol, Jerusalem, they discovered life in a foreign land, and they mourned.

By the waters of Babylon we sat down wept when we remembered Zion...How can we sing the songs of the Lord in a foreign land? (Psalm 137:1, 4)

The word foreign in the Hebrew has for its root a word which means to recognize or acknowledge, and carries a sense of being able to recognize an object or place which one formerly knew. For people like Carter Barker of the Pratt United Methodist Church, foreign is any place but where he sits in church, and God help the poor foreigner who doesn't know that. In this particular passage it pretty much refers to a strange, unrecognizable place.

What Isaiah is giving reference to, is that for the Jewish people living in exile in Babylon; they recalled the wonderful story of the Exodus from Egypt, and their ancestors dwelling in the Promised Land that would be their ancestral home for generations. Now they were exiles in a foreign land with a hostile desert between them and their homeland. Chapter 43 begins with the powerful words, "But now, this is what the Lord says," and is followed by some of the most dramatic lyrics in the Hebrew Scriptures. It's a song of deliverance and salvation, and a new way to the future. Those former things the prophet is asking them to forget seem to be indicative of the exodus with its long and arduous sojourn through the wilderness. God will do a new thing for the people of God. They are being asked to replace their reliance solely upon memory with a hope in God; from the epochal events of the past to the redemptive events of the future; a divine route to the still to come, or yet to be. This is how it is when God does a new thing.

Serving as the Dodge City District Superintendent and living in the great southwest corner of the state, I have become acutely aware of others in our midst, like Mennonites. I didn't know there were so many

Mennonites in Kansas. I thought they were all from around Newton and Hutchinson. These folks however have been well established for a number of generations throughout the entire District. There is one aspect of the presence of others in the undeniable data regarding the growing population of Hispanics in Kansas. The communities of southwest Kansas like most communities throughout the heartland of the United States were pioneered, settled and developed as pretty homogeneous places. The major differences within the makeup of most towns were whether folks were mainline protestant or Roman Catholic, Democrat or Republican. People feel secure in consistency and familiarity, but change begins a process of perceived loss; loss of identity and acquaintance, loss of comfort, and perhaps most of all, loss of power and control.

Loss is never easy to adjust to, let alone accept. I remember at Harmony Church in Mankato the UMW had an annual Chicken Noodle Supper with homemade pies of all of my favorites. Now just speaking of pie, I can see a change of apocalyptic proportions in the near future when the last of the good old pie bakers are gone, and our only choices come from the frozen food section of the store. Anyway, with many of the women in leadership positions in the group aging, they decided to allow let the young women plan, prepare, and serve the next dinner. The women had everything set up, dining tables and serving table. They had the wooden pie shelves that were only used for this purpose set up in a place where they would be out of the way for the traffic flow. One of the elderly church matriarchs came by and I helped her carry some salad or a pie to the church basement. There was no one else around when she noticed where the pie shelves were sitting. "Oh dear!" she exclaimed, "We've never had those shelves over there; they belong over here." And she proceeded to drag the tables on which the shelves sat across the room to the place they always had been. It is very difficult for people to see change or give up control of their environment.

So it is with the traditional populations of southwest Kansas. If we just take Dodge City, where the district office is, and several of our boys either have, or will finish high school, this becomes a profound issue in terms of demographics. In 1970, the non-white population was under ten-percent. In 1990 it had jumped to over twenty-percent. By 2007 the figure would be right at sixty-percent non-white. This represents a pretty rapid demographic change. This type of change would be fairly accurate for any of the larger communities in southwest Kansas, including Garden City and Liberal. If you are a person who grew up in one of these communities as a part of the traditional, (white/Anglo) population, you would be very much aware of how your community or neighborhood has changed. The place where this is most dramatically observed is in the school system. As of the beginning of the 2010-11 school year for the Dodge City School District, the figures are quite telling.

School	Hispanic/Latino	Total Students	Percentage
Beeson	297	347	86%
Central	286	323	89%
Linn	249	338	74%
Miller	265	328	81%
Northwest	264	336	79%
Ross	264	448	59%
Sunnyside	316	346	91%
Wilroads	87	109	80%
Comanche	552	637	87%
Soule	233	322	72%
DCMS	616	790	78%
DCHS	1198	1662	72%
Bright B	343	381	90%
TOTAL	**4,970**	**6,367**	**78%**

The historical statistics listed above are from Ford County, and the school statistics were provided through the office of William R. Hammond, Executive Director of Business and Operations for Dodge City Public Schools, USD 443.

What does data such as this tell us about Dodge City or any city that is experiencing this type change in ethnic, cultural, and demographic makeup? A question like that is so open ended it can be answered in a lot of variant ways, many of which are not positive or helpful in moving into the future. I think if we are looking at this information from the standpoint of the Isaiah passage recognizing that God is doing a new thing, the question then becomes more focused. Framing the question as, "What as the church do we do with data such as this?" should lead us to eventually arrive at an answer which will be faithful to the Gospel, even if we have to walk through some wastelands.

I know there is a lot of grief that goes with the sense of loss. I'm sure there are many persons throughout Southwest Kansas, in Wichita, or anywhere the demographics are indicating the rapid increase of a particular ethnic group who were just like me growing up. In high school, they taught a Spanish class. I didn't take it because I couldn't for the life of me think of any reason I would ever need it. Everyone I knew spoke English. Today, my ministry as a district superintendent reaches out to a lot of people who either speak very little, or no English at all. I preach to these congregations with the use of an interpreter; or when just bringing greetings, I type something up from a translator service on the computer. This is indicative of a remarkable societal change. People grieve change and they do so in many ways. Some of the ways the demographic changes are being grieved is by simple denial, for others, it is flight, and then of course there is racism. We've all heard comments about folks speaking Spanish in public, or regarding the immigration status of persons, or stereotyping a group for exhibiting particular behavioral traits. It's wrong; but I guess the best we can hope for, is that it comes out of the sense of perceived loss, and the high anxiety people are experiencing, rather than unashamed bigotry.

When it comes to the church finding itself in the midst of change of just about any kind, the natural tendency is to circle the wagons and be protective of what we have and who we are. However, there are some who are pioneering into a new future, just like the generation that established the church on the wilds of the prairie. If you want to talk about Ebenezer moments, that conversation for the United Methodist Church in Southwest Kansas would largely center on Liberal, Garden City, and Dodge City. These Churches are bringing themselves into this new reality of the twenty-first century by seeking to find ways to be representative of and relevant to the changed community around them. How do we do church in this new reality? Dodge City First United Methodist Church has its roots going back to the earliest days of this town when it was the western most "Sodom of the Plains." It was a time when Wyatt Earp, the cattle drives, cowboys, and the accompanying social industries were alive and well on Front Streets, (both of them). It could not have been easy to start a Methodist class, let alone a church. According to Volume I of the *History of the Southwest Kansas Conference of the Methodist Episcopal Church*, it must have been deemed so bad, that in those very early days, there were a couple of preachers who were appointed to come here "who never showed up." [23]

Well, today, and for many years previous, the Dodge City Church is viewed as one of the strong, flagship churches of the Kansas West Conference. However, like the community around it, it has experienced change, mostly in the decline of the Anglo population over the last twenty years. This congregation has challenged itself to seek a direction for the future which will eventually be reflective of the current ethnic makeup of Dodge City. Again, it's never easy. Power is hard to share; control is just as hard to relinquish, and familiarity is difficult to lose. But God bless em! They are doing something. They are doing a new thing; God is doing a new thing in and through them. They are framing the question as "what do we do?" rather than simply "What does the data say?" Tom Colvin's hymn really lends itself to this subject; the refrain of which says:
Jesu, Jesu, fill us with your love; show us how to serve the neighbors we have from you. [24]

Several years ago the Senior Pastor, Lance Carrithers, invited a small independent group of Hispanic persons who found they needed to secure a different place to worship, to come to First United Methodist Church. They were given the use of the Chapel in which to hold their worship services. Following this, their pastor left town. They were encouraged to stay together as a congregation even without a regular pastor. They would later be encouraged by Sergio Tristan to become members of the United Methodist Church, and on a given Sunday, they were received into membership and enrolled in a membership class. This would be the catalyst for what would become Casa de Oracion, or House of Prayer. For a number of years, Pastor Carrithers has been speaking toward the need to reach out to, and invite in the Hispanic people. His prophetic vision of what the church would look like in twenty more years if it remained solely an Anglo Church was accurate, but stark at best. That vision however included a hope for the future; and his sense that God was calling this traditional church into a new paradigm of being—that of a bi-lingual, bi-cultural congregation.

In conjunction with the Kansas West Conference Hispanic Ministries, church growth, and development, leadership from the national level of Hispanic ministries, and God, a national search for a bi-lingual associate pastor was advertised. There were some who were hesitant about the process, and some who were doubtful if any responses would be received; but remember I said, "And God." The response was phenomenal. There were so many quality responses that a couple of other Hispanic and bi-lingual appointments were able to be made in the Kansas Area. For Dodge City, a wonderful, vibrant, spirit-filled and spirit-led Cuban born Pastor Tania Monterro was appointed after the church made the official decision to move in this direction, and the interview process was complete. We now stand on the threshold of having a multi ethnic, bi-lingual, growing, flagship church in our Annual Conference.

I can now see many hopeful signs and even fruitful progress that the Churches of Southwest Kansas are 'perceiving' the direction God is moving. Garden city is pressing forward in partnering with our Conference Mission Church, Nueva Evangelica, in reaching out to an equally growing Hispanic population there. Liberal First UMC currently shares facilities with a Spanish component of the congregation and is in the process of becoming one congregation with English services and Spanish services and two pastors. The Bridges to the Future Capital Campaign which our Conference undertook to fund such ventures along with a number of other valuable Conference ministries are helping to be a vehicle for moving us into the future. There are currently two pastors appointed there, one who speaks English and one who speaks Spanish. Now if we could get both of them to become bilingual that would be helpful. Again, I am not one to talk. Still, if my Grandmother Utt could learn how to start a car at age eighty-four, then surely I can learn to become more acquainted with the Spanish language. I don't think churches are being asked to necessarily replace their memory with hope, but rather to live out of their memory and their history into a hopeful future. That's the Ebenezer moment.

 I realize that for many parts of the country homogeneity has long been a thing of the past, if it ever really existed to begin with. A New Yorker, Philadelphian, or San Franciscan would be hard pressed to understand our concerns about ethnic or cultural change. Still even in these great cosmopolitan cities where there are wonderful ethnic and cultural neighborhoods, with local foods, drink, customs, and even churches, there must be people who are ready to perceive the new things God is doing. Bishop Jones, in his book, <u>The Evangelistic Love of God & Neighbor; a Theology of Witness & Discipleship</u> writes:

> *When homogeneous units are culturally formed by ethnicity, language, and other factors, they can be a valid starting place for a Christian journey. But the character of the community must make it clear that the new believers will be shaped in ways that will help them appreciate the diversity of God's people...It is not necessary that every congregation be multicultural. However given the prevalence of racism in American culture, it is necessary that each congregation become a tool for discipling persons to become the inclusive, loving persons God has called them to be.* [25]

A couple of years ago, I started every Charge Conference, the basic unit in the connectional system of the United Methodist Church which gives the local church its organization and vision for the coming year, with a devotion that centered on the Native Americans who once occupied the area. I asked them to imagine an evening campfire one-hundred-forty years ago with members of an Indian tribe sitting around enjoying the quiet of the evening. Perhaps a tribal elder is telling an epoch story of their past, regaling them with heroic deeds and spiritual wonders. Suddenly the stillness is shattered by the rumbling, clanking and clomping of horses, oxen, wagons and white settlers passing nearby. The Elder looks at those gathered around the fire with him and says sadly, "Well, there goes the neighborhood."

There are not many Native Americans still living in this part of the state anymore. However, that sentiment about the neighborhood changing is alive and well. The traditional populations of our communities, the fourth, fifth and in some cases sixth generation of the European descended white settlers who came west, sense this change. They articulate it especially as they see their numbers declining as a new migration has been part of the demographics for a couple of decades now. There is difficulty in recognizing many of the places we formerly knew. What the church has as choices is either to sit down, weep, and sing a dirge or lament, such as, "By the waters of the Arkansas we sat down and wept for thee Dodge City, or Garden City, or Cimarron, or Deerfield," or anyplace beside any river, or with no river at all. Or we shall learn a new song; one God is leading for all of God's people. We will perceive what new thing God is doing, engage it as faithfully as we can, and in so doing bring honor to our past which we will blend into a still emergent future.

Reflection:

Where do you see God at work in new and maybe unfamiliar ways?

How have you responded to change that may not always be comfortable?

What are some positive, forward looking ways to be faithful to God's new things?

Are we willing to sing a new song even if the words are not in a familiar language?

What is Good?

He has shown you, O man, what is good. And what does the Lord require of you? To act justly, and to love mercy, and to walk humbly with your God. (Micah 6:8)

In his book Good to Great, Jim Collins starts off in his first sentence by saying,
> *Good is the enemy of great. And that is one of the key reasons why we have so little that becomes great. We don't have great schools, principally because we have good schools. We don't have great government, principally because we have good government. Few people attain great lives, in large part because it is just so easy to settle for a good life.* [26]

While Mr. Collins' book is primarily secular in nature and geared to developing stronger businesses and corporate leadership, I believe he right on target with society in general. How is it not like the church? How is it not like any of us who are willing to be satisfied with just being good; or good enough? When we read this book for Incubator, one comment I made about it was that if we were to add the spiritual dimension, it could well serve as a twenty-first century compliment to Mr. Wesley's A Plain Account of Christian Perfection. Collins makes an interesting comment in Chapter 6, A Culture of Discipline,
> *Few successful start-ups become great companies, in large part because they respond to growth and success in the wrong way...What was once great fun becomes an unwieldy ball of disorganized stuff...In response, someone (often a board member) says, 'It's time to grow up. This place needs some professional management.* [27]

I think the "great", which Mr. Collins speaks of in terms of professional management, is in fact the 'good' of Micah 6:8, the better way, the beneficial way, the best way. The Message Bible I have, which was given to me by the Seekers Class, reads the verse like this,
> *But he's already made it plain how to live, what to do, what God is looking for in men and women. It's quite simple: Do what is fair and just to your neighbor, be compassionate and loyal in your love, and don't take yourself too seriously-take God seriously.*

For Christians, that professional management should be the Holy Spirit, moving us to grow up. The power of the Spirit in conjunction with the means of grace we Wesleyans understand as worship, the Sacrament of Holy Communion, prayer, searching the Scriptures, and fasting or abstinence is the way we move to be a great follower of Jesus and to mature into the persons God has called us to be.

Over the years I have heard several people testify to being sanctified. I think what they were referring to was having a definite, second work of grace, subsequent to justification; which is one way some in the Wesleyan tradition have sought to define sanctification. I believe in sanctification and I believe in being sanctified; although in this day and age I feel one should be careful about the use of that particular word. I am mindful of a person's need for sanctification in light of Mr. Wesley's belief that it, or Christian perfection, is the Grand Depositum which God has lodged with the people called Methodist.

In Wesley's A Plain Account of Christian Perfection he quotes from an earlier tract, "The Character of a Methodist"

A Methodist is one who loves the Lord his God with all his heart, with all his soul, with all his mind, and with all his strength...And loving God, he 'loves his neighbor as himself. [28]

While I know what it is that I should probably be striving for in my relationship with God, I think it is a much more powerful witness to be sanctified and not necessarily be aware of it, or at least feeling a need to draw attention to the fact.

One of the few people I have personally encountered who I would say exhibited a sanctified life was my Uncle Howard Hunt. About the time I was struggling with God's call on my life which would eventually lead me into ordained ministry, our pastor Reverend Keith Dudeck allowed several of the lay persons in the church the opportunity to deliver messages during Sunday evening services. One of these persons was Uncle Howard. He had been very active in church all of his life; serving as Sunday school superintendent for many years and teaching classes. The text for he chose for the evening was Micah 6:8,

He has showed you, O man what is good. And what does the Lord require of you? To act justly, and to love mercy, and to walk humbly with your God.

His message shared about how a Christian life should revolve around these qualities. From that point on, I have never been able to read or speak on this lofty passage of scripture without being mindful of Uncle Howard. I believe, and I think anyone who knew him would agree, that this Bible verse captured the essence of his life; with his natural sense of justice, mercy and humility giving him a genuine Christian dignity. He really was a person you wanted to listen to when he spoke.

Howard Hunt; a really good person to listen to

He wasn't born that way, however; no one ever is. There were times he wasn't good or someone you wanted to listen to. The story is told about a particular incident in which he and his younger brother George were playing and Howard coaxed George into the barn. Then he convinced him to follow him out of the hay loft through a loose piece of siding and then up a section of roof that took them to the very peak of the barn. When they decided to climb down, George got scared of falling, and refused to move from his perch. Howard went ahead and got down, went into the house and told his mother, "George is up on the roof of the barn and he won't come down!" They went outside and pointing upward he said, "There he is and he is not coming down." The sight of seeing her youngest son up on the top of that barn led Grandma to surmount any fears she had of height, or danger, and go up and get him, but once she got up there, she too got scared and couldn't get down. Realizing the serious, if not desperate nature of the moment, he ran to the field where his dad was working ground, and said, "George got stuck up on top of the barn and Mom went up to get him and now she's scared to come down, so they're both just sitting up there." Well Granddad came in from the field and went up and helped them down one at a time. I'm not sure what happened to Uncle Howard when the full story got told, but I recall Mom talking about Granddad's willingness to use the razor strop.

Every kid has at least a propensity for orneriness as well as childish behavior; and some more than others. That is pretty typical. However, there does come a time to grow up. Regardless of the fact that our society seems to have a growing population of rapidly aging adolescents resisting any inclination to maturity, Paul writes in I Corinthians 13:10-12,
...but when perfection comes, the imperfect disappears. When I was a child, I talked like a child, I thought like a child, I reasoned like a child. When I became a man, I put childish ways behind me.

Mr. Wesley says in his Notes on verse 11 of that passage,
I put away childish things-of my own accord, willingly, without trouble. [29]

There should be at least a harmonious, and willing, transition from the child to the mature adult; albeit at a pace which is peculiar to each individual. For Howard Hunt, it was fairly trouble free as well, that is to the best of my understanding.

Intelligent and witty as he was, the last Christmas we had with Uncle Howard, he was still able to recite the ABCs backward from Z to A faster than his great nephews and niece could do it forwards. As long as I can remember, he gave the prayers for all family functions. It just seemed the natural choice. Still, I'm sure he never thought of himself in terms of sanctification, and most likely never thought about the concept beyond a preacher's sermon or Sunday school lesson. What he thought about was from the perspective of justice, mercy and humility; "The matured person." Now that's a good way to phrase it. In an age where maturity does not appear to be a high priority with al lot of people, Christian maturity in the Wesleyan theological tradition is a concept worth rediscovering.

Bishop Jones, in his book on United Methodist Doctrine commenting on Mr. Wesley's 'Notes on the New Testament' writes,
Wesley rephrases 'perfect man' as 'spiritual manhood,' and then refers to 'maturity of age and spiritual stature.' That "Wesley is aware that the word translated perfect also means mature." Following this, he writes, "Wesley makes it clear…that there is a gradual process of growth in the Christian life as well as natural…Part of the reason for this process of growth is the awareness that God's grace is shaping the human heart. Sanctification is divided into two types of holiness, inward and outward. Wesley's understanding of human psychology was that outward behaviors are the result of inward tempers. [30]

This is a very practical description for a sanctified life; maturity, and temperament which grows over time through a relationship with Christ, and appropriate social, and familial environments. The key word here is growth, not plateau, or peak; especially on barn roofs.

When he died, his funeral service music being provided by a well known jazz band from Winfield to fulfill a desire of his, it was said of him in his eulogy that he fulfilled that which God had asked of him; and indeed it was good. I seem to be very aware of the need to play catch up in this sanctification process, but I am so appreciative of those who leave a witness of loving God and neighbor naturally and seem never to need to call attention to it. That steady, controlled maturity I have seen in his living has been an Ebenezer to me.

Charles Wesley wrote a hymn based upon the Micah 6 passage,

and I have taken the liberty to paraphrase a few of its ten stanzas from Wesley's Hymns into a slightly more contemporary language.

> *With what, O Lord, shall I draw near,*
> *And bow myself before your face?*
> *How in your purer eyes appear?*
> *What shall I bring to gain your grace?*
> *Will gifts delight the Lord Most High?*
> *Will multiplied oblations please?*
> *Thousands of rams your favor buy,*
> *Or slaughtered opossums to appease?*
> *For those who would to you approve,*
> *Must take the path yourself has trod;*
> *Justice pursue, and mercy love,*
> *And humbly walk by faith with God.*

Reflection:

Are there areas of your life in which you feel satisfied with just being good?

How can Micah 6:8 become a theme for your life?

What are the aspects of your life, and your relationship with God that you see, or are working on, in terms of growth and maturity?

What progresses do you see in your Christian walk?

Do you have difficulty in using the word 'great'?

What do you think about the Wesleyan doctrine of sanctification? How could it be reframed for this day and age?

There's Nothing Morbid About It

Brothers we do not want you to be ignorant about those who fall asleep, or grieve like the rest of men, who have no hope. (I Thessalonians 4:13)

My first job of any regularity was working for the Belle Plaine Township at the cemetery under the supervision of the long time Sexton, Frank Zumbrun. Most of my responsibility was pushing a heavy, three wheeled edger (this was before weed eaters) around every tombstone, marker, tree, flower, and fence post; up and down, back and forth, row after row. I also did all of the other cemetery stuff, like help set up for graveside services, spray for bagworms with arsenic and lead, (that might answer some questions) and pick up old flowers. Whatever it was we did, it was a lot of hard work for a fourteen/fifteen year old. Dad always had fun in telling people, "Yes, working at the cemetery is a pretty good job for Kendal, he's over about three-thousand people in his position."

There was no running water in the cemetery. There were however, two wells with the old fashioned pumps with the long handle. Early on Frank said, "If you ever want to get a drink of water, go up to the pump by the north gate. The ground water flow is from the northwest to the southeast, so you shouldn't be drinking any water from under the cemetery itself." There was an old wrought iron bench to sit on and rest and the proverbial tin cup hanging from a wire hook on a fence post beside the pump.

One hot, humid afternoon, I shut off the edger and walked up to the pump to rest for a few minutes and get a cold drink of water. There was plenty of shade. My great-Grandmother Schwyhart and other members of the Grand Army of the Republic Ladies Auxiliary, had years ago planted elm trees and put in a sidewalk from the corner north, along with a bridge across the Euphrates, to the south end of the cemetery. Sitting there, I watched as two girls, a couple of years behind me in school came walking down the sidewalk. I don't know where they were going but they stopped and we talked for a little bit. One of them said, "I didn't know you worked down here." The other one quipped, as they started on down the sidewalk, "That's kinda morbid, isn't it?"

Morbid? I had never thought about it like that. I had been coming to the cemetery for as long as I could remember; funerals, Memorial Day, and Sunday afternoon drives. And now I was there almost every day working. It did take a little while to get comfortable with going against mother's prohibition regarding actually stepping on a grave, but ya gotta do what ya gotta do, and I figured they wouldn't mind since I was keeping their final resting place neat. Beyond that, I had up to five generations of family from three different branches buried there, so who was going to give me a hard time? To me it was a peaceful place; sacred ground; and I had a privileged role in keeping it that way.

Going up and down the rows of stones time and again, I tried to pay attention to them; who they were, when their time in life and death was, what information was included on their grave. One of the saddest was the Gilchrist family. During the course of two days during August of 1888, three generations of the men in that family died. "It was typhoid fever" Frank said in answer to my query. He was a tremendous resource of knowledge about people as he had worked there forever and was from one of the old families of Belle Plaine. So I made it a point to ask questions about the things I thought of as I worked.

As far as I know there was only one haunted grave in the whole cemetery. I had heard this story from my great-Uncle George. He had been around forever too. A veteran of World War One, he was for years the post master and then rural mail carrier. He was a very intelligent man for having gone only to Meeker Country School. He had ponies that could count and dance, a magic show that he did at schools, and could solve almost any mathematical problem in his head. So it was only natural that I trusted his story about this certain grave. It looked like it was a crypt set above ground; a highly carved piece of limestone that was about eight feet long, and covered with a heavy, solid marble slab. Uncle George said, "Anyone who touches this tombstone will die a horrible death!" He continued by adding, "Her two sons were ornery sorts, and one night they went to the cemetery and shot craps on the top of their mother's grave. One of them died within several days and the other a little later on, horribly too!" Then he gave one final caution, "Don't ever touch it, nobody knows just how many people have died from it." I remember trying to be very careful around that particular grave as I operated the edger.

One day while eating lunch in the old cemetery office (a former chicken house with a dirt floor and an old wood stove for cool days), I decided to ask Frank about the haunted grave. Following a long knee slapping laugh, he said, "I've heard that old story myself, but it isn't true. First of all, she's buried in the ground just like everybody else in this cemetery; that whole thing is just one solid tombstone. Secondly" he continued, "she never had any sons because she was never married; she died pretty young."

While Frank's response pretty well destroyed my only sense of the mysterious, and macabre, I was still intrigued by symbols and words on so many of the older stones. Some had the figure of a hand with a finger pointing upward. There were little lambs or cherubs, indicating the loss of an infant or young child. There were cloth draped urns and hewn logs symbolizing death. Then there were the epitaphs; those words carved into the stone to leave a lasting message. I used to read the words on the large granite stone of Mr. and Mrs. Frank Forney. Frank was a brother to my great-Grandmother Hunt, and was murdered by a hitchhiker back in the early 1920s. People from all over the county were out with dogs and guns looking for this person. Fortunately for him, the sheriff caught him. Anyway, the words read, "These words are dedicated to my parents in memory of their many kindnesses to all: Mable Forney." I didn't know any of these distant relatives, but every time I would go by this stone and read what was written, I would ask, "What words? It doesn't really say anything descriptive about these people!" There is one stone in particular which has always stuck with me. It was for a young woman, certainly a wife, maybe a mother to someone who probably moved on following her death. It reads:

Beneath this stone we place in trust,
Not the immortal but the dust;
Of one on Earth to us most dear,
Who learned in youth, her God to fear.

What a context for understanding; what a statement of faith and comfort. What a way to grieve as Christians, with the hope we have in Christ. Time and time again, these words have passed through my mind. I have had the pleasant occasion to repeat them at a few graveside services. It was certainly someone's Ebenezer to have left those words for the ages to read.

Reflection:

Are there views of death which hinder persons from living a resurrection faith?

What could someone write on your tombstone which would indicate that concept of resurrection faith lived out in you?

Focus

Since you have been raised with Christ, set your hearts on things above, where Christ is seated at the right hand of God. Set your minds on things above, not on earthly things. (Colossians 3:1-2)

Like many small communities in times past, Belle Plaine had a movie theatre, pronounced, "theeaterrr". It was built as an opera house and converted into a movie theatre in the early 1900s. Going to the show was something almost every kid in town did almost every week. Westerns, comedies, science fiction, horror (pre Jason type), war, and even love stories; whatever was showing, we went and watched it. Dad gave me thirty-five cents every week to go to the show. It cost a quarter to get in, and the dime was for discretionary spending. I could spend the dime at the concession stand by buying a nickel box of popcorn and a candy bar, small milk duds or pack of gum. Or blow the whole thing and get a cup of pop, usually a Green River from one of those old pop dispensers where the little cup falls down into a holder, you push the button for the pop you want, and the syrup, followed by the carbonated water was dispensed into the cup. For years, it was owned and operated by the "old man and old lady". I didn't know they even had names, just that they were cranky when it came to noisy kids. Almost weekly, at some point in the show, the movie would stop, the lights would come on, and the old lady would walk down to the front and start yelling, "If you kids can't keep quiet, we'll shut the movie down for good, and send you all home!" Now there was one nice thing they did, (beside put up with all of us kids on a weekly basis) every year they would give a free show on the Saturday afternoon one week before Christmas. Every kid in the country would show up for that. There would be kids sitting in the aisles and clear down front on the floor. As soon as the show was over, there would be a mad, bone crushing stampede for the door, and the wagon of goodies in the street, which would be passed out by Santa Clause, who was really Uncle George.

    By the time we got into eighth grade, the old man and old lady sold the theatre to some cousins of mine. They operated it at least until I left for college. One of the good things about having cousins running the show was getting in free when you helped out. I enjoyed helping operate the projectors. Up a steep, narrow flight of stairs, you entered the projection booth which contained two antique movie projectors. They were lit by burning rods like you find in a welder. Movies came in tin boxes usually two reels per box. You could tell how long a movie was by how many reels it was. The first reel, including previews of coming attractions and the cartoon, and the second reel began the movie. You had to keep watch for the little circles that would appear in the upper right hand corner of the screen; that was the signal to start the next reel to keep things moving smoothly. You couldn't horse around up there. While you could watch the movie, you had to know when to start paying very close attention for the signals to start the other projector. If things went bad on the screen, they went bad pretty quickly, and people usually started to yell, "FOCUS! FOCUS!" Now it usually wasn't a focus issue as much as it was the arc rods burning down and needing to be readjusted. There was a heavily colored glass in the side of the projector through which you could "see the ark (arc) without going blind" that is almost biblical or at least Indiana Jonesish. Anyway, there were knobs you turned and pulled to get the two rods back into a properly aligned position for optimum light so the people down stairs would quit verbalizing their discontent with the folks in the projection booth.

In the very first reel, there were a set of frames which had the word FOCUS inside a circle with cross hairs on them. It was at that point you should be paying attention, and if needed focus the lenses on the projector. There were knobs for that purpose too, adjusting the lenses so the picture was crisp and clear with no distortions. Even today, when I find myself being distracted, I can hear that crowd of frustrated theatre goers yelling, "FOCUS! FOCUS!" and I see that word with the cross hairs inviting me to realign whatever is needed in my life. The chorus, "Turn your eyes upon Jesus, Look full in his wonderful face, and the things of earth will grow strangely dim, in the light of his glory and grace" seems to be a little more helpful than listening to people hollering "FOCUS!" I'm really glad Dad never picked up on that word. He was always saying "Buckle down" or "Tidy up." Thankfully, I never heard him say "Focus!"

While we are called to "set our minds on things above," there is another aspect of focus. Psalm 8:1 is quite eloquent in this regard:
O Lord, Our Lord, how majestic is your name in all the earth! You have set your glory above the heavens.

When we were kids, there was no air-conditioning for the upstairs. On some really hot nights, we would be allowed to sleep on the living-room floor in front of the air conditioner in the window. Many times Dad would let us sleep outside in the backyard. He would lay out there with us until we fell asleep. He would help us find satellites moving across the sky. Satellites were a big thing in the early 1960s. When we watched really big news events, we knew they were "live via satellite" because the TV screen said so. It allowed us to feel like we were really seeing something important; something we should know about or pay attention to. I still go outside many nights and sit in the lawn swing, or lie in the hammock, and look for satellites moving across the sky. But more than this, I just look at the stars. I never tire of pondering the unfathomable depths, and distances, the immeasurable vastness of the space out there, the possibilities that exist beyond earth's vision, and the God who spoke it all into being. Psalm 8:3-4a goes through my mind and spirit each time;
When I consider your heavens, the work of your fingers, the moon and stars, which you have set in place, what is man that you are mindful of him, the son of man that you care for him?

John Wesley writes in his sermon, "What is Man?"
How is it possible that the Creator of these, the innumerable armies of heaven and earth, should have any regard to this speck of creation whose time 'passeth away like a shadow'? [31]

So it is quite appropriate that any of us should ask, "Who am I that you, O God, will from the farthest spun galaxy, at the very edge of this incomprehensible universe, focus down so specifically, that I am known, cared for, and loved by you, Lord?"

We may need to realign our focus from time to time on the important things of life; like relationships, family, work, discipline, the future, and Jesus. This is a good avocation to take seriously. The good news however is that God is already focused on us without the need for realignment. The one who set the boundary at the edge of the universe, who surpasses that boundary, has focused down to the foot of the Cross, and is mindful of you and me.

Reflection:

In what ways could God help you realign or sharpen your temporal and spiritual focus?

How do you understand God's focusing upon you?

What persons do you know for whom you can be a focusing mark?

Burnt Beans

...being confident of this, that he who began a good work in you will carry it on to completion until the day of Christ Jesus.
(Philippians 1:6)

The whole time I was growing up, all I ever wanted was to be a farmer. For years I wouldn't entertain any other thought in terms of my life's vocation. I remember being scolded by my sixth grade teacher, Mrs. Orrell, for doing poorly on an English assignment to which I responded (and she never let me forget for the rest of her life), "I don't need this stuff! I'm going to be a farmer." I really enjoyed being with Granddad and helping him around the farm. I loved livestock, working ground, planting and harvest. I got my chance to farm, first as hired help starting my junior year in high school. Seems I had been fired from my job at the cemetery. Frank passed away after a short illness. That left just me who knew anything about the cemetery. Well they weren't going to leave a high school kid in charge. To make a long story short, the excuse they (one township trustee who shall remain within the same venue as game wardens) used to terminate my employment was that I took the now wilted flowers from around the graves following Memorial Day, like we always would do, and hauled them to the land fill. Pretty darn flimsy if you ask me. But it got me to farming, the thing I wanted more than anything else. The two farmers I was working for had ancient tractors with no cabs, umbrella, or buggy tops, just sunshine, wind and dirt. Still I didn't mind at all.

Later, when I had graduated from Cowley County Community College with an Associate's Degree from the Agri-Business program, I went to work for the Johns. Mr. John had a fairly large, farming and cattle operation. He had a horse he used for cattle work that usually grazed around the barn in a very pastoral mood. He decided that farming and cattle were not enough so he got into the hog business. This meant that I had to rebuild a lot of fence from simple barbed wire to woven wire. The first sows to have litters were kept in a part of the barn before the hog sheds were built. When it came time for the baby pigs to be weaned and moved into another lot, they had to be escorted down a lane which was still fenced only for cattle. Well those little pigs ran everywhere. Several of them got into the lot where the horse was. This was the first time this horse had ever seen a baby pig, and it went to jumping and snorting and kicking. It actually tried to kill the small pigs. Without thinking too much about it, I jumped into the pen and began shooing the little piggys out. There was just one left when suddenly that horse wheeled around and gave me both hooves in my right hind quarter and put up on the top of a gate. That really hurt and I wore those hoof prints for several days. Still I saved the pigs. This would be my one and only bout with any serious messianic complex.

When I started farming our east place, the eighty acres Granddad left Mom, I used Mr. John's equipment. I raised wheat, grain sorghum, and soybeans on it. In my spare time, I was still helping one of the farmers who I had worked for earlier. I had in my mind that when he was ready to retire, I would purchase his equipment and farm his land. During the summer of 1975, while working many fifteen and sixteen-hour days, it became clear that he was going in a different direction. What I saw was some pretty significant doors beginning to shut. I began to question what I was going to do with my life. In the mean time, I had preached several times at our church as an uncertified, untrained lay speaker. It seemed that while my life's plans were beginning to be in a state of flux, my spiritual life was taking on a more serious nature. On one particular Sunday morning in July, I had gone to the field to work ground about 5:00 a.m. for several hours prior to church.

While this old John Deere two-lunger didn't have any physical amenities, it did have one of those old box radios. I was listening to music for a while and then changed the dial until some radio preacher came on. I don't know who it was or what he was speaking about, but the sun was just getting ready to pop over the horizon and what few clouds there were in the eastern sky became a brilliant purple, red and gold. For some reason I turned the radio off for a while. Now I didn't see anything but what I have already described. I didn't hear anything but the johnny-popping (the sound made by a two cylinder John Deere) of the tractor. Still there was something suddenly going on that led me to shut off that tractor, get down on the ground on my knees, and bow before the Almighty God and cry out, "Lord, I don't know what you want out of me. I don't know what it is you want me to do. But whatever it is, I'll do it. I'll be whatever you want me to be." I got up, started the tractor and took it in and parked it. I drove straight to the church, still in my overalls. The pastor, Keith Dudeck was there. I walked in and said, "Reverend Dudeck, I think I have been called into the ministry." He didn't hesitate in his response saying, "I wondered how long it would take." I don't know what he, the church people, or even God saw in me, but there I was, having a life changing moment.

I was at a church meeting and was sharing about going into the ministry and that I would probably work until the end of the year, save some money and then go to Southwestern College in Winfield to get my bachelors degree. One of the old saints of the church asked me, "Do you believe you are called to go into the ministry?" "Yes" I responded. "Then don't wait, you get started right now. God will take care of what you need." So for the next three years, Southwestern College was my academic home.

Following graduation with my Bachelor of Philosophy, Ph.B., (yes they actually offered this degree), I had this one last summer to farm Mom's eighty acres. I decided to put the whole thing into soybeans. Even with a modest yield, I figured I could pay for a couple of years of seminary. In preparation for planting, I was working the field one morning when I noticed the man who owned the farm to the north and east of us. He was a very wealthy man who lived in Wichita but came down a couple of times a week to make sure things were going right on his property. He was out walking in his field. Suddenly, he climbed over the fence and started out for me. I stopped the tractor and got off. Now in my mind I was thinking, maybe he is going to hand me a check to pay for seminary expenses. Goodness knows he wouldn't miss a few thousand dollars any more than I would a nickel. We had always got along pretty well. I had done some work for him over the years, and he had been a good friend of my Granddad. In reality, what happened was, he walked up to me and after a little small talk, he grabbed me by the suspenders on my overalls and said, "Boy, you've got faith and that's alright I guess, but my life has always been a game to see how much money I can make before I die. If I have eight, nine, or ten more years, who knows how much I can have." Sadly, as he walked back toward the fence, I thought of Jesus' words about the man who built bigger barns, and those words from Luke 12:20,

You fool! This very night your life will be demanded from you. Then who will get what you have prepared for yourself?

I also thought that was a pretty silly game, because you will never know the final score. Well, not getting any money out of our neighbor, I went ahead and planted the soybean crop. They came up good; they looked healthy and began to grow. Then the hot dry July and August hit. There were too many days of 100+ temperatures. There was too little rain. Now given the nature of isolated showers, our wealthy neighbor got some rains on his beans. But do you think it could rain on mine? Noooooo!

When it came time for me to leave for seminary, I had written off the beans in my mind, but not in my heart. That first semester at Asbury, I was in the preaching class of Dr. Lewis. We were to prepare our first classroom sermon. In the meantime, Mom called and said, "Francis and your Uncle Howard cut your beans yesterday. They hauled in eighty bushels." Now, that translates to one bushel per acre. That was so pitiful that Francis didn't charge me anymore than the eighty bushels for harvesting them, although I know the bill would have been a lot more had there actually been a crop. Then Mom said, "Oh by the way, the beans to the north made over forty bushels." My heart sank. "God, all I needed was a little rain." Are you serious about me being in ministry?" I was counting on those beans to help with my seminary you know!" Now what was I going to do? I was eight-hundred miles away from home and broke.

As I prepared for my first classroom sermon in Preaching 101, I don't recall the text I was given but it had to have been appropriate to the moment, for the message of the sermon was this. In my field of burnt beans, God was saying in a rather dramatic way that, "If I have called you, I will provide for you." As I thought through that concept, I came to the conclusion that I was relying on my own initiative too strongly. I shared this in the sermon I preached to my classmates and Dr. Lewis. I received an A+ for it. While I was still a little disappointed about the way things turned out, I didn't feel so desperate about the burnt beans and the loss of their income.

Shortly before we graduated, we were all supposed to stop by the business office and check our accounts. When I went in, they showed me my account ledger sheet. I didn't owe a dime, but that wasn't what really caught my attention, nor brought the deep sense of gratitude to the fore. It was the total amount paid. Those thousands and thousands of dollars my education had cost. I thought, "I've never had that much money. That money never went through my hands." God had provided in God's marvelous way, through God's marvelous people; and God still does!

Reflection:

In what ways has the leading of the Spirit changed the direction of your life?

How have you witnessed God providing the things which are needful at various stages in your life?

Can you recall some specific times where God took care of you?

Just an Old Steel Chair

That if you confess with your mouth that Jesus is Lord, and believe in your heart that God raised him from the dead, you will be saved. (Romans 10:9)

Remember Mrs. Bowlby, the lady with the pretty legs? As I said, I used to mow her lawn. I also mowed her next door neighbor's lawn, Mrs. Pearl Treakel. She had millions of iris plants also. Besides those two widow ladies, I mowed for Lestle Hollingsworth's Beauty Shop at the end of the alley across from the funeral home. I charged them $1.25 apiece for the two women's lawns and $1.00 for Lestle's. Dad let me use his lawnmower and gas. I saved my lawn mowing money so I could pay my way to summer camp. I had finally gotten old enough to go to Camp Horizon. I had never been there before, but we went by it every time we made the trek to Granddad Utt's at Silverdale. This would be the first time I would be away from home by myself. I was very excited.

Camp Horizon was the Methodist Camp near Arkansas City. It was on top of the high ground, a bluff overlooking the Arkansas River below. You could see clear into town and all the way to Oklahoma from up there. Mom had gone there back in the late 1940s shortly after the Conference had taken over the place. There was a boys' dorm and girls' dorm. The girls' dorm was down at the bottom of a long set of steps below the dining hall, (kind of handy for them). The boys' was quite a way off to the south, down below Inspiration Point, and over a rocky road. They were both actually old Army Air Corps barracks from Strother Field. As I remember it, there was a row of bunk beds, (wooden frames with canvass stretched over them) on either side of the building with restroom and showers at one end. My bunk was near the main entrance; for ants that is, who crawled back and forth all day and night.

It was a typical church camp with the singing of songs like Waltzing Matilda, and Zum Gali Gali; games, campfires, crafts (I think I made a belt), and bible lessons as taught by our counselors. There was the morning hike, afternoon nap, evening hike, and swimming pool time. There was a trip to the old abandoned (actually never used since it was a scam from the early 1900s) cement factory. Then there was the hike to the sandbar on the river for an evening of bonfires, hotdogs, marshmallows (pre smores), and swimming in the river. Every night we would have some type of service in the big room above the dining hall. One evening, there was to be a movie. I am sure it would have been appropriate for the kids at camp if we had gotten to see it; but there was a problem. The film that was sent wasn't the one that was ordered. There we all were seated in the dining hall, the lights went off, and everyone became quiet. The film started and there were people talking about things that fifth and sixth graders in the 1960s weren't accustomed to. It wasn't vulgar or nasty, just inappropriate for the age. When they started discussing breast cancer, the projector was shut off, the lights were turned on, and we started singing Waltzing Matilda again.

Now this "Big Room" had wrap around windows on three sides so you had a panoramic view of the river and inspiration point where the large wooden cross stood high above the valley. On the last night of camp, we had service. There was singing and then preaching. The preacher gave an invitation for anyone there to accept Jesus as their Lord and Savior. We were to divide up into little groups with an adult and share and pray. I remember sitting on one of the old steel folding chairs in a small circle. The leader was talking about the subject the speaker for the evening had used, committing your life to Jesus Christ. Now I had been a part of the church all of my life. The folks had me baptized by Reverend Major Parker when I was about a month old. I have no memory of a time in which I didn't believe in God. I never missed church or Sunday school since the only acceptable excuse in our home for not going was death. I went to Bible school every summer whether I wanted to or not. So what was this about me needing to do something else? It must have been, at least in part, a response to the question of my parents in the old Baptismal ritual of the Methodist

Church where it asks them, "Will you endeavor to keep this child under the ministry of the church until he by the power of God shall accept for himself the gift of salvation, and be confirmed as a full and responsible member of Christ's Holy Church?

I believe this was the first time that I would have my own say about my relationship with God. This was totally my decision to make. I wasn't being made to say or do something, put on a bowtie, have the top of my hair piled up in a big curl, wear a jacket, or be nice to the Sunday school teacher, or anything else that was beyond my control when it came to church. Whatever was or wasn't going to happen in the next few minutes would be totally up to me. The leader of our group said that if we wanted to accept Jesus Christ as our Lord and Savior, we could right now, tonight. If we thought we were not ready to do that, we didn't have to. Of course there is that little thing called group dynamics and peer pressure that might play into a moment like this. But I really wasn't aware of it. I remember kneeling down on the floor, and putting my arms and head into the seat of that old steel chair, and praying, "Dear Lord, I repent of my sins." Now at this point you need to understand that at that time my sins were pretty limited to things like sticking my sister in the eye with a pencil, or dropping a water meter lid on her big toe, or laughing out loud in church when the preacher used the word Leviticus. I continued my prayer by asking Jesus to be my savior, to come into my life and help me to do your will. *Amen.*

Well I got through that. The service closed and I spent my last night with the ants in my bunk. The next morning we packed up to go home. Mom and Dad came to get me. It had been a great time. I would return the next year. Now while I have not always lived like a child of God, I was always mindful of God. Over the years, when I have wondered for one reason or another if I really have gotten it right with God, or used the right formula, or said the right words, or said them in the right order, or questioned whether or not I was even accepted by God, that's when I remember. I remember that sacred moment, not at some highly polished alter on padded cushions in some well cared for sanctuary or chapel, but hovering over an old steel chair in the upper room of a dining hall. Where, with the encouragement of a camp counselor, I prayed my first prayer of commitment to Jesus Christ. And I am given that assurance that God heard and honored that prayer; and in God's unlimited grace and longsuffering (patience) God would hold me faithful to that commitment made early on in my life. It was an Ebenezer moment.

Several years ago, I was asked to preach a revival at the Protection United Methodist Church. On Monday evening, the church hosted Youthville from the Dodge City Campus. These are children and youth who have been placed there for various reasons including not having any parents. After a nice meal the church put on, we began gathering in the Sanctuary for the service. That night I had my youngest son, Taylor with me, so I sat out in the pews with him until time for me to preach. There were several Youthville kids sitting in front of us. One of the young men turned around and said, "This is the first time I have ever been in a church." So we began a pre-service conversation. His mother had died and his father was in prison on drug charges. He went to live with an uncle in a rough section of Kansas City, who was sent to prison on virtually the same charges. He would be returning to Kansas City to appear before a judge as to what would happen to him, and probably not return to Youthville. Now this young man was all alone except for the other students, adult leaders, and Reverend Kip Ryherd, the Chaplin.

It came time to go up and preach the evening message. I preached for about forty minutes and then gave an invitation for people to come to the communion rail if they felt God leading them. I was also quite focused on anyone who had never accepted Christ as their Savior to come and pray. We began to sing an invitation hymn and several folks came forward and knelt for prayer. Soon, I noticed this young man coming and kneeling down. I walked over and knelt down beside him and asked him if I could help. He said, "I don't know what to do." "What do you want me to help you do?" I asked. "I want to accept Jesus into my life." "Alright, I will pray a few words, if you believe, you repeat them, okay?" "Okay," he said. We prayed a very simple prayer of faith, forgiveness, and asking Jesus to come into our lives.

This wasn't all that different from forty-two or three years earlier, when I had a little guidance in praying virtually the same prayer. The only difference was I was heading back into a stable home environment. He didn't have a clue where he was going. My prayer for him is that God will put a hedge about him wherever he goes, and hold him faithful to that commitment he made that night at an alter in a strange church.

Reflection:

What are the faith commitments you have made to Christ?

How has God, and others helped you to keep that commitment over the years?

You Need the Fruit of the Spirit!

But the fruit of the Spirit is love, joy, peace, patience, kindness, goodness, faithfulness, gentleness and self control. Against such things there is no law. (Galatians 5:22-23)

I learned to drive out in Granddad Hunt's alfalfa field. Mom could turn me loose in that old 1949 Dodge pickup, that infamous survivor of the 1970 Halloween mishap. But out in the field, there was no road, no trees or other obstacles, no pedestrians or other vehicles to get in my way, so I was able to concentrate on learning how to shift gears and stuff. Then, Mom would sometimes let me drive down to Mrs. Lawless's, our egg lady, or Mr. Stunkle's for milk. By the time I was in drivers' education the summer following my freshman year, I was doing pretty well at driving. Even out on the main highways at speed approaching 70 mph, I was holding my own. The problem was that there wasn't a lot of traffic in those days, and almost all of our roads in South Central Kansas are flat and straight, and if you did get behind a slow driver, you could usually pass within a few seconds.

Taking weekly turns driving to Ark City for junior college classes, we made good time over several routes we had to get there. The same was true for going to Southwestern; though living in the (pre-renovation) Broadhurst Hall, I went home a lot for farming. Then I went to Kentucky for my seminary education and southern Ohio as a student pastor, and my driving world was suddenly turned upside down. Dad had bought a 1973 Chevrolet Impala from a buddy at work and traded that to me for my pickup. It was a huge car that you could launch aircraft off of the front hood. It would go at least, well pretty fast, and could get as much as fifteen miles to the gallon going downhill with a tail wind. This cruising machine was build for the long straight roads of Kansas. This car had a real problem with the curves and speed restrictions of the eastern part of Kentucky and southern Ohio. This was still during the days of the federally-mandated, (however unconstitutional) Richard M. Nixon 55-mile-per-hour speed limit. So my question became, "why can't those people at least do the speed limit?"

US Highway 68 through Kentucky and Ohio should never have been given any federal designation beyond that of snake path. There was nothing but hills, curves, and slow drivers. These people would actually squall their tires, burn rubber, throw a cloud of dirt and smoke into the air to pull out in front of you to drive forty-seven-and-a-half miles an hour. I couldn't take it. Riding in a van with another student one day, he had the rare opportunity to actually pass one of these people. I started to roll down my window to give him a good driving manners object lesson, when I felt a hand gripping me by the shirt and pulling me to the center of the vehicle. He said, "Don't you do anything, I have a 'clergy' bumper sticker on the back of this van! Do you want to give us a bad reputation?" he added with a scolding tone. Between Lexington and Paris, Kentucky back then, there was only one good place to pass. I was heading to Bentonville for the weekend and found myself behind a string of cars and truck going about 40 mph. This was really eating at me. I don't think the word road rage was too common then. I could see a clear way for passing when a vehicle came over the top of the hill a ways off. Could it be true? The vehicle pulled off to the side of the road. "It's now or never," I thought. I floored that old Chevy and started around the offending cars. One, two, three, and nobody was coming over the hill in the opposite lane. Four cars down, and as I was nearing the hill I passed number five. The double lines had just started when I caught up to the semi and started to pass him. The old girl hadn't seen 80 in a long time. "Oh please don't let there be anyone coming over the hill!" I prayed and I started to pull in front of the truck. "I made it;" but I no more than got those words out than I saw the reason the oncoming car had pulled off to the side of the road. He had been stopped by a Kentucky Highway Patrolman who at this time was motioning him on and getting into his car. He'd probably never seen anything like that before because he was coming after me. Still, he was behind a lot of vehicles. Wouldn't you know it; there wasn't a single dirt road to pull off on; nowhere to hide, so I just plugged along at 55. Just as I hit the city limits of Paris, he pulled me over. After a few moments he walked up to my car and asked for my driver's license. "I didn't think I was speeding officer" I said gently. "I didn't stop you for speeding boy; although I am a little surprised I caught up with you this quickly." I stopped you for passing five cars and a truck on a hill and a double yellow line and you had to be going ninety or a hundred when you got around that truck." He then headed back to his patrol car and stayed in there for what seemed to be an eternity. Finally, he walked back up to my car. He handed me the ticket and said, "Here! Sign this." I looked it over and read where it actually had down for an infraction, "Passing five passenger cars and one semi on double yellow line at high rate of speed." I signed it. He then said, "You need to follow me to the Bourbon County Courthouse and pay the fine." "I don't have any money on me officer, can't I just send in a check?" "From Kansas?" he blared. "Well I go to school in Wilmore," I responded, trying to make myself sound more like a local. "So where are you headed now?" he asked. "Well…..Sir….you see, I'm the student pastor at the Bentonville United Methodist Church." I couldn't tell just what it was he was saying through that glare he was giving me, but I'm sure God wasn't being highly honored right at that moment. "Alright!" he exclaimed. "I'll let you get your money sent in by the date on the ticket. But let me tell you something mister!" he added. "You might be able to pass like that in Kansas, but you can't pass like that in Kentucky!" Embarrassed? Highly! Angry? Indeed! Convicted? I don't think so.

 I was put into a group for a class entitled Supervised Ministry. We were to go to the Veterans Hospital in Lexington one day a week and work under the hospital chaplains. They would give us each a floor to roam and call on patients. We would then write up an experience in a theological reflection paper and discuss it in a group setting at the seminary. We took turns driving, but one of the men was from Nigeria and he didn't have a car. One of the other fellows had a Vega, so I did a lot of the driving. I couldn't help myself. It made me feel better to discuss the poor driving habits of the exceptionally slow people in front of me and point out their rude and self-centered attitudes. "Get out of the way Sister?" That has always been one of my personal favorites. "Move it or milk it, buddy!" was another classic.

One morning we were on the road to Lexington, and behind the usual string of slow drivers. I really believed there was a network in which people would call each other and say, "Utt's on his way, everybody get out there and drive slow and make as many left handed turns as you can make in heavy traffic." This particular day, Joe, the guy from Nigeria, was sitting in the front seat with me. As we pulled around the corner to head into the hospital parking lot, he looked at me and said in his strong African accent, "Brother Kendal, you need the fruit of the Holy Spirit to help you drive your car." A ton of bricks just hit me. No one had ever spoken to me like that. I have no memory of saying anything in response. Embarrassed? Definitely. Angry? Yes; at myself. Convicted? To the core of my soul; real Holy Ghost conviction that says, "Take notice of this moment and the message you just heard." Had I been selective in the ways I was allowing the Holy Spirit to work in my life?

In order for a fruit tree to bear good, healthy, and abundant fruit, it needs a lot of sunshine, variant temperatures, continuous moisture, and lots of various types of nutrients to draw up through the roots. The fruit of the Spirit is a list of character traits which should be present in the Christian life. This fruit hangs in triadic clusters from our tree of faith. The first three, love, joy, and peace tend to be present due to the fact that we have a personal relationship with God in Christ. The second cluster, patience, kindness, and goodness seems to be the natural outgrowths of that relationship with God as it becomes directed towards others and how we live our lives in relationship with them. The third cluster, faithfulness, meekness, and SELF CONTROL would indicate responsibilities we each have to ourselves, and a high quality of life.

If I am to be faithful to my Lord and "Bear much fruit", and I think he means good fruit, one of the nutrients that seem to be most important to me is the ability of the Holy Spirit, through whatever means, to apply appropriate conviction to my life. Like the time a Sunday school class Justin was in went to Wichita for some activity. When they got home, his Sunday school teacher said, "Kendal, we were sitting at a stop light and when it turned green, your son hollered, "Hurry up sister!" Now where did he hear that at?" The alternative to being convicted is not a pleasant thought. I have learned to appreciate God's conviction; it is usually pretty near an Ebenezer moment.

Reflection:

Where have you been caught not exhibiting the fruit of the Spirit?

What have been the challenges which have made bearing fruit difficult?

Which ones would you say need to be produced by your relationship with God?

>by your relationship to others?

>by your relationship with yourself?

It's About Home

I would rather be a doorkeeper in the house of my God than dwell in the tents of the wicked. (Psalm 84:10)

I carry fond memories of all of the parsonages we have lived in during our pastoral ministry. They have all been a part of our memory as a growing, developing family. I think we enjoyed living in all of them, considering the making them our home, not just a house. Well that is with the exception of the house in which we currently live, the district parsonage. This is the nature of the itinerate ministry peculiar to the United Methodist pastor, that is to those United Methodist pastors who still itinerate.

The parsonage at Bentonville, Ohio was a small trailer house. Under no circumstances would it ever pass any Conference's minimum standard for a dwelling, but it was my very first away from home, home. It had everything I needed; there were lovely green sinks, counter top range, oven, and refrigerator. I had never lived in a home with colored appliances before. It was heated by propane which would usually run dry on the coldest Saturday night of the year. It had a mouse problem. The first time I noticed the first little mouse, it didn't bother me too much, but when they went to using my silverware drawer for a restroom, I declared war. Traps, got a bunch of them, but their cousins moved in faster than I could kill them. I had heard about mothballs having an offensive smell to mice. I went to the store and bought a case of mothballs. I opened up the skirting around the trailer and spread several boxes under the trailer. I removed the covering over the water pipes from the bathroom to the kitchen and filled that with moth balls. I strung mothballs under the sink and cabinets; behind the divan and television, and anywhere else I believed a mouse might go. It must have worked to some degree. Who knows what lasting effects the fumes had on the mice or me.

It had a water problem. The water supply was a large cistern located under the front step and vestibule of the church and received water drained from the north side of the church. This cistern had a habit of running dry during showers just as shampoo was applied to the hair. The fire department would have to haul a tanker load of water down to the church, and dump it into the cistern to get us by until the next rain, or the next shampoo incident. The cistern's capacity had always been quite adequate for the church, but when they added the trailer house on the system that really strained it. While it had no leaks, it was certainly becoming unreliable. The men of the church cleaned out the cistern once. There was about two feet of a fowl, mucky sludge covering the bottom. When one of the ladies of the church saw that and realized that was what they were making coffee out of, it wasn't long before the Trustees voted to upgrade several aspects of the utilities. Not only were we going on county water, we were going to get natural gas at the church and parsonage. They dug a big trench to run both lines from the road to the church and on to the parsonage. No more cold nights waiting for the propane truck and no more shower outages. We were looking forward to the technological updates including new furnaces.

The Geneseo parsonage was a large two story house which was built by a couple just in time for them to die from the Spanish Flu during World War I. It had huge rooms, with colonnades and beams in the ceiling and sliding beveled glass doors partitioning the living room from the dining room. It was purchased by the Presbyterians who later became Methodists, so we got a nice parsonage. It had a fire place with a gas log. I took the gas log out, the church put in a fire place insert, and we started heating with wood. This came in real handy during the ice storm of 1984. By this time, Justin and I were keeping house together, and with all the power off, we lived by the fire. I cooked potatoes, macaroni, canned corn, and boiled water for oatmeal and coffee. We got along just fine. It was probably the most elegant house we lived in.

When Justin and I moved to Wellington, they didn't have a parsonage for the associate, so we moved into a house vacated by a church member. It was a huge rambling ranch style with two fireplaces and two dining areas and, well it was just real nice. But it sold, so we had to move into a small house the church bought for us. It would become our first home for Joyce, Justin, and I. I remember climbing the large TV antenna tower so I could watch a tornado go by to the west the night Hesston was hit by one during the same storm system.

The most family friendly parsonage we lived in was the big house in Mankato. It was built in 1906, and was itself quite elegant for a Methodist parsonage of that era. There was an entry hall with a large formal living room or parlor off the north and a large dining room to the south. It also had a small living room and a nice sized kitchen. Also they had converted a small closet into a toilet. No bath or shower, just a toilet with a little sink. It was so small you had to go outside to change your mind. Then there were four nice bedrooms upstairs and a large attic which we insulated and made into two additional rooms. Justin claimed one of them for his room.

While it was a good place to raise four boys, it was not very economical to heat or cool. Another problem, the street out front was probably the busiest one in town with the exception of the highway. Joyce had this concern about the boys running out into the street, or onto the highway, or anywhere she could not see them out of a window. We built several different pens in the back yard to keep the boys from running off. Each successive pen was a little more formidable, but I don't think Leavenworth could have kept those boys in, and I know that people would have objected to the use of barbed or electric wire. Joyce came in one afternoon just as I got in from the office and said, "Kendal, you better get out there in the back yard; those boys are digging a hole." "Boys always dig holes," I said reassuringly. "This is what boys do. They're not going to hurt anything in 'that' back yard." I continued with fond memories of several of my own attempts to dig to China with some of the neighbor boys. Some of those holes are still used to this day as burn pits. Anyway, it wasn't long before she came back in and said, "You'd better get off your butt and go out in that yard and see the hole those boys are digging." So I got up, right during the news, and went to the back door. There to my shock and surprise was the biggest, deepest boy dug hole I had ever seen. Somehow, and God only knows, they had discovered a cistern which was put in when the house was first built. It was brick lined and because it had been filled in at some point with sand, they had easily excavated a hole to about a four-foot depth. If that had caved in, it would have been pretty serious. I walked out and told them to stop digging. I grabbed each one of them and set them up on the level. I then proceeded to tell them how dangerous it was and why they could not dig here anymore and that we needed to fill the hole in right after supper. Well, by the time supper was over, they were all zonked out and asleep from their sand hogging all day, so I had to fill in the hole.

    I walked out of the front door, off the porch and down the walk heading to the car one afternoon when I noticed my neighbor, Mr. Grout, standing in front of his garage door looking upward. He had one of those 'I can't believe my eyes' looks with a good dose of horror mixed in. So I turned around to see what he was looking at. Now the house had a large bay window that ran from the dining room on the lower floor to the main bedroom on the second floor. Its roof was level with one of the dormer windows in the attic. It had a little white wooden railing around it for decoration. What caught my eye resulted in much the same look as I had noticed in my neighbor's. There about thirty feet above the ground was our then two year old Adam, standing, rather leaning on this fragile railing. He had crawled out the dormer window and was enjoying the view. Needless to say, I ran back into the house as quickly as I could, up two flights of stairs, then quietly and calmly made my way to the window, reached out and grabbed him by the tee shirt he was wearing, and pulled him back into the house. Later in the evening I visited with Mr. Grout in his garage which he used as a wood working shop. He said "Kendal, I was so scared seeing that boy hanging on tat rail I couldn't even holler at you. You ought to nail them dormers shut up there to keep them darn boys from doing that again." Well I couldn't do that as the north one was where the old swamp cooler fan was located. This was our 'whole-house fan' we used to cool the house down at nights. The south one actually had one of those rolled up fire escape ladders that would reach almost to the ground for Justin to use in case of fire. I was just glad the other boys never figured out that there was a ladder there. All in all, we had a great time there. Mankato was a place where I never took the keys out of the cars, and we never locked the doors to the house.

The Pratt parsonage was probably the finest parsonage in the old Hutchinson District with five bedrooms and three bathrooms. The west end of the large living room/dining room had a large stained glass window in it from the old church. We had died and gone to heaven. The church was really inclined to take care of their property. Anything we needed was done.

Several years ago, Mom called one morning and said, "Your Aunt Dorothy is going to sell the house and about five acres out at the farm. We need to think about this." Now this farm is where Mom was born, in the old house, and where my granddad and his brothers and sisters were all raised. It has been in the family for nearly one-hundred-twenty years. The "new" house was built in 1937/38 by Granddad, Uncle Henry, and a few others. The "old house" was a two-story structure with no electricity or running water, but it did have carbide lights in it.

During the 1935-36 school year, mom's older brother, George who was named after Granddad's brother, was seriously injured in a football game when his helmet came off during a play. He graduated later that school year but was not well He suffered from terrible headaches. They had him to several doctors but nothing was helping. This was during the Great Depression and the Dust Bowel, and George (besides the continuous pain) obviously had some understanding that there was not a lot of money for doctoring and supporting a young man who was not able to do much. We might call this severe depression today. George asked his Mother to go into town and get him some new batteries for his radio. Grandma and Mom headed into town. Granddad was working ground up on the Conklin place. George, obviously having planned this out for several days and knowing he was alone, got his

Dad's "Anti-Horse Thief Association" pistol, shot himself through the heart and died. Grandma found him lying on the bed; she knew he was dead. She called up to the Conklin place where Granddad was working and said for them to send Art home at once. Grandma said to Mom, "Marjorie, Don't go in there!" speaking of the south bedroom where George lay. Well you can't say that to an eight year old and not have them go ahead and go in. It wasn't long before the house and yard were full of people trying to make some sense out of the terrible tragedy which had just occurred.

In the days and months after George's death, and subsequent funeral, when the house and yard had long been vacated by family and friends, Grandma would be out in the yard, just walking and probably crying, with a distant and searching look in her eyes, as I'm sure countless parents have done following the death of a child. I am sure that the horror of George's suicide and Grandma's difficulties in dealing with it was the major reason for the building of the new house. The kitchen was separated, pulled off and set out east for them to live in while the old house was torn down, and construction was underway.

Now the Hunt way to do everything is inexpensive. Granddad used all the usable lumber from the old house he could. All of the framing; studs, floor and ceiling joists and rafters as well as some of the flooring and doors were from the old house. I think it is genetic. His brother, Uncle George's favorite saying at the domino table in the old pool hall was, "Make a nickel every chance you get." I was driving down Linden Street one afternoon and saw Uncle George sitting on his front porch of the large old Victorian house they had lived in for years; so I stopped to visit. He was about eighty-five years old and one of Belle Plane's last World War I veterans. I said, "Hi Uncle George" as I walked up on the porch and sat down in the other chair. "How are ya boy?" he asked. "Fine" I responded. We made a little small talk for a few minutes. Aunt Hallie came to the front door and said "Well hello Kendal. I thought I heard somebody out here. It sure is a nice day." Then she continued "I'm going to get a new cement porch. Warren, (one of their sons) is going to have it poured. Then we'll have a nice place to sit instead of this dirty old porch." Uncle George chimed in by saying, "We're not getting any cement porch! There is nothing wrong with this one. Besides, I just fixed it here a while back." "You sure did!" Aunt Hallie snapped. "You took four rotten boards off one end and nailed them to the other end. Someone is going to fall through these old boards and break their leg!" "Well you can fall on cement and get hurt too," Uncle George retorted. "How well I know that!" she quipped. "I fell down there on the sidewalk and you didn't lift one finger to help me George Hunt." "Well I figured you were old enough to help yourself," he said with an ornery wink and a smile. With that she headed back into the house, and I figured I had better be getting on down the road.

Well Mom decided to purchase the property we always called, "Out Home." Joyce and I have a strong hope to live there by the time we retire if not before. It certainly isn't fancy, being a depression era farm house, but it's home.

Reflection:

Where is home for you?

What was unique about it?

How has it nourished your growing up, your character, your living today?

How has God been present in your home?

It's About Directions

Thy Word is a Lamp unto my feet and a light unto my path.
(Psalms 119:105)

The day I left home to head for seminary, I had decided to drive all through the night. I started about 3:00 p.m. and headed up the turnpike. I knew the coffee in my thermos would not last too long, so I had bought a bottle of NO-DOZ pills. I had never used them before but I thought they might be helpful especially in keeping me awake through the bigger cities. When I got close to Kansas City, I took a couple of pills. Just before St. Louis, I took a couple more pills; then again north of Evansville, finally at Louisville, a couple more. Needless to say, I stayed awake. I didn't know about the Circle-4 bypass around Lexington, so I drove right through the heart of town and found myself on US Highway 27 to Nicholasville. When I got into town, I stopped and filled the car up with gas. I asked the attendant how to get to Wilmore. He said, "Well the fastest way to get there is to go down to the stoplight at the courthouse and turn. It will be a pretty narrow road so you gotta be careful." "Much obliged!" I responded. I got to the stoplight at the courthouse and realized there were two ways I could turn. "I don't remember him saying anything about right or left," I thought to myself. "Which way do I go?" I wondered. The light turned green and my sense of direction having long been obliterated by the lack of a straight road, I turned left, and headed down the road. It went on for quite a while just as he said—a pretty narrow road. But when I started noticing grass growing up in the middle of the road, I became concerned and wondered if I was going to get to Wilmore before the road ended. Finally, I saw a woman out in her yard burning a pile of brush, so I decided to stop and ask her for additional directions. I got out of the car and said "Excuse me, but is this the road to Wilmore?" She leaned her rake against a tree and started to laugh. "Lord, boy! You're lost!"

Now I had heard something like that before. The first time I ever flew on a plane was the summer of 1977. Mom took me to the airport in Wichita for a flight to Columbus, Ohio to visit my then girlfriend and her family. I had spent much of the summer in old Walt Duvall's barn where he had a woodworking shop. Walt had worked at the post office for years. As a little kid, he always had a stick of gum for me. He had grown up with my great-Uncles Harrison and George and went to France with them to serve in the First World War. I made, with no pattern or plans, a wooden silverware case for the silverware set her grandmother had given her. I asked my Uncle Wayne, the head upholsterer for Beach Aircraft to put a felt lining in it. I had it all packaged up to give to her when I got to Columbus. When they started to board the plane, I was one of the first persons to get on. I made the right angle turn and walked down the aisle a little ways and saw a seat that looked nice, so I sat down. There were a lot of people getting on the plane and they were all heading further on beyond a curtain into another part of the plane. Pretty soon a very well dressed lady with a mink stole around her shoulders sat down in a seat across from me and a row ahead. Finally, a stewardess came by and I stopped her and said, "Am I supposed to be in this seat?" She looked at my ticket and said, "Oh my no! This is first class; your ticket is for coach. Follow me and I'll find you a seat." The only seat left back there was in-between a rather large, but suited man and a woman who couldn't get to one of the smoking section seats before they were all filled and had a nicotine fit all the way. When the plane landed in Chicago, we all had to get off. There was another plane I would have to get on to go to Columbus. I had never been in such a large place before. I wondered about my luggage. I saw a TWA person and asked, "I'm going to Columbus, where is my suitcase?" He said, "Well, it's probably through that door and down stairs." What he should have said was, "It's being transferred to your next flight; it'll be there in Columbus for you." But he didn't. I went through the door thinking I should find my suitcase so I could get it to the next plane. I walked down the stairs into a huge area with lots of machinery, but no luggage. I walked through a door and found myself outside where all the planes were. A man approached me and asked, "What are you doing out here?" I explained to him that I had gotten off a plane from Wichita and was going on to Columbus. I was looking for my suitcase and a man upstairs told me to come down here." "Son!" the man said, "Your luggage is automatically transferred from one plane to the other. It's probably already on board. All you need to do is go to the baggage claim in Columbus and pick it up. You're really not supposed to be out here!" He was kind enough to let me in a door with a stairway that led me pretty close to the gate I was supposed to be at so I could wait for the next flight. Thinking about that experience today, I'm just glad it happened before everybody got so concerned about airport security.

Anyway, the woman I was talking to about directions to Wilmore said, "What you need to do is turn around and go back the same way you came. When you get to the stoplight at the courthouse in Nicholasville, go straight on until you get to Highway 68. Turn left and watch for the sign to Wilmore." Feeling rather embarrassed and aggravated for wasting so much time, I thanked her and headed off from whence I had come. It was late in the evening when I finally drove into Wilmore, found my dorm, located the person who had a key to my room, unpacked the car, and went to bed as I was exhausted. It was either the excitement of finally getting there and being on campus, or a residual effect of all those No-Doz pills I had taken, but I couldn't sleep a wink that night.

C.B. Davis was an old farmer I had gotten acquainted with while at Geneseo. He wasn't a member of the church but was one of the areas more colorful, even flamboyant characters. One of his great passions was the history of the area. On several occasions, he took me to places I would have never gone on my own. He showed me the petro glyphs on the old Peverly place. These were carved into the exposed sandstone along a creek that was part of the headwaters of the Little Arkansas River. This was a major area for the Quivera Indians who had occupied the land prior to and during the explorations of Coronado. There were many symbols and drawings there including what would have to be one of the earliest Native American depictions of a European horse. There was one symbol carved there that looked like a warriors shield with a spear laying on it, and this, according to C.B., was what many had thought it represented including the Smithsonian Institute which had done several surveys of the area. However, he said they were all wrong. This symbol had a series of concentric circles. "This is not a shield, but a symbol of water," he said. "What do you see when you drop a stone into water?" he asked. "Little ripples working their way out."

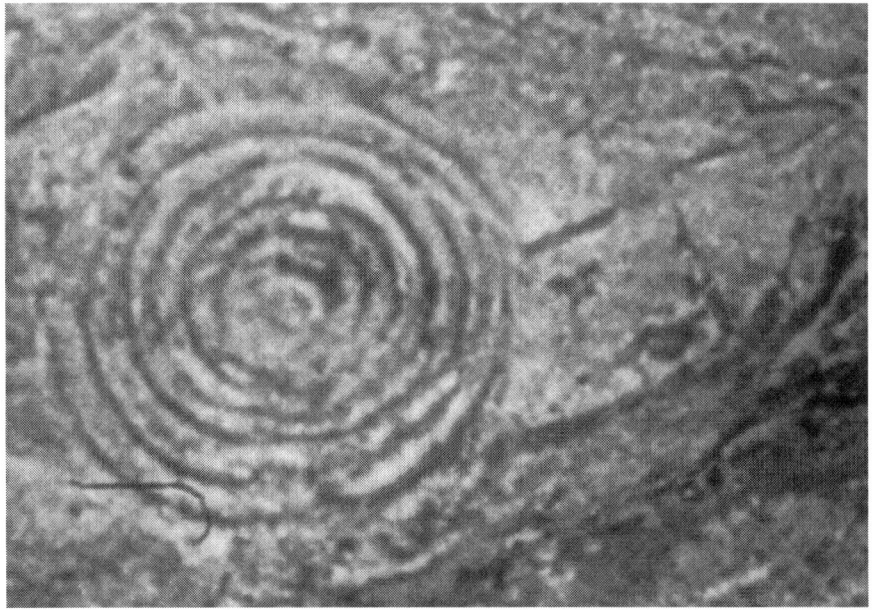

Pointing the way

"This" he exclaimed, "is the symbol for water and that is not a spear but simply an arrow pointing the way to the next good source of water." Here was a man who showed me how to find old military trails by looking at how the snow melted, and where to see guide rocks pointing the direction to head going out of valleys. He had a good eye for this kind of stuff. He knew how to look for things and see them. I have no reason to doubt his interpretation about the water source direction symbol.

He even showed me a buffalo stairway; a series of steps carved into the sandstone hillside by millions of hooves as a way migrating bison could gain access to the water in the Smokey Hill River Valley.

I remember the first time I went to the Big Dam on the Arkansas River north of Oxford. It was a diversionary dam to get water to the Little Dam controlling the flow to the old Oxford Mill. It was a place where people fished. Some folks could even catch 20 to 30-pound flatheads if they knew what they were doing. I didn't. Several of us boys went down there to go fishing, and the first thing I did was to head out on the dam. Now water flowed over parts of it and there was a dry spot about thirty yards out. I figured that would be a great place to sit and fish. As I headed out there through the running water, a man on the bank started telling me something, but the sound of the falling water was pretty loud. I just looked at him and said, "Okay!" (Whatever you said) and headed on. About a half a dozen steps later, I fell into a deep hole in the top of the dam and scratched my leg up pretty good, floundered around till I got my balance back, and was able to crawl out of that hole. What that man was undoubtedly saying to me was, "Watch your step kid, there's a big hole in front of you!" In a few minutes, several of the other boys started out and I said, like the expert I was, "Watch out! There's a big hole there!" They were able to avoid it.

I am learning that if I want to know where I am going, I need to listen to those voices that give me direction and look for the signs along the way. "The Word of God for the People of God" is a lot more than a response to close out the Scripture reading during a worship service. God's word is exactly that, the Word of God, and it will let you know just who, and what you are and where you are going in pretty plain language if you listen to it. A college professor once asked me about my old worn out Bible saying, "Is that wear from reading and studying, or just toting it to Sunday school?" I can read, listen to, and preach from the same passages over and over again, an find , no, receive brand new insights into the wonderful truth God has for us and the directions it can lead us.

Reflection:

When people give you advice, or instruction, what attention do you give them?

In what ways have you seen the Scriptures, through worship, study, and devotion give direction to your life?

Where could you pay better attention to the guidance offered in the Word?

The Mystery of Faith

…the mystery that has been kept hidden for ages and generations, but is now disclosed to the saints. To them God has chosen to make known the glorious riches of this mystery, which is Christ in you, the hope of glory. (Colossians 1:26-27)

Before we had dial telephone, you could just pick up the receiver and a voice would say, "Number please." Now I knew our number was 202, but I didn't always know other people's numbers. I could usually say I need to talk to Grandma Hunt or Aunt Dorothy and get connected anyway. Out at Grandma's they still had a large wooden telephone mounted on the wall. Whenever it would ring, Granddad would say, "Is that our ring?" Two longs and a short was the signal that the call was for them and not someone else on the party line. It had a crank on the side that you turned if you wanted to make a call. This let the operator, "Central," know you were placing a call and it also made the bells on the phone ring.

One of the things I liked to do when no one was watching was turn the crank and make the bells ring. If I got caught, the response was, "You better not do that. Central will come and get you!" "Who was Central?" I would ask. "It's the voice in the telephone. It gets mad when you ring it and don't make a call," Grandma would say. I wondered, "Did Central live inside the phone?" As to what would happen to you if Central ever caught you, I had a pretty good idea. In the office building of the old Ninnescah Valley Telephone Company, was a hole in the floor with a metal lid on it. I don't know what it really went to, but probably the myriads of phone lines coming into the switchboard. What I was told by my Mother, as we would go in there to pay the phone bill, "That hole is a bottomless pit where Central throws people who turn the cranks on telephones." Well I certainly didn't want that to happen, so I tried to be careful whenever I turned the crank and stand back as far from the phone as I could. The world got a lot smaller when I finally learned that Central (the operator at the switchboard) was either Aunt Helen, dad's oldest sister, or Gladys Thompson who lived just two houses south of her.

In the backyard of our house growing up was the smokehouse. It was a building about 10x12 and originally was where they smoked meat. We just used it for the dog house and a place to play. We had some neighbor kids, the Reed twins, Ronnie and Donnie, who were several years older than I was, but they would come up and play once in a while. One of the things they liked to do was tell me they were going to go into outer space. They would go into the smokehouse and shut the door. Then when I would go in, there was nobody there. They had really gone into outer space. Then pretty soon, they would emerge and tell me about all the things they had seen up there. That was so fantastic! "How do you do that?" I asked, "When do I get to go into outer space?" "You're not old enough yet" they said. One day when they had gone into outer space, I went in and sure enough, they were gone. I don't know why I did what I did next, but it really changed my life. I looked up; (perhaps this is why the old Epworth League motto was 'Look Up, Lift Up') and there in the open joists above me were Ronnie and Donnie, hiding and waiting for me to leave so they could continue the mystery. Now however, it was over. No one would ever be able to go into outer space from our old smokehouse again.

In the house, we kids slept upstairs. There was no heat up there except what came up the stairway or through an iron vent in the floor in the hallway. This vent was right above the large gas stove in the living room. It allowed heat into the hall, but the only way to get warm in our bedrooms was to have Mom cover us up with a stack of blankets and quilts.

Our house did not have a fire place; just narrow chimneys that ended in that gas stove. I was smart enough to know that Santa Claus could not get down our chimney because of the size and the blazing stove. He had to come into the house through the front door. Now I had sung "Santa Claus is Coming to Town" for the Odd Fellow and Rebecca Christmas Dinner so I understood about being good, and

Santa watching you and all that. But I thought that if we got our blankets and pillows and camped out around that iron vent in the hallway floor, that was close enough to being in bed, and we would be able to see Santa come in with our presents. There were a couple of years that my sisters and I tried that, but somehow we always managed to wake up in our beds on Christmas morning, rush downstairs and see the presents Santa Claus had left for us. I don't remember the year that particular mystery (the Santa Claus thing) was solved for me, but thank goodness Christmas always continued to come.

As parents, it was always fun when the boys were little and still had that sense of mystery about it; except for that one year. This was our first Christmas after moving to Pratt, the largest church I had served in my career. It was December 24 and I was at the church with my vestments on ready to begin the Christmas Eve Service. The church was filled to capacity with about five-hundred people in attendance. Suddenly there was a last minute phone call. It was Joyce using one of those tones that I never like to hear. "Kendal, you need to get over to the house, the police are there; somebody called 911." "Who called 911?" I asked. "Just get over here" she ordered. Well I threw off my robe, took off the mic, and headed over to the parsonage. Sure enough there was a police car out in front. As I walked into the house, I saw two officers. "What's the matter?" I asked. "One of your sons called 911, and we are required to respond. We haven't figured out just which one made the call yet," one officer said. "Okay! Who called 911?" I asked the boys. Finally, Adam said "It was Taylor." He was our four-year old. "Taylor Jacob Utt, what did you call 911 for?" He looked like he was about to cry and finally said, "I just wanted to check on where Santa Claus was." I tried to be as caring as I could in stating that, "You boys are to only call 911 in real emergencies, right officer?" The police then gave them a brief warning about the misuse of the 911 system and told them to never do that again. We finally got everyone to church. I got re-vested and put my microphone back on. The service started a couple of minutes late and all 500 persons there knew what had happened.

Fifty years from now, the people of Pratt will make reference to my time as their pastor as, "Wasn't he the Preacher whose boys called 911 to find out where Santa Claus was on Christmas Eve?"

In the liturgy of the United Methodist Church for the Sacrament of Holy Communion, there is that familiar phrase that speaks to our "proclaiming the mystery of faith" with the response, "Christ has died, Christ has Risen, Christ will come again." Mystery is essential to the people of faith. Through it we understand the reality of the Divine; the Messiahship, and Lordship of Jesus, and the unstoppable fact of the coming of the Kingdom of God.

Really I am not a huge mystery fan; in the sense of the classic who-done-it plot, but I do have a favorite mystery movie, Alfred Hitchcock's 1959 suspense thriller North by Northwest, staring Cary Grant and Eva Marie Saint. I must admit that one reason for this is due to the scenes in the movie that show the interiors of New York's Grand Central Terminal and Chicago's long demolished LaSalle Street Station along with scenes on board the old Twentieth-Century Limited. I can watch that movie over and over, along with a few others like The Wizard of Oz, She Wore a Yellow Ribbon, and Casablanca. I am a big believer in the idea that children need mystery for healthy development, and I wonder sometimes if our high tech world is robbing them of that aspect of their lives. I really appreciate being allowed to grow up with a sense of mystery about life; the fact that there are things we can't explain, we just know. Like faith itself, it's the "substance of things hoped for, the evidence of things not seen" Hebrews 11:1.

Reflection:

How did Santa Claus get into your house?

What were the mysteries you entertained as a child?

In what ways does mystery affect, even strengthen your faith?

It's About Wrestling

So Jacob was left alone, and a man wrestled with him till daybreak. (Genesis 32:24)

From the fifth grade on, a boy by the name of Leonard was the fastest, strongest, and the oldest kid in our class. By the time we got into high school, he was pretty formidable. There was a group of us boys who took PE all four years. There were several reasons for this. The first was that PE didn't have any homework. The second was that for non-freshmen boys PE was third hour, the one right before lunch. The south door of the gymnasium was as close as we could get to the cafeteria from high school property. The third reason was it was an easy A. All you had to do was be able to climb the rope and touch the ceiling of the gymnasium once during the year, develop a little tumbling routine, and do a few sit ups; oh, and take your turn wrestling with Leonard.

I don't know why for sure, but as we picked on each other over the years, Leonard was at least as easy of a target to pick on as anybody else. We didn't bully each other. Certainly not in the context with the vicious manner youth treat each other in this day and age. The fact was we didn't really have any bullies in our school after the last one, a boy by the name of Tinker, had moved away. Besides that, how could you bully someone who could snap your neck, back and leg all in one powerful crunching action? I think a more accurate term would be "annoy." Anyway, the word one of my teachers used when he wrote a note on the down slip he sent to my parents was "Kendal seems more interested in 'pestering' Leonard than paying attention in class." That took some creative explaining.

Leonard was always very easy to get along with, and he never bothered, pestered, or annoyed anyone. If you made him mad however, he would usually do that neck, back and leg thing on you. Whatever any of us received at the hands of Leonard was certainly well deserved, and our PE teacher, Mr. Wilson, knew it. Every year during a particular week we would study wrestling, and since Belle Plaine did not have any wrestling teams in any competitive system, we just wrestled with each other. There was a caveat however, and that was that every boy in the class was required to wrestle with Leonard at least one time, and Leonard really looked forward to it. Now I knew that any serious attempt to engage him in an actual wrestling match would result in a lot of pain. The wrestling strategy I developed was called the "the immediate spread eagle." As soon as Mr. Wilson would blow his whistle to begin my match with Leonard, I would do the immediate spread eagle on the mat. Knowing what I was doing, Mr. Wilson's count seemed to have taken a lot longer than it should have.

I have found that it is pretty easy to just do the spread eagle in a lot of circumstances in life. Maybe it's just human nature to try and avoid pain or conflict. It seems like we try to sanitize so much of life anymore and seek the painless way through or out of it. On days I have exhausted myself working down at the farm or around the house with a lot of sweating, I crawl into bed at night, put my head on the pillow and try to get comfortable, stretching and relaxing my body for a well deserved night of sleep. The next thing I know is a Charlie horse in my leg. I don't know why, but I seem to be prone to severe cramps in my legs and feet. I'll try to move the other leg and get a Charlie horse in that one also. You can't spread eagle a Charlie horse. With muted screams and moans, the only option is to force yourself to get out of bed and begin to walk, and walk, and walk,: until the muscles start to relax and the pain gradually leaves your body.

I have always said, "Pain hurts!" but sometimes that is the only way to go forward. If I had to do it over again, I probably wouldn't do the spread eagle thing. There is something missed in avoidance. There is a purpose in effort and struggle whether one is seeking forgiveness or redemption, grace or mercy, or simply to accomplish a difficult task, or overcome a complicated situation. I have heard some old timers say, "It's a rough road to Jericho!" I've also heard them refer to a form of prayerful struggle as "praying through." Don't give up; don't give in until you have fully dealt with the spiritual, personal, or relational business at hand. Forgiveness is not for the weak and timid; after all, where would any of us be had Jesus done that spread eagle thing in the Garden of Gethsemane?

Charles Wesley wrote a hymn which today might be called a ballad of sorts. Come, O Thou Traveler Unknown, or Wrestling Jacob, #386 and 387 in the current United Methodist Hymnal, is referenced as, "…one of the grandest sacred lyrics in the English language:" and "This is doubtless the most celebrated lyric poem that Charles Wesley ever wrote. It is founded upon Genesis 32:24-26." This biased, yet valid comment is according to the companion to the 1905 edition of the Methodist Hymnal, <u>The Hymns and Hymn Writers of the Church</u>. I'm not going to use all 14 stanzas of the hymn as a few will suffice to describe the struggle that people honestly dealing with faith and relationship issues may experience.

> *Come, O thou Traveler unknown,*
> *whom still I hold, but cannot see;*
> *My company before is gone,*
> *and I am left alone with thee:*
> *With thee all night I mean to stay,*
> *and wrestle till the break of day.*
> *I need not tell you who I am,*
> *My sin and misery declare;*
> *Thyself hast called me by my name,*
> *Look on thy hands and read it there:*
> *But who, I ask thee, who art thou?*
> *Tell me thy name, and tell me now.*
> *What though my shrinking flesh complain,*
> *And murmer to contend so long?*
> *I rise superior to my pain;*
> *When I am weak then I am strong:*
> *And when my all of strength shall fail,*
> *I shall with the God-man prevail.*
> *Tis Love! Tis Love! Thou diedst for me!*
> *I hear thy whisper in my heart;*
> *The morning breaks, the shadows flee;*
> *Pure, universal love thou art: to me,*
> *to all, thy mercies move;*
> *Thy nature and thy name is Love.*

One astounding thing about wrestling is that it is not just a creature activity. It is also a divine activity.

The Prophet Hosea writes,
> How can I give you up, Ephraim? How can I hand you over, Israel? How can I treat you like Admah? How can I make you like Zeboiim? My heart is changed within me; and all my compassion is aroused. I will not carry out my fierce anger, nor will I turn and devastate Ephraim. For I am God, and not man; the Holy One among you. I will not come in wrath. (Hosea 11:8-9)

These verses containing four "rhetorical" questions God is asking precede the earlier portion of the chapter where God discusses Israel's unfaithfulness and rebelliousness and what His response would be. Dr. Bruce C. Birch, a graduate of Southwestern College and member of the Scholars Hall of Fame, is a well known professor of Old Testament studies and Dean Emeritus at Wesley Theological Seminary in Washington DC. He writes concerning this passage,

> *Elsewhere in Hosea, the fate of Israel reflected in verses 5-7 would seem a perfectly appropriate expression of God's judgment on Israel's apostasy. But in verses 8-9 of this speech we find, not a portrait of divine wrath and judgment, but a remarkable and impassioned divine self-questioning that leads to compassion and mercy as God's response to Israel's sin. Verse 8 opens with a dramatic glimpse into the internal life of God. God engages in an intense self-questioning...But when God asks, 'Can I do or allow these things?' the implied answer is 'I cannot!' God's internal inventory finds not the expected final execution of divine judgment. Instead God reports, 'My heart recoils within me" He closes the section in a dramatic tone, "Israel's sin will not end the relationship because God's love will not allow It, and God's divine power will enable a future where human powers alone could not prevail.* [32]

Here is the good news; our God is a wrestling God! God wrestles with us, and for us. So in the long run, maybe we only think we are the ones doing the wrestling. Anyway, aren't you glad God has never decided to just do the spread eagle thing on us?

The thing I appreciated even then, and admire now about Leonard was his predisposition to forgive and forget, and move on as your friend. That should be a characteristic we should all seek to develop and maintain. No, Jacob couldn't avoid facing his brother Esau. He was quite fearful of vengeance and even for his very life due to his perception of the state of their relationship as brothers. Neither could he have avoided the wrestling match with God. It was his conversion experience. He went from Jacob to Israel. John Wesley had his heart strangely warmed; Jacob had his hip put out of joint. The good news for Jacob was the overriding power of forgiveness. As I said, Mr. Wilson knew what I deserved; I knew what I deserved. Leonard knew what I deserved. I suppose if I were to be totally honest, I have never received anything that I didn't deserve, with that one exception being the amazing grace of God.

O to grace how great a debtor,
daily I'm constrained to be.
Let thy goodness, like a fetter,
bind my wandering heart to thee.

Reflection:

When have you found it easier to simply give in to a situation, rather than to struggle with it?

How do you see God's wrestling with himself, as a struggle on your behalf?

How predisposed are you to being a forgiving person?

If you were to get what you really deserved, would you want it?

Changing Boundaries

There is neither Jew nor Greek, slave nor free, male nor female, for you are all one in Christ Jesus. (Galatians 3:28)

Grandma Utt, who rarely was seen without a full apron on, and a paring knife in her hand, used to make some really great sand plum jelly. Now there have been sand plums around our part of the country forever, but Granddad Hunt brought some home from his brother Jesse's place up in Rooks County that were supposed to be very hardy sand plum bushes which were known to bear good fruit. He planted them along the north fence of the east place. By the time I could remember anything about them, they were well established along that fence. Grandma Hunt used to say, "We'll never get any plums from out there because as soon as they are ready, Doris Cox calls the neighbor ladies and they get them all picked before I can get out there!" Doris and Asa Cox, (Asa was Morris the undersheriff's brother) were our neighbors out there, and they were good neighbors and always very helpful except when the sand plums were ready to be picked. Years later their place sold and the new neighbors had their property surveyed. It must have been the first time since the original survey of the county, because suddenly, the sand plums were on the other side of the new fence which had been put up. What had happened was, over the years, the blowing and shifting sand and dirt, especially during the dirty thirties, had literally pushed or moved that portion of the fence, several feet north of the actual surveyor's line.

It is inevitable that boundaries will change over time. Most boundaries are natural or legal divisions or partitions. For many of us, the classic example of a changing boundary is the fall of the Berlin Wall and the reunification of Germany. Another is the development of the former Soviet States into independent countries. However, there are still a lot of boundaries which follow ethnic, cultural, racial, and religious lines. Some boundaries are placed for behavioral purposes and appropriate conduct, which when moved or transgressed, may cause a lot of harm to individuals. However, as mentioned above, the boundaries which disconnect and the dividing walls of separation and hostility need to change. This dividing wall is a reference in Ephesians 2:14 to the wall which once divided the Court of Israel from the Court of the Gentiles in the Temple at Jerusalem.

When Justin was five years old, he and I took the train to Chicago for a little vacation. This was the first time I had ever been in a really big city. We stayed in a hotel by the Merchandise Mart and spent the few days there going to the museums. On our first full day, we walked over to State Street and picked up a bus to go to the Science and Industry Museum in the far south side of town. As we boarded the bus, I noticed there was hardly anyone on it. It let us off a couple of blocks from the museum, and we spent most of the day there.

Now I am not an expert on mass transit never having been around it except for the school bus I rode as a kid. I was smart enough to know that busses were on routes, and if I walked back over to where I got off the bus, I could get back on, and it would take us back down town. We headed in that direction, and just missed the bus. I knew another one would come by soon so we just waited. Justin sat down on the curb and was playing with a piece of trash when a man who was out walking his dog approached us. He stopped and looked at us then said, "Have you been over at the museum?" "Yes!" I answered. "Where are you from?" he asked, obviously perceiving we were not locals. "Wellington, Kansas" I said. "Waiting on the bus?" he inquired further. "Yes, we're staying in a hotel downtown," I responded. "Well that's what I thought," he said. Then continuing in an advisory manner, he shared, "You don't want to get on the bus at this stop. It will take you into a very bad neighborhood. You need to go across the street and get on there. Then it's a straight shot uptown." "Much obliged." I said and grabbed Justin and headed for the bus stop sign across the street.

It wasn't long before the bus came to a stop and the door opened. No one got off, and we were the only ones who got on. I noticed two things, one, there was only one open seat on the whole bus, and two,

Justin and I were the only white people on board as everyone else was African American. As a general rule, this should not have bothered me to any great degree; although I was a little anxious. While I grew up in a totally white town, (with the one exception of one Hispanic family which made us a truly inclusive community) my parents taught us to respect all persons, and they wouldn't tolerate speaking badly of others especially regarding racial slurs. I remember hearing a "new" word at school one day, and when I got home my sister Kenna made some remark I didn't like and I called her that new word. It only took Mom one step to get from where she was to where I was and deal with my new vocabulary issue. Anyway, after sitting down on that bus and placing Justin in my lap, (in those few seconds of absolute silence between the shutting of the bus door and the pulling away from the curb) Justin, in a voice loud enough for everyone on board to hear quite plainly said, "Daddy, is this bus going to take us into a bad neighborhood?" Dear God in Heaven, please take me right now into thy eternal kingdom!" I prayed. There wasn't even a decent crack in the seat to try to crawl into. I could only hope that my fellow passengers were sensing my extreme embarrassment and displeasure with one loudmouthed child. I've never understood where he got that from.

 I didn't know any African American people until I went to college. As I said about racial slurs, we were not allowed to use the "N word" in our home, and we were not even supposed to use the word Negro. We were to say "Black People" that's how polite white people who didn't know any African American people referred to them back in those days. In the early 1960s, my Father needed to have surgery. He was in the old Saint Francis Hospital in Wichita. Children were not allowed to go onto the wards or rooms back then, so I had to sit out in the waiting room. I had brought my most recent issue of my scouting magazine, Boy's Life, to read. I noticed at one point that there were only two of us in the whole waiting room; myself and an African American boy about my age. I had finished reading the Pee Wee Harris comic strip for the fourth or fifth time, so I walked over to where this other boy was sitting and handed him my magazine and said, "Would you like to have this magazine to read?" "Sure! Thanks," he answered. Later, feeling as though I had done a great thing to promote race relations, I told my mom what I had done. "That's nice." She said.

During my senior year at Southwestern, there was an African-American student who lived across the hall from me. He was a member of the Church of God In Christ, a traditionally black church. The only one in the area was at Arkansas City. Since I was serving as senior pastor of Fifth Avenue Presbyterian Church in Arkansas City, (it sounds impressive anyway) he would often ride down with me and I would let him off at his church and head over to mine. Someone would usually take him out for dinner and he would get a ride back to the dorm.

One Saturday evening there was freezing rain. It made travel hazardous, and with the steps at Fifth Avenue, and the elderly nature of the congregation, they decided to call off services. Sunday morning rolled around and he was wondering how he would get to church. He was in the choir and felt he needed to be there. I said, "Well I don't have anything else to do, I'll just go to church with you." "Great" he said. We pulled up to the church, and surprisingly there were a number of cars already there. We went inside where he began to introduce me to several people including the pastor. He told me to just sit down somewhere as he would be with the choir. I found a place and settled in for the service. When it started, they sang a familiar hymn, but I quickly found that I couldn't sing it the way they were singing it. Pretty soon, they sang another hymn and again I just couldn't follow them. Finally they announced, "We were going to sing Amazing Grace." I thought, "Now I can sing this one!" No, I couldn't. They just didn't sing like any of the Methodists, Presbyterians, or even Baptist that I knew. I must say however, it was very inspirational singing, and I enjoyed listening to it.

Pretty soon the pastor got up and made a few general remarks, and then in a booming voice declared, "Bless God! We got us a Presbyterian Preacher here today." With all eyes firmly fixed on me he said,

"I'm going to ask the good brother to stand up and share a few words with us." "Well, uh, thank you. It's really nice to be here with you folks this morning and I'm glad the weather didn't keep you away. I'm not where I usually am this time on Sunday morning, but I'm glad to be here and worship the Lord with you." Then I sat down. A long time later, when the service was over, I was heading down the center isle for the door. I stopped to shake hands with the pastor. "I really enjoyed the service this morning." "Well!" he said, "We were glad to have you. You come back and get some more holiness!" That was the first time I had ever worshiped in an African American Church.

Joyce and I were privileged to go to Montgomery, Alabama and attend a seminar at Frazer United Methodist Church. While there, we went down town. It was interesting to see the place where Rosa Parks refused to give up her seat on the bus. I also was struck with the proximity of the Dexter Avenue Baptist Church, where Reverend Martin Luther King, Jr. was pastor, to the Alabama State Capitol building where Governor George Wallace presided over a segregationist government, and the first White House of the Confederacy. Then around the corner is the National Civil Rights Memorial sponsored by the Southern Poverty Law Center. Upon this circular black granite sculpture, with water flowing outward to its edges, are listed in a chronological order of their martyrdom, the names of those who gave their life in the struggle for civil rights in this country.

We also found ourselves in Memphis, Tennessee following the United Methodist Congress on Evangelism. We had about seven hours to kill before our train, the Amtrak rendition of the "City Of New Orleans," arrived to take us to Chicago and home. We had decided to walk from the train station to Beale Street and see the sights and eat supper. As we were walking down the street, passing various store fronts, we passed an open area. I looked to my right and stopped dead in my tracks not saying a word. I saw the building and noticed the two antique automobiles sitting in front and was just seized with a deep sense of awe. Joyce stopped and said, "What's the matter with you?" "Do you know where we are?" I asked. "We are in front of the Lorraine Motel. This is where Martin Luther King, Jr. was assassinated." We proceeded to walk over toward the motel and discovered it is now the National Civil Rights Museum. We were on our way home from a major continuing education event so that meant we didn't have any money left so were not able to go through the museum. I did however manage to by a small picture in the gift store there. It is framed in black plastic and is a photograph of a group of slaves. The caption simply says "Strength" and the words beneath read, "The strongest people in the world aren't those most protected, they are the ones that must struggle against adversity and obstacles—and surmount them—to survive."

I keep that picture on the wall in my office. It is helpful to have it in view. It reminds me of a couple of things. One is, I do not know what real struggle or adversity is. The second is that whatever mild struggles I do face from time to time, they are surmountable. It is also helpful to honestly recognize that the prejudices I, (and I think many people) have are born out those things which we simply do not know or understand, as opposed to those whose bigotry stems from the things they perceive and distort.

We seem to be living in a day where there are new attempts to redraw the old boundaries, and raise the old walls that seek to separate people; rich from poor, black from white, brown from everybody else. If we would stop and listen to ourselves as a nation, and the debates raging over the still active race, and immigration issues, they clearly seem to indicate the old walls are not as destroyed as we would like to think. When the Sons of Confederate Veterans, an organization which probably seeks to legitimately honor soldiers who fought on the side of the South in the Civil War, seek to honor a Confederate General who became the first Grand Wizard of the Ku Klux Klan on state license plates in a place like Mississippi with its diverse racial population, that should say to us that indeed, the walls are still there. Anyone who has stood at that black granite fountain in Montgomery forming that timeline memorial understands what the nearly overwhelming effort they gave their lives for was all about. And raising that stone was a real Ebenezer moment, name by name.

The National Civil Rights Memorial, Montgomery, Alabama

Reflection:

What are the boundaries which need to be kept in place?

What are the boundaries or walls that need to move or be brought down?

Where have you experienced discomfort in changing boundaries?

All I'm Asking is for a Little Respect

He who gives to the poor will lack nothing, but he who closes his eyes to them receives many curses. (Proverbs 28:27)

That line from Otis Redding's (made famous by Aretha Franklin's voice) RESPECT is most certainly taken out of context in light of Proverbs dire warning of those who close their eyes to the poor, but it sure lends itself well. For years on the South end of town stood an old wooden mill. It was on the north side of the Missouri-Pacific Rail Road tracks across from the alfalfa mill. It was originally built in January of 1880 by my great-great-Grandfather A.G. Forney and his brother J.W. out east of town on the Cowskin Creek. Somewhere in the early 1900s it was moved into town by two steam tractors and block and tackle. At one time, when Granddad Hunt was young, they even played basketball in it. I was told as a kid never to go in there because it was dangerous and full of hobos, or as Grandma Hunt used to refer to them, tramps. Now that might sound a little disparaging to call someone a tramp, but that's what they did; they tramped up and down the rail roads and highways of America. When people used to bake bread, they would often bake an extra loaf or two and set aside to give to persons who were making their way through the country. I never saw a hobo that I know of, although there was a place called the hobo camp out on the river by the "Old Maids Bridge."

Despite the prohibition, the way we used to get into this old mill was to crawl under a dilapidated loading dock on the west side, squeeze through a hole in the foundation, and you were in a room full of old wooden pulleys and idlers that at one time turned the belts which operated the machinery on the floors above. If you could work your way up an inclined chute, you could gain access to the upper floors. There you could see an area that seemed to be used for someone to occasionally stay, like a hobo. Sitting next to the mill was an ancient wooden boxcar. It was the home of an old bachelor by the name of Jimmy Shinn. He had been a hired hand for a lot of the farmer's years ago. He was a tall and slender man who would go into Ansel Lawless' barber shop every now and then for a haircut and a shave. I knew he didn't have much money, and living in that old box car couldn't be very comfortable for him. I always tried to greet him when I saw him on the street, "Hello Mr. Shinn." He might have been poor, but he always seemed to have the disposition of a dignified gentleman, tall and erect; and I think everyone tried to treat him respectfully.

I think the first time I ever saw a truly homeless person, at least that I know of, was in Saint Louis, Missouri. I remember taking a picture of that person with his little bag of things. Several years later, I was sitting in the magnificent waiting room at Chicago's Union Station, one of the last of the truly majestic train stations. I was waiting for a train in the early evening of a very cold January day. In spite of the one-hundred-foot-high ceiling, the marble floor and granite columns, the long wooden benches offered warmth to the few people choosing to sit in there and not in the crowded, livestock pens Amtrak calls its passenger waiting area. On a bench across the way from where I was sitting, there was a man and his wife and what appeared to be a college-age daughter each with a few pieces of small luggage. I also began to notice another man, quite slender and tall, with a beard. He looked to me to be a professional type person. He had a small bag that he placed beside him on the bench, and almost immediately got back up and started to walk around the great hall at a pretty brisk pace. When he stopped at a trash receptacle and took out a bag of unfinished French fries, I knew I was looking at a person who for all purposes could pass for anyone he wanted to, but was homeless. It was bitterly cold outside and he had come in to warm up and find some food. He probably would find less harassment from security in this older section of the station. He didn't bother anyone, he didn't ask for anything, he just took his supper back to the bench and sat down. The other folks I had described earlier were sitting at the far end of that same bench. When they saw what the man had done, they gathered up their things and moved on, presumably to one of the interior waiting areas.

Now this was so foreign to anything I was used to. I didn't know what to do or how to react to what I was witnessing. I'm sure the gentleman sitting across from me knew all too well what he was doing. One thing I did know; I was ashamed for the way those people had behaved. Not just in their moving, but in the unconcealed manner in which their disgust was being made known to the man who shared their seat. I also knew that my heart went out to him. I thought about him. I wondered what his story was. He certainly looked as though he could be part of an affluent family. Did he even have a family? Had he lost them, or had they left him; had he lost his home or job? Would he be okay in Chicago's January? I thought of the words of Jesus:

Then the King will say to those on his right, 'Come, you who are blessed by my Father; take your inheritance, the kingdom prepared for you since the creation of the world. For I was hungry and you gave me something to eat, I was thirsty and you gave me something to drink, I was a stranger and you invited me in, I needed clothes and you clothed me, I was sick and you looked after me, I was in prison and you came to visit me.' Then the righteous will answer him, 'Lord when did we see you hungry and fed you...' The King will reply, 'I tell you the truth, whatever you did for one of the least of these my brothers of mine, you did it for me.' (Matthew 25:34-40)

We need to read just a little farther and be reminded of the words spoken by the King to those who did not do for the least of these.

In that beautiful hall located on top of two enormous Corinthian marble columns flanking either side of the passageway from the waiting room to the concourse, and inscribed with the words "To All Trains" are large statues. These figures were part of the original 1925 design of the building. One is looking out holding a rooster; the other is hooded and has an owl sitting on its arm. They represent Day and Night. The significance of these figures is they mark the recognition that humankind is on the move twenty- four hours of every day. In 1925, nowhere was this showcased in a grander manner than the great city train stations. Today while most of the people who move across the polished floors of this magnificent relic from the great age of passenger trains pay little heed to those stoic beings high above them or are even aware of their original symbolic nature, those statues continue to speak out to the general movement of humankind. There is a relentless 24/7 movement of a humankind that is going somewhere. Many are just looking for a place to rest, warm up, or locate a little food; some who may not know where they are going, just that they need to go somewhere on the 'midnight train going anywhere.' Some are lost, hiding, escaping, searching, or displaced. Day and Night call out for us to be cognizant of those we encounter; and that at the very least they deserve our respect and whatever else we are able to do to help them find an Ebenezer if only for a moment. "Dear God, like you help us never to close our eyes or feel the need to change seats."

Night and Day in Chicago's Union Station keeping vigil over a moving humankind

Reflection:

In what ways were you taught respect for others?

How should respect for all persons motivate your behavior?

In what ways should we allow respect for the 'least of these' to result in action?

Even God Takes Amtrak

Now an angel of the Lord said to Phillip, "Go south to the road-the desert road-that goes down from Jerusalem to Gaza." So he started out, and on his way he met an Ethiopian eunuch... (Acts 8:26-27a)

This story deals with divine intervention and direction, and making the most of a travelling opportunity to share the Christian faith. Underlying all this is a notion that wherever we are travelling, God goes with us in our witness and testimony. Phillip, like a person dear to United Methodists, Mr. Harry Denman, the great lay evangelist, understood the power in simple conversation shifts that leads from small talk to faith talk in very unassuming ways. Some may have noticed that I have referred to train travel several times and flying only once. There is a reason for that. I hate to fly. It's not because of any fear of flying; it's that I get sick. I can get really car sick if I'm in the back seat. Dad used to love to go to the Ozarks for brief vacations. Invariably I would get sick. "Kenny, Kendal's getting car sick!" Mom would say. "Well there's no place to pull off here. Roll your window down and hang your head out." was Dad's response. When I got old enough to stay by myself, I just remained at home.

Being in an airplane is worse. There are no windows that roll down. All I can do is close my eyes and hope for the best. I usually try and get as doped up on Dramamine as I can prior to flying. Once, I was so sick that I said to the flight attendant, "Lady, if you could just pull over and let me out so I can lay in the ditch for a while, I'd appreciate it." I know that in some yet undiscovered manuscript there is a Biblical passage that reads, "If God wanted man to fly, he would have given him wings."

Now the passenger train is a different story. I still take a Dramamine or two while traveling but you can get up and walk around, go to the lounge car and get a pop or coffee, or sit at a table, especially in the dining car with fellow travelers and strike up a conversation. This is a personal opinion, but I believe the demise of long distance rail passenger service is a poor management of resources. For people who do not have to be somewhere as quickly as possible, it is still a viable, ecologically sound, and socially connecting mode of general transportation. A number of years ago the Bush Administration was attempting to end long distance travel with the exception of the Northeast Corridor between Boston and Washington DC. Now I have never been a protester, or an anarchist about anything, but I was upset with the government's desire to end my trains. As I had earlier alluded to, I wrote a protest song and emailed it to the White House. Here is my one attempt at political activism.

A Rail Passenger's Lament
They're not singing Hail to the Chief on Train number Three,
But God save Amtrak from GWB.
No trains full of people crossing the land, Just highways that choke
and can't meet the demand.
Billions and billions for highways and planes,
But not one red cent for our passenger trains.
No! They're not singing Hail to the Chief on Train number Three,
But God save Amtrak for you and me.

Now if I could only set this to music, it could rank right up there with Arlo Guthrie's, version of 'Riding on the City of New Orleans.'

I was sitting at a table with a younger person on one trip. It was for breakfast, so we had the table to ourselves. We were talking about ourselves and where we were from. He was from Georgia and worked in Atlanta. I told him I was from Kansas and was a United Methodist Pastor. He said, "Really? I was confirmed in a Methodist Church in the sixth grade. But I haven't gone to church since I was in high school." Now there's an open door for further conversation for you. A comment like that is akin to saying "Sic-em" to a terrier. We talked about church and the difference between faith and religion while we ate our breakfast. I didn't see him after that, but hopefully the conversation we had will percolate in his spirit for a while. This is just the kind of place you should expect to engage others in non-intrusive, undemanding conversation about spiritual matters, faith, and God. It seems that if you are observant, you will engage people quite pleasantly and, as the Message Bible puts it in Acts 8:30, "running up alongside" share in their journey.

I think this is the Holy Spirit way. Oh to be sure, there are times when there is nothing that will get hold of a person like strong spiritual conviction, but Jesus also refers to the Spirit as Paraklaton: "And I will ask the Father, and he will give you another Counselor to be with you forever—the Spirit of Truth." And again: "But the Counselor, the Holy Spirit, whom the Father will send in my name, will teach you all things and will remind you of everything I have said to you" John 14:16-17a, 26. In using this term for the Holy Spirit, Jesus seems to indicate that one primary function of the Spirit in relating to people is in coming along side of them as a comforter, counselor, or as Mr. Wesley, in his Notes on the verse says, "or encourager."

Brandon, Taylor and I took the train to Albuquerque several years ago. If you want some beautiful mountain vistas, Raton Pass, and the unsurpassed, high plains panoramic sights, then trains #3 and #4, The Southwest Chief, offer some of the grandest left in the country. As we prepared for our trip home, the train was actually early into the station for once. We were able to board, stow our luggage, and get our seats. Shortly after this, a man in shorts and a Hawaiian shirt was making his way down the aisle asking people questions. At first I thought maybe he was just entertaining himself or under some delusion of being a real police officer. It wasn't long and there he stood beside me and asked to see my identification. I looked at him for a moment while he produced a genuine police badge indicating he was with drug enforcement department of the Albuquerque Police. I showed him my driver's license. He asked if I was travelling with anyone else, and I pointed to the boys across the aisle. I told him they were my sons. He asked where we got on and where we would get off. It seems they were looking for people using the train to smuggle drugs. Suddenly, a highly excited voice came on his communicator and off he ran into the next car forward. This was followed by a muffled pop. "Great!" I said. "Now we're going to get behind schedule before we even leave." Suddenly, there were vans from the local television stations showing up. I first went to the window in the door that separated the cars and looked in to see several men leaning over a seat doing something. I then walked outside and began to visit with other passengers. It seems they tried to take someone into custody and he produced a weapon and it discharged (that explains the muffled pop) with the bullet going up through the luggage rack and into the ceiling. "Wow" I thought, "I've never been this close to a shooting before."

Finally, the police and news crews left and the train began to roll out of the station. The conductor came by getting reservations for dinner. I turned in ours for three persons at the 5:30 seating. The train got up to speed and we passed the massive Sandia Mountains, the narrow Apache Canyon, and rode over Glorieta Pass. Finally, the announcement was made for the 5:30 folks to make their way to the dining car. As we passed through the car ahead of us, I noticed the hole where the bullet had gone through the luggage rack. The steward placed us at a table and gave us the menu. Now I knew there would be one more person seated with us so they could fit in as many folks for this time slot; and that was one of the delightful aspects of eating in the dining car; getting acquainted with fellow passengers. Shortly after we were seated, he returned and in a low voice said, "You are probably aware there was some trouble at the Albuquerque Station earlier. There is a young man who was sitting next to the person who fired his gun, and he is pretty upset about it. Would you mind if he sits with you?" I said, "No, that would be just fine." "Thank you," he said as he went to bring him to his seat.

It was just a few moments until our college-age table companion joined us. He sat down and remained very quiet for a while. Finally, I introduced myself and the boys to him. He gave his name, and a general conversation commenced dealing with everything except the earlier incident. Finally I asked him about what had transpired and how he was doing personally. He then let it all out. He told how he had ridden for hours with this person who seemed to be asleep the whole time under a coat. When the officers came by and tried to question this person, he suddenly produced a gun and acted like he was going to shoot it. In the reach for the gun the man discharged it, and then things got physical for a few seconds. In less than an instant this poor fellow was right in the middle of a situation not of his own making, and with nowhere to hide. "It's very fortunate that neither you nor anyone else was hurt through it all," I said. Our conversation centered on the unforeseen and unscripted happenings in life for a while before turning to typical table talk. We had a very peaceable conversation over our meal. I think he had a calm spirit by the time we parted. I don't pretend to have had any effect on this young man, except that he was placed at our table and we engaged him in conversation at a critical moment in his life. Perhaps we were called alongside of him just for that moment. Like Phillip, or Harry Denman, we should see any casual conversation as an opportunity to come alongside folks where they are and shift it in ways that the Spirit can be present for them. There is a verse from an old hymn by William M. Bunting in Wesley's Hymns that draws upon this paraklaton concept:

> O could I always know thee near,
> Midst means and ministries of grace!
> Thy footsteps in my closet hear
> Thy finger on my Bible trace!
> My God! Here find, here grant thy rest,
> Pleased inmate of my peaceful breast!
> Nor me alone instruct, rejoice;
> All souls are thine, teach, comfort all!
> Let each soon recognize thy voice
> In every evangelic call,
> Then feel thy halcyon rest within,
> Calming the storms of dread and sin.
> Thus, searching the deep things of God,
> And witnessing his mind to us
> Where'er peace dwells, or truth hath trod,
> Reveal thy glorious person thus!
> And, with all majesty divine,
> All praise, blest Spirit, shall be thine. [33]

A halcyon rest, now there is one description of train travel I dearly love—calming and peaceful. Hurry up and wait is the theme of airports where people, like cattle or hogs in a meat packing plant, are forever moving toward the head of the line only to be eventually stuffed into a plane where everyone seems to be pretty much into themselves; hurried, rushed, tired, dehumanize, or just plain rude. If you have the time, Amtrak is the way to travel; to come alongside others in your journey. A simple train trip, (and let me be magnanimous, any journey including flight,) can become an Ebenezer moment for the unsuspecting traveler. Next time, take Amtrak; I know God does.

Reflection:

When have there been times you were thankful someone came along side of you at particular moments in your journey?

In what ways have you experienced being such a person for someone else?

How do you experience the Spirit as one who continually does that for us?

Boys Will Be Boys

Sons are a heritage from the Lord, children a reward from him. Like arrows in the hands of a warrior are sons born in one's youth. Blessed is the man whose quiver is full of them. (Psalm 127:3-5a)

Justin was six years old when Joyce and I were married. He was looking forward to having a mother around. He needed to have a mother around. When you get called into the school for a kindergartner, you could be in for a long twelve more years. I don't know where he got his orneriness, but it surfaced every now and then. When we decided we were ready to begin adding to the family, Joyce wanted to find a woman doctor who could help her with "female stuff" and babies and the like. I called up to St. Joseph Hospital in Wichita and was told of a fairly new doctor who was receiving patients in a clinic associated with the hospital. "Doctor Greenwood will be real good for you" was the response on the phone. She was right; Dr. Greenwood was a very good, efficient, understanding doctor who just happened to be married to a United Methodist pastor. Joyce took to her very quickly. She said one day, "I really don't care where the Bishop sends us, but please promise me I can keep my doctor." That was a promise I made sure to keep no matter how inconvenient it would get.

Joyce was pregnant with Adam when we moved from Wellington to Mankato. The church was really excited about it as our baby would be the first one born into their parsonage. We signed up for Lamaze classes at the hospital in Superior, Nebraska. Joyce was pretty faithful to them. I had to miss a couple of classes due to scheduling, but all in all I think we felt pretty confident about having this child with the process we had learned. The due date was September 12 so we made arrangements for Joyce to go down to my folks a few days prior to this and stay, and I would come down at the first hint of a baby. Well the days passed and nothing happened. She would call and let me know how bored she was. The due date came and went. I finally went down and spent a couple of days trying to encourage her to go into labor. We went out to the farm and I walked her through ploughed ground for a while. We walked down the old Missouri Pacific Railroad track. I took her to a Mexican restaurant. Nothing seemed to work. Finally the doctor said, "Just bring her in and we will induce labor."

On September 21, 1990, we got up early and headed for the hospital, got checked in, and were given a room in the birthing area. Lo and behold, she started to have labor symptoms. The nurse came in every now and then to check on that dilation thing. I would say to her, "Okay Joyce, now just do a few good deep breaths and we'll get this kid out." It is amazing how men use the 'we' word during labor. The problem was that nothing was happening except that Joyce was starting to experience a lot of pain. They finally gave her something for it and the doctor put a monitor on her for the baby. All of a sudden, bells and whistles started going off; the baby's heart rate was dropping and he was becoming stressed. I don't know what his little problem was, but people were running into the room like "Katie bar the door." The doctor called for the emergency delivery room to be prepped, and down the hall they ran with Joyce in her bed. Dr. Greenwood and another doctor performed a C-section on Joyce and delivered the baby. Adam Wesley Utt was born at 11:00 a.m. We named him Adam for his paternal sixth great-grandfather who served in the Pennsylvania North Hampton County Militia during the Revolutionary War, and Wesley for the founder of Methodism, John Wesley. They got him cleaned up and Dr. Greenwood handed him to me.

One year later we were expecting Brandon Wayne. We were not going to have any surprises this time. Joyce was NOT going to go down and stay two weeks in Belle Plaine. We decided to have another C-section and schedule it several days prior to the due date, which was about August 28. On Sunday morning, August 25, about 3:00 a.m., Joyce woke me up and said, "Kendal, I think you better call Dr. Greenwood." "I'm not calling her at this hour of the night and getting her out of bed!" I said still half asleep. I never sleep well on Saturday nights in anticipation of Sunday worship services. "She quickly responded,

"She's a doctor! She's used to getting called in the middle of the night. I think the baby is coming!" I got up and called the doctor. She said to get everything we needed in the van and head for the hospital. "If you think you need to, stop in Concordia or Salina on your way down," was the doctor's advice.

I called Freddie Murphy to let folks know that we would not be in service, and to have someone to keep an eye on Justin and Adam. I put Joyce in the back bench seat of the Caravan and off we headed. She was real quick to let me know about any pains she was having. "Keep breathing!" I said. "Just do that breathing thing and you will be okay." I said reassuringly. Every time she would have a contraction, I would try to time them and the time in-between. "You know, if I was smart, I would have at least tried to renegotiate this doctor promise I made prior to be sent to the far northern border of Kansas," I thought to myself. I took all the county road shortcuts I could think of to the Interstate, like the Delphos cutoff, to avoid any non-church-going state troopers. We did make it in exceptionally good time. Part of that had to be God's answer to my prayer to clear the road of cops and deer. They had the delivery/C section room ready for us. Brandon Wayne was born on his own terms and at his own time. Little did we realize, at that happy, relieved moment that this would be the manner in which he would live his life everyday from then on. Brandon was a name Joyce liked and Wayne was after a brother of my dad.

The last one to come, Taylor Jacob, (Taylor being another name Joyce liked, and Jacob another of the old Utt names) did everything exactly as he was supposed to. We scheduled him to be born while we were in Wichita for Annual Conference. This would save the need for making a special trip. On a beautiful May 29, 1993, while Bishop Mutti was leading the Annual Conference in the sanctuary of First United Methodist Church several miles away, our fourth son was born. I was thankful that God, who had really been active in the previous deliveries as unpredictable as they were, allowed this one to go on schedule without any difficulties or surprises.

Now we had Justin Ryan, Adam Wesley, Brandon Wayne and Taylor Jacob. These names were phonetically perfect for those times in which we needed to use both names in addressing them. They sort of rolled off the tongue as you spoke them in anticipation of a serious discussion or disciplinary action. I have learned that it is important to refer to children by their names and not by other terms unless they are terms of endearment. When they were little, they were close enough in age and abilities to create a lot of trouble. Several times, stretching the limits of my patience, I referred to them as "little heathens." They could make such messes. It never ceased to amaze me the things they could conceive of that would create a mess. There were no door knobs, safety latches, hooks, locks, screws, or nails that could keep them within any enclosed area or out of any restricted area. One afternoon, Joyce and I had to run to the Jewell County Fairgrounds for a few minutes. In that half hour we were gone, Justin had gotten distracted by a television program and Adam and Brandon made it to the basement, an unfinished area where the washer and dryer were and where we had a lot of our stuff in storage. In one corner was a shelf of stuff that either belonged to the church or to a broad array of former pastors. I had never paid much attention to what was there. The boys did. They discovered a fifty-pound bag of old bird seed that was lying on the bottom shelf. With super-human strength, they were able to pull it out into the middle of the basement area where they proceeded to have a bird seed fight. When we got home, Taylor was sleeping on his little pallet on the divan beside Justin. "Where are the other boys?" Joyce asked. "I don't know, I think I heard them down in the basement a little while ago," Justin said. "Kendal, you better go see what they are up to and get them upstairs," Joyce commanded. I headed for the basement. When I got to the bottom, I almost slipped and broke my neck from stepping on something. I looked, and there was the floor, a washer and drier, the furnace, the freezer, the work bench, everything covered with bird seed, and two boys standing in the middle of it all. As I surveyed the damage, the only thing I could say was "You little savages!" Then, before

I could say anything else, Adam said, "No Dad. We're not savages; we're heathens!" Now that remark from my son really spoke to me. It is a good thing it spoke to me. It moved my emotions from what the boys had done, (the cleanup of which would occupy most of the rest of the evening) to what I had been saying to them. Was this a self-fulfilling prophecy every time I referred to them as heathens? I tried really hard to never again use any derogatory language with the boys. Well that is until we had moved to Pratt and had a nice finished basement with a large play/recreation room, two extra bedrooms, a third bathroom and a huge storage room.

Our neighbor across the alley was an elderly couple. It was her second marriage but his first. She had grown kids but he didn't have any children. They were very nice people, kept a lovely yard, very friendly, and watchful. But I know the boys made the husband very nervous, and occasionally cranky. Brandon especially would go over and make a nuisance of himself, asking lots of questions. Their propensity for winding up in the street made him nervous also; that and climbing onto the roof of the parsonage to retrieve balls. But I grew up with cranky neighbors. I think it does a kid good to have at least one cranky neighbor to keep you in line.

Adam decided he wanted to get into archery. One day while we were in Wichita, I got him a "Big Chief" bow and arrow set. I got a bale of straw, pinned the accompanying target to it and placed it out in the back yard against the shed. I explained how they could only use this while I was with them and made several other safety related comments. That arrangement seemed to work pretty well for a while until they got tired of it and the bow and arrows were put up in the storage room and forgotten about. Sometime later, on a Saturday morning, while Joyce was at work at the Doughnut Shop, I was sitting in the recliner and watching TV. I started to feel a dull vibration. It was accompanied with a little thudding sound. I figured the boys were just playing in the basement so I didn't think much about it. Soon, one of them walked by me heading toward the refrigerator, so I asked, "What are you guys doing down in the basement?" "Shooting the bow and arrows," he said. "WHAAAAATTT!" I screamed as I jumped out of the recliner and headed for the basement. "What in the Sam Houston are you people doing with that? Didn't I tell you to only use it outside with me around?" I asked. "YOU'RE PUTTING HOLES IN THE WALL!" I screamed. "No Dad! No we're not" Adam said. "We're shooting them into this box." "YAH! THEYRE GOING THROUGH THE BOX AND INTO THE WALL!" I said. When I moved the box, there were several dozen holes through the sheetrock. "Give me that dad burn thing right now," I ordered. "I don't want to ever see either of you touching this bow ever again! I hope you know I'm going to have to pay someone to get these holes fixed. You realize that when I retire, the only thing I will be able to afford is enough gas to get to your homes and mooch off of you people for the rest of my life!"

I did hire a drywall man to come in and cut out the old piece where the arrow holes were and put in a new piece and mud it in so I could paint it. If I remember right it cost almost as much as the bill for the plumber and backhoe at Mankato when the boys took a hammer and beat off the cast iron lid to the sewer vent outside the house and filled it up with rocks and toys which caused the sewer to back up into the basement. Given all of that, Joyce and I are very blessed with our four sons. I wouldn't trade any of them for less than a fifty-pound bag of bird seed.

There are a number of persons who have never had children. Just because someone is not a biological parent, doesn't mean there aren't little people looking up to them as well. I believe everyone is called to parenthood, even if they are only befriending or influencing someone else's children; even if they are occasionally cranky, even though good neighbors.

Reflection:

How have you looked through the events of being responsible in raising children and been blessed?

Where have you needed help in accomplishing it?

Where has God been involved?

How Shall We Escape

We must pay more careful attention, therefore, to what we have heard, so that we do not drift away. For if the message spoken by angels was binding, and every violation and disobedience received its just punishment, how shall we escape if we ignore such a great salvation? (Hebrews 2:13a)

The year after the Halloween 'rolling of the pickup' tragedy, Joe and I decided to try and have a quiet, mild observance of the holiday by soaping a few windows around town and eating candy. Since everyone soaped the windows down town and at the school house, we thought we would go soap a place that never got any attention; the elevator. After it got good and dark, we walked down to the south end of town. When we got to the elevator, we walked up the four or five steps to the platform in front of the large window in front of the scale, and proceeded to soap it up real good with messages for the guys who worked there. Suddenly, around the corner of the elevator a police car came sliding sideways out of a cloud of dust, the red light came on and out jumped one of Belle Plaine's finest; a volunteer cop on extra duty for Halloween. I took off running across the scales and headed south as fast as I could go. I thought Joe was behind me. I heard the words, "HALT" and I thought, realizing this was one of the auxiliary police officers who rarely got to deal with real criminal activity, "Dear God, please don't let them shoot me." I was also aware that there was a hedge row coming up real fast and if I could just make it through there without butting heads with a tree, I was in the clear. I put my hands up to protect my face and flew through the hedge without a scratch. I continued to run for about three-hundred yards into an alfalfa field and finally stopped to catch my breath. Joe was nowhere around, but I had escaped the long arm of the law.

I walked back into town and headed for the show, which was the best place to meet up with anyone. It wasn't long and I saw Joe. I said, "Where did you go?" "I didn't think I could make it, so I just froze," he responded. When I asked him what the cops did to him, he said, "They just took my soap and told me to go home." I have an idea that if he (the cop) really wanted to, he could have gotten hold of me.

We like to escape, get away, maneuver through, or around any given situation. Escape is a multibillion dollar industry which offers people a chance to get away, be free of the responsibilities of life, if only for a brief time, and this can be a very healthy activity for people. But the writer of Hebrews isn't really dealing with the issue of escape. The actual concern here is neglect. The word neglect used here in this passage means to be careless, to make light of, or to not take something serious. Many polls have the number of people who believe in God, or a universal spirit somewhere in the ninety-percent range. So where are they? The Prophet Isaiah, in Chapter 6:9-10 just following his dramatic "Here am I. Send me." call to ministry, is told by God to say to the people,

Be ever hearing, but never understanding; be ever seeing; but never perceiving ...Otherwise they might see with their eyes, hear with their ears, understand with their hearts, and turn and be healed.

Granddad Utt was very hard of hearing. He had one of those old-time hearing aids that looked like a small transistor radio which he kept in his shirt pocket. It had a long cord that ran up to the ear piece. Many times when you would walk in, he would pull it out of his pocket and turn it on so he could hear. I never knew if he was saving the battery, or just tuning Grandma out. I think tuning out it is a human trait of insensible proportions that is not always beneficial unless you are sure you can tune back in at the right time. A number of years ago, Adam and I had taken the train to get Justin from a visit with his mother's people. Given Amtrak's propensity for being very late, we missed our regular connection, and wound up riding on one of the very last runs of the old Broadway Limited from Chicago to New York, making a complicated train change to Washington D.C., and then into South Portsmouth, Kentucky where we would pick up Justin and bring him home. While we were in New York City for this long layover, we stepped outside and could see the King Kong building down the street, but returned to the caverns of Pennsylvania Station to wait, and wait, and wait. I remember an Orthodox Jewish family entered the waiting area. There was the father, dressed in a black coat and pants, with a black hat on. You could see his prayer shawl under the coat. Then there was his wife and a son and daughter who were all very chatty, laughing, and talking with each other. The father was reading a newspaper and seemed totally oblivious to the family conversations next to him. Whenever an announcement about trains came over the speakers, he would put down his paper, raise his arm, and hold up one finger into the air. At this all animation and verbalization by his wife and children ceased, immediately, totally. When the announcement was finished, the father would bring down his arm and return to his paper, and the conversation amongst the others would resume. This happened several times before the announcement for their train was given and they finally walked off. I thought, "What a marvelous ability; to be able to command an entire family to absolute silence with just an elevated finger." Where can I get that kind of power or authority?" I find that if I try to tune out, I miss something. There is nothing that aggravates Joyce more than for her to be talking and hear me say, "I'm sorry, what did you say?"

 I know I've been in that sort of tuned out frame of mind with God. There are a lot of things which would be different, more positive, beneficial, and easier, if I had not been neglecting my listening to others throughout my life, especially God. I also know that some of life's greatest blessing and surprises come from people who are not neglecting their relationship with God, but are doing their best to stay tuned in. While a student pastor at the Bentonville/McColms Chapel Charge, it came time for Annual Conference. The West Ohio Conference always met at Lakeside, a church facility on the shore of Lake Erie. This was clear across the state from Bentonville. I was really hoping to get to go. At this time, this was the largest Annual Conference in the denomination. Over three-thousand clergy and lay members would meet in historic Hoover Auditorium not far from the lake. This would be a great experience as the preacher for the conference was Dr. Zan Holmes, one of the premier preachers in the church. There was one problem with me going; my car absolutely had to have a new battery, and I didn't have the money for one. Several days before the Conference was to begin, I went down to the post office to get my mail, and there was a letter from Dick Smithers, a member of the church back home in Belle Plaine. When I got back to the house, I opened it up and out fell a fifty-dollar bill. The letter read something to the effect, "I was just sitting here when the Lord brought you to mind. I thought this might come in handy for you. Use it for anything you need." Well that paid for my new battery and off to Conference I went.

I knew that what I had just experienced was a God thing. God provided a way for me to get to Conference that year and be a part of a great part of United Methodism first hand; plus swim in Lake Erie since they said it was now clean enough for people to get in if they didn't swallow too much water. All this was because someone was not insensible or distracted in their daily life, but actually paying attention. Mr. Wesley's sermon On Dissipation, where he uses the text I Corinthians 7:35 "This I speak...that ye may attend upon the Lord without distraction." He writes:

This expression of the Apostle...is exceeding peculiar: (Greek). The word which we render 'attend upon' literally means sitting in a good posture for hearing. And therein St. Paul undoubtedly alludes to Mary sitting at the Master's feet, Luke 10:39. Meantime Martha was 'cumbered' with much serving, was distracted, dissipated...And even as much serving dissipated the thoughts of Martha, and distracted her from attending to her Lord's words, so a thousand things which daily occur are apt to dissipate our thoughts, and distract us from attending to his voice who is continually speaking to our hearts-I mean, to all that listen to his voice. We are encompassed on all sides with persons and things that tend to draw us from our center. [34]

The aspect of being centered in God is important to Wesley, and should be important for any Christian. I suppose one of the chief ways to become not centered, is the neglecting of our faith and living distracted lives.

The other chief means of neglecting our salvation, our relationship with God, as well as our relationship with others is procrastination. I remember once during a sermon asking people to raise their hand if they ever procrastinated. Nobody raised their hand. I said, "You are all just procrastinating in raising your hands!" One of the saddest passages of scripture in my mind is a story related in Acts 24:22-25.

> *Then Felix, who was well acquainted with the Way, adjourned the proceedings...He ordered the centurion to keep Paul under guard but to give him some freedom and permit his friends to take care of his needs. Several days later, Felix came with his wife Drusilla, who was a Jewess. He sent for Paul and listened to him as he spoke about faith in Christ Jesus. As Paul discoursed on righteousness, self control, and the judgment to come, Felix was afraid (convicted of his behavior) and said, 'That's enough for now! You may leave. When I find it more convenient, I will send for you.'*

Part of the reason for keeping Paul around and not deciding his case was not just procrastination but the hope of bribe money. Still, he had this Apostle of Christ in his midst, and knew something of the faith Paul preached. He had special audience with Paul. When he was perhaps at a point of being convinced of the things of Christ, he procrastinates. "Some more convenient day on thee I'll call." as the old song says. Living on convenience is an expensive way to live. Writers differ on his career but all agree he continued to live as though he was above impunity. There is no tradition of him ever coming to faith. Outside of scripture he is only remembered as part of the background for the song Almost Persuaded.

There is a poem I have only on copy paper now, but I at one time had an old book with it printed in it. The poem is entitled "Put Off Town" and I have no knowledge of any author.

> *Did you ever go to Put Off Town;*
> *Where the houses are old and tumbled down*
> *And everything tarries and everything drags*
> *With dirty streets and people in rags?*
> *On the street of Slow lives old man Wait and his two little boys*
> *named Linger and Late,*
> *With unclean hands and tousled hair,*

And a naughty little sister name I Don't Care.
Grandmother Growl lives in this town,
With her two granddaughters, called Fret and Frown;
And old man Lazy lives all alone
Around the corner on the street Postpone.
Did you ever go to Put Off Town
To play with the little girls, Fret and Frown,
Or go to the home of old man Wait,
And whistle for his boys to come to the gate?
To play all day on Tarry Street,
Leaving your errands for other feet?
To stop, or shirk, or linger, or frown,
Is the nearest way to this old town.

I have been fortunate to get out of a lot of situations I wouldn't want to be stuck in. But no one can go through life just escaping one state of affairs after another. The good news is we don't have to. In Christ, God has already provided a marvelous way for us, the way of the Cross, not through a hedge row. We don't have to worry about the escape part. It is however, the neglecting piece that is ours to be mindful of through our not being distracted or deferring of the relationship we have with God.

Reflection:

What are those aspects of modern life which can become distractions in a person's relationship with family; with friends; with God?

Where do you see procrastination in your life; especially your walk with God?

What are you 'putting off' today?

"Ya'll Come Back Now, Hear?"

Let the Wise listen and add to their learning, and let the discerning get guidance. (Proverbs 1:5)

Anywhere I have ever been I have enjoyed the opportunities to teach. Bible studies, comparative religion classes, theology classes, confirmation, and church history classes have all been an important part of my career. I've been blessed to have taught philosophy and New Testament courses at local Community and Bible colleges. This has helped give me an appreciation for those who spend their lives in education; especially those who tried to teach me a thing or two. One of the most entertaining, no that's not right, I think comfortable classes I ever taught was the Seekers Sunday School Class at the Pratt Church. It was basically made up of late-forty and early-to-mid-fiftyish persons who would be considered in a professional category such as educators, farmers, medical and dental folk. The Seekers were usually game for anything in terms of 'structured' learning. After completing one of our usually in-depth and scholarly lesson series, we were wondering what to do next. I believe it was an attempt to lighten up a little bit that someone suggested that we should try the new Beverly Hillbillies Bible Study.

I can remember when Filmways production of The Beverly Hillbillies first aired in 1962 on Channel 12, the Wichita CBS affiliate. I started calling Grandma Hunt, "Granny". Well, that didn't last very long. "I'm not a granny!" she would say. Many years later, Steven Skelton and Entertainment Ministry would produce Sunday-school curriculum based on some of the classic sitcoms of TV's golden age.

Well, we got a TV and DVD player down in our classroom and spent several weeks watching Jed and Granny, Ellie Mae and Jethro. Following the episode, there would be several scripturally related questions which we were to discuss. I couldn't believe I was actually leading spiritual discussions based on Jed's homespun wisdom, Granny's temperament, Jethro's ability to cipher, Ellie Mae's love of critters, or the banker Mr. Drysdale's insatiable greed. Somehow, God's word and instruction came through the characters we were studying. We went on to use several other studies, like The Andy Griffith Show. Still, I was greatly relieved when our next study was the Rick Warren book, "The Purpose Driven Life." Even so, the closing admonition of the old Beverley Hillbillies every week was, "Ya'll come back now. Hear?" There is a lot of truth in that when you stop and think about the fact that we were using that series for a Sunday school class. Proverbs 16:22 says:

Understanding is a fountain of life to those who have it.

Those who have it? That sounds like there are some that do and some that don't; which seems to be a rather sophisticated notion about intelligence and humankind. If the sophists were the first professionally paid educators, teaching those few who could afford to pay the tuition to learn those things their teachers had witnessed firsthand of other places, cultures, values, science, and laws, then they are right to say that some have it and some don't. This would appear to be a rather elitist view of the world. This is like the current effort of some politicians who seem to be trying to devalue public education, and move to a more 'for profit' educational system. To me, it seems that this sophistication, or being worldly wise, and general scholasticism, "to devote ones time to learning" are complete opposites, with one being quite exclusive and the other totally inclusive. When it comes to wisdom, understanding, or learning, it is obvious there are some who for one reason or another just don't get it, or should we say aren't concerned at having it. But I wouldn't say I've ever met one in that category in any class I've ever been a part of; well except for maybe… well, never mind. This devoting one's time to learning is taking on a peculiar and new paradigm for me lately. With the instruction of some unlikely teachers, I am striving to gain a few new skills for my own life. If I stick with it, and the instructors don't become frustrated, I will have a new Ebenezer to raise; but that will be a story for another day.

There is a Far Side cartoon by Larry Larson, and I'm sorry I can't recall where it came from other than the humorously brilliant mind of

Mr. Larson. But there are two guys in the middle of a great desert with nothing but sand dunes and vultures flying in the sky above them. They find a drinking fountain. One man pushes the button to release the water and get ready to drink what is perhaps his first libation in many hours or even days. The second man says, "Now hold on there, let it run for a few minutes and see if it gets any colder!" For years, there was a drinking fountain on the corner in front of the city building in town. It was just a porcelain fountain that ran 24/7 except during winter. It wasn't chilled, but it was wet. Many times, coming home from school, or after the show at the theatre, it was a good place to quench your thirst, especially if you didn't have a dime for a soda at Roy's Rexall Drug Store at the other end of the block.

If wisdom or understanding is a fountain, it is there for all of us. It is consistent with its content, and it is a place where we can keep returning time and time again. I've always said, whether about ancient, classical, or contemporary people, "It's usually not an intelligence problem, it's a knowledge problem." Those who penned the Scriptures and developed the doctrines and teachings of the church were not people bereft of understanding. They were not Ordovician primitives. They were not ignorant fishermen or shepherds, nor were they bound by superstitious fears and myths of the unknown. They walked in all the light they had or could attain. You add that to some Holy Ghost leadership and inspiration, and you have some pretty intense thinking going on. Proverbs 1:7a says that

The fear of the Lord is the beginning of knowledge.

This seems to be a good overarching theme for the life of any seeker after wisdom and understanding. It is the continuous, consciousness, comprehension, and confirmation of our starting point—fear (or reverence and awe of the Lord). It should remind a person, at least from a Christian perspective, that every encounter one has with inquisitiveness, every question asked, and each answer sought out, must take God into account. To be sure of the beginning or starting place is to know that Source of all our wisdom.

Today, given the explosion of knowledge, there is no reason outside of availability or personal desire to attain as much of that knowledge and understanding as possible. If one of the boys who stood with me in that backyard pit trying to dig a hole to China, could become one of our nation's leading physicists, and he did, then wisdom is there for all of us. While we are on the subject of physics, let me just say that I know the person who wrote the "Laws of Physics." His name was Murphy, and most of us would understand physics as Murphy's Law.

If we want to grow in wisdom and stature, in the knowledge and grace of our Lord Jesus Christ, and in wisdom for the practical aspects of life and living, then we return to the fountain as often as possible. This is the very nature of the meaning of wisdom in the Hebrew Scriptures. It's beyond simple science, theory, speculation, classroom lectures, exams, or experimentation; it is grounded in the revealed principals of God, the why rather than the how of creation, and the meaning of life and how to purposefully live one's life out of that understanding on a daily basis.

And let those learn, who here shall meet,
True wisdom is with reverence crowned,
And science walks with humble feet
To seek the God that faith hath found. [35]

The above is the final verse of a hymn written in 1871 by Charles T. Winchester, a professor at Wesleyan University, Middletown, Connecticut for the dedication service of the Orange Judd Hall of Natural Science.

No one will ever be able to attach the moniker 'sophisticated' to the members of the Seekers Sunday School Class; though whether it is a scholarly curriculum developed by a well known theologian, or an adaptation of the Beverly Hillbillies, they will continue to learn and get a heart of wisdom; and they will have a great time doing it. I miss that community of learning.

Reflection:

Is your wisdom sophisticated or scholastic?

Where have been the fountains of wisdom for you?

How can a small group, such as a Sunday school class be a source of wisdom for a person?

In what ways are you a seeker of wisdom and understanding more than just knowledge?

Breaking Up is Hard to Do

On that day, says the Lord, you will call me, My husband,...And I will take you for my wife forever; I will take for my wife in righteousness and in justice, in steadfast love, and in mercy. I will take you for my wife in faithfulness; and you shall know the Lord.
(Hosea 2:16, 19-10)

As we have seen earlier, Hosea is a book of relationships. From Gomer's promiscuity and predisposition to break away from Hosea, to the names which are given to their children; Jezreel, for "God Scatters;" and Lo-Ruhamah, "I will no longer show love to the house of Israel." It reflects the relationship Israel experiences with God. Perhaps it would be better to say it is the relationship God experiences with Israel. It is similar to relationships we find ourselves in throughout the course of life with others as well as with God. Its message gives the reader, especially one who is moving through a difficult time in a relationship or under the threat of a relationship ending, some hope even if it is only through an exhaustive and non guaranteed effort. It deals historically with Israel's closing days of existence prior to being overrun by the growing power of the Assyrian Empire. God's word through the prophets seems to be saying, "Stay in the relationship. Keep faith with my Covenant. I am your God, I am your best friend, I am your parent, I am your lover. We never communicate anymore." Countless people struggling to hold on to a relationship, especially those attempting to save it without any assistance from the other side, have turned to Hosea's example of hanging in there despite the difficulty; regardless of the odds.

The fact is that nearly everyone breaks up. I don't know of anyone who in growing up hasn't experienced a break up from a girlfriend or boyfriend, and rarely is it a mutual decision. Someone is hurt or even crushed and finds they are suddenly unable to see any point or meaning in life anymore; that is until someone new comes along. I didn't have to worry about it all that much in high school since I couldn't get an honest date with any girl in my class with a hundred-dollar bill hanging out of my shirt pocket. Did I say that already?

When I got to Southwestern, I made a few rather vain attempts to develop a relationship but to little avail. Then, a fellow Broadhurst resident's sister came to campus. We got acquainted and started hanging out and then dating. We dated steadily until she transferred to a much larger school in southwest Ohio. That didn't deter me. I wrote several times a week, called often and even visited. We maintained our relationship even when I began to attend seminary. I really hoped, no I believed, that she was the one with whom I would spend the rest of my life. She was beautiful, intelligent, and from a really good Christian family. Following my first spring break at seminary and a trip to Kansas to meet with the Board of Ordained Ministry, I headed to her home prior to going back to school. I drove all through the night and arrived early in the morning. I don't remember anything being different when I first arrived, but by that evening I knew things were heading south really fast. She was in fact, breaking up with me. She told me that she hadn't spent any time in a relationship except with me and needed to do that. I didn't buy that for a moment and felt there was probably strong pressure from another source on campus at her school, namely the religious group in which she was participating. But I would never have any proof of that, just as I would never have any viable answer as to what was suddenly happening. "Don't call, or write, or come by anymore," is a pretty good paraphrase of our closing moments together. She stood with me beside my car in front of her home as it began to lightly rain. I gave her one last, brief kiss, told her goodbye, and got in the car, and drove off into a rainy night wondering what in the world had just taken place. As I headed down the interstate, I finally had the wherewithal to turn on the radio; the first song that played was Willie Nelson singing, "Blue Eyes Crying In the Rain." I kid you not!

I hadn't felt so alone, so deserted, so unable to make sense out of things since my Grandfather Hunt died thirteen years earlier. It was a pretty tough way to get back into the academics of seminary. I actually blamed this breakup on my not being able to pass my first attempt at New Testament Greek which was required to graduate. Now I knew how legitimate the emotions of others really were as they experienced breakups in their lives.

In his sermon entitled "The Wilderness State" Mr. Wesley says,
God never repents of what He has given us or desires to withdraw them from us. Therefore God never deserts us, as some speak; it is only we that desert God. [36]

Wesley speaks of estrangement from God and a 'darkness that may be felt.' Whether immediate or gradual, the culprit in this separation is humankind's old nemesis, SIN. The primary force that would wedge us from our relationship with God is the cessation or marginalization of prayer, which for Wesley is a primary means of grace. This would also strongly infer that the primary force in degrading or destroying relationships with each other is our communication or the lack thereof.

One of the classiest lines from any movie, ranking right up there with Humphrey Bogart's, "Here's looking at you kid" from Casablanca, or Judy Garland's, "Toto, I've a feeling were not in Kansas anymore." is a phrase from the movie Cool Hand Luke. It's when the Captain of Road Prison 36, played by Strother Martin, says to the reluctant member of the team, Paul Newman "What we got here…is a failure to communicate." Isn't that the truth? Regardless of the hundreds of millions of cell phone conversations, text messages, twitters, and tweets, one of the most prevalent and growing issues in human relationships is that we don't really communicate. It's like my old seventh-grade teacher, Mr. Daniels, once said, "Kendal, you talk more and say less than anyone I know." If you listen to any of the TV counselors or read any current research on parenting or marital/relational problems such as divorce or other difficulties in human interaction, communication is a key component. If you don't want to break up or feel separated, it's the way to make up or better yet to always stay connected. Instead of attempting to be a better lover, a higher wage earner, or make others see life through the perspective of self, perhaps we should be praying to be dearer friends, closer partners, dearer soul mates, more supportive companions, and better listeners.

Could it possibly be that was the ending of my relationship from college days, that while we shared dozens of letters, we really weren't saying anything anymore, and therefore couldn't hear each other anymore. I now believe that it was just me not wanting to listen to what she was trying to tell me about herself, and what she wanted, or needed, or felt she had to do for some reason. As traumatic as that was, I must wonder, no affirm that God was there at work, doing in my life, and I must believe hers as well, amazing things that certainly could not have been seen at that present time. Perhaps "Blue Eyes Crying in the Rain" was more than an emotional tear jerker on a dark, lonely, and rain-soaked interstate highway; but an Ebenezer moment that just took a long time to see, or appreciate. When any of us find ourselves in that 'darkness that may be felt,' that sense of aloneness, even the unassuwaged grief in moments of great loss, as people of faith we communicate the loving patience and presence of God when we affirm that at every turn of life, God is with us; and from God's standpoint, breaking up is really hard to do.

As Hosea gives the Word of the Lord, these earlier chapters deal with marriage as much as the later ones deal with parenting. Through the prophets, God is constantly communicating the divine character of covenant and commitment to God's people. Birch writes,

The issue behind the marriage metaphor in Hosea 2 is the conflict between the worship of Israel's God, Yahweh, and the practices of Canaanite religion, particularly the appeal of the Canaanite god, Baal. To those defending the purity of Israel's religion, any practices or trappings associated with Baal...constituted idolatry...The final verses of chapter 2 move us from harsh indictment to hopeful vision. They express a driving resolution for renewed and loving relationship...In this reframed context, verses 14-23 can be appreciated as one of the most moving portraits of divine love, reconciliation, and hope in the prophetic literature. The divine response shifts away from judgment. God resolves to woo Israel again. [37]

I'm really glad that God is God and not mortal, the Holy One in our midst, as my paraphrase of chapter 11:9b. We cannot find ourselves in a broken relationship with God, because God refuses to give up on us. Still there are ways we can step out of the relationship, walk in a different path, and choose not to give or receive communication, or even openly rebel. But God remains faithful, and acknowledgement of that affirmation can lead to Ebenezer moments.

Reflection:

How important is communication for you in maintaining your relationship with others; with God?

What encouragement do you find in the notion that God never withdraws from us what he has given; that is God never breaks relationship with us?

In what ways have you tested your relationship with God?

It's about Tension and Stress

The Eternal God is thy refuge and underneath are the everlasting arms. (Deuteronomy 33:27)

I made reference to "The Old Maids Bridge" which was an ancient, iron, one-lane truss bridge over the Ninnescah River. It was really called the Walton Bridge because it was located beside the old Walton Place, but we often referred to it as the Old Maids Bridge because of the two sisters who never married and lived out their lives there. One of them would don a pair of denim pants, boots and an old time sun bonnet, carry a 410 shotgun, and walk up and down the river collecting money from people fishing on their property. Now while that was true, they really were very nice, Christian women, and had gone to the Meeker Country School with my Granddad Hunt and his brothers and sisters. That old bridge was one my favorite places to hang out, fish, swim, shoot turtles, and just sit and watch the river go by. When a car or truck would cross the bridge while you were on it, you could feel the deck move up and down, hear the wooden planks rattle and the iron shudder as it accepted the additional load and movement. Would it collapse from weight and age? I know when we were little, Mom would say, "Hold your breath while we go across the old bridge." From a distance, looking at the bridge framed by the trees of either side of the river bank, it was one of the most beautiful sights in the area. It never collapsed and withstood many floods, but it could not evade the power of the county commissioners to replace it with a new, unassuming, non-esthetic, concrete bridge.

Truly, one of the most elegant and graceful forms of engineering is found in the truss. And in my humble opinion the through Pratt truss bridges are the most beautiful bridges anywhere in the world. While there are several variants of such structures, the one thing they all have in common is the use of triangles for support. Now I am no structural engineer, but I know that there are really two major energies at work in holding up a truss bridge, and its load. One is tension. The other is stress, or compression. One pulls and one pushes. Without these forces at work, the bridge, for all its elegance and grace, would collapse. For the non engineering, and bridge-loving world, stress and tension are not usually positive concepts, but they are regularly used terms describing our society. One of the main complaints people have today is that we are under too much stress and tension. If you Google the word stress, you will get about 142,000,000 results. Tension will give you about 71,000,000. That says something of the role they play in our culture. Some of the classiest pain relief advertisements of the sixties and seventies were Excedrin's tension headache relief. An older woman tries to be helpful in the kitchen when her daughter explodes saying, "Please Mother, I can do it myself!" "Sure you're tense, irritable, but don't take it out on her," says the announcer.

There are tests for understanding the amount of stress we might be experiencing in our immediate life situations. The higher the scored number the worse off you are for stress, and it often becomes a contest or badge of honor to see who can be suffering with the most stress and the highest number as if that gives us some special validation of our personhood. We take stress tests for our heart to see what shape it is in or what degree of stress it will handle. I took a cardiac stress test several years ago. I was having some discomfort in my chest. Doctor Fowler said, "Kendal, you got the heartbeat of an 18 year old runner." "Wow!" I exclaimed with pride, "That's great." "Well not really," the doctor said. "You are not 18 and you are not a runner. That heart beat should be a little more age appropriate." He continued me on my blood pressure medicine and even gave me a bottle of liquid nitro glycerin, and said, "If you experience chest pain that won't go away, put a couple of drops of this under your tongue, and make sure you don't ever shake the bottle." I never said anything about having it to anyone and kept it well hid and fortunately, I never had to use it.

How many people would say they have stress in their job, or lack thereof; in their marriage, or personal finances? There is even a disease called 'Inner Urban Stress Syndrome' which is a catch all for the ills of modern society, such as crime and drug abuse. While Joyce says I should have been a doctor, with my ability to self diagnose, and ability to see the problems in others, I'm really not, nor do I know anything about medicine or psychology from a professional point of view. But I think stress and tension in our lives, at least the kind we ascribe negativity to, are just reactions we create when we experience particular events or challenges which may be difficult, discomforting, or even threatening.

One thing Joyce loved to do was work at the doughnut shop. From the time she was a young girl helping her uncle and aunt and later her cousin in the Wellington Daylight Doughnut Shop and later at the one in Pratt for Darrell and Dena Henke, she was at home. Being a very shy, introverted person, this was a place she could flourish and develop strong relationships in a safe environment. When we moved to Mankato, and she found herself without a job for the first time since grade school, and the first time she really ever lived away from her family, there was a growing stress on her. Having two babies within eleven months, added significantly to that stress. To go back a few years to when we were still dating, Joyce, who has always been a very honest person, shared with me that she had an eating disorder and had had some counseling regarding it. As her stress level increased, I became aware that behaviors common to persons living with such disorders were more and more prevalent.

When the little café closed next to the old hotel where the parish office was located at the time, she thought about putting in a Daylight Doughnut Shop. She called her cousin in Wellington, who told her of places where equipment could be located. It really became a dream for her to accomplish this. I thought it would be good because I had a door in my office that led through a small hallway to the building in question. I thought how neat it would be to sneak in unseen for a doughnut or long john or bear claw. We sat down and figured what would be needed in terms of time and energy, how would Justin and I fit into the responsibilities, and then the financial side of the equation. I had a District Superintendent tell a group of clergy one time, "Very few Methodist preachers retire wealthy." I have certainly found that to be true. Of course, there are not a lot of wealthy Methodists period. When we realized that there would be no way for us to secure the needed amount of financing for this venture that pretty well sealed the fate of Joyce's dream of having a doughnut shop.

What I noticed almost immediately was a significant change in her moodiness. Her energy was gone, there was no serious communication, and there was a marked increase in her irritability. I was walking on eggshells all the time. I began a conversation with Doctor Greenwood about her health, both physical and mental. I still remember the day I decided something had to be done for Joyce's sake and for our sake as a couple and a family. Her doctor felt that some isolated time and space away from everything and everyone and in the context of a medical/physiological atmosphere would be very helpful for her. I fully believed, or at least had convinced myself, that Joyce would not agree to this on a voluntary basis; that she would move into a sense of denial and would resist strongly. The doctor and I developed a plan to have her hospitalized in the psychiatric department located in the old St. Joseph Hospital in Wichita. I was scheduled to have an endoscope to check on my stomach issues, which were getting worse (I wonder why?). I was to tell Joyce that Dr. Greenwood wanted to see us briefly on the day before for some preliminary stuff prior to the test. We headed down to Wichita; I was nervous, and frightened. I felt that my wife's life was about to change real fast and that our relationship could do the same. I just didn't know in what manner.

We arrived at the hospital, and went into a small examination room in the emergency department. Dr. Greenwood came in and began a conversation and slowly drew Joyce into it. Finally, the subject just centered on Joyce and what we felt needed to be done. Well, needless to say, Joyce would have no part of our little plan and was quite upset. The doctor had a couple of people come into the room with a wheelchair and a restraining system. As I sat on the examination table, I began to cry hard as I looked into a pair of angry eyes that seemed to communicate a sense of betrayal. All I could say was, "Joyce, I love you and I am afraid of losing you!" "I don't ever want to see you again!" was her response as she was wheeled out of the room and through the tunnel which led to the high security area across the street. I took the two babies and headed down to Wellington feeling like I had indeed betrayed Joyce. We went to Joyce's folks, where I told them what had just happened. They were very concerned but very understanding. While we talked, the boy's great-Grandfather Brownlee pulled them around the yard in an old wagon.

Later that evening I went up to Belle Plaine and stayed at the folks' for the night. The next morning was my test at the hospital. I drove myself up there and checked myself in and waited for the doctor to come and run that thing down my esophagus. They put you to sleep while they run that test. They also blow a lot of air into you to inflate the stomach so they can see what's going on. As I lay in the recovery area, I awoke to the realization that all of that air needed to be expelled and there wasn't any modest way to do it. I recall a person whom I could see through a partially closed curtain looking over at me from time to time. I am sure I was still somewhat groggy from the anesthetics, but I do remember raising my head and saying to this person, "It's just air."

The next day, the third day into Joyce's hospitalization, I got the nerve to call and see if I could talk to her. They put me through to her and we spoke for the first time in those days. I could tell she was glad I called but still pretty angry. I said, "Are you alright?" "Well I had better be! I can't go anywhere," she exclaimed in a soft but forceful voice. "Can I come and see you?" I asked. "That would be nice," Joyce said. "But you had better bring me some clothes because I didn't come prepared for this!" I didn't have any idea how long Joyce would be in the hospital, so I went home and got some clothes gathered up for her. I also got a picture of the boys to take to her.

The following morning, I went to the hospital with her clothes. It was a feeling I had never experienced before as I walked down the hall to the security doors to see my wife. I wondered, "What will she say? How will she receive me? What will I say to her?" Still, I walked until I came to the speaker phone on the wall, pushed the button, waited for a response, identified myself, waited for the click, opened the door, and moved to the nurse's station where they examined the things I had brought. Following this I was shown the way to Joyce's room. I knocked, walked in, and there she was. She looked a little disheveled, vulnerable, confused, and angry; but oh so very beautiful. I wanted to hold her but refrained from trying. I gave her the bag of clothes, and then took out the pictures of the boys. This was the first time she had ever been away from them. I could tell she was happy to have them.

We made a lot of small talk about what she was doing there; talking with a counselor, writing a lot of things down on paper about her life. I think, even at that stage of her stay there, Joyce was realizing this would be life changing, and benefit her greatly. However, I believe that if she could have articulated it, she would have said that she should have been afforded the opportunity to have been asked to make this decision on a more positive level. I should have trusted her with that opportunity. Regardless, she moved past any denial or avoidance, she was finding a system of support and trust, discovered that it was okay to be assertive, and was learning to reflect upon the nature of various relationships throughout her life.

Robert E. Quinn, in his book <u>Building the Bridge As You Walk On It</u>, writes,

> *When we commit to a vision to do something that has not been done before, there is no way to know how to get there. We simply have to build the bridge as we walk on it.* [38]

Quinn is speaking of transformational leadership for institutions, corporations and other like organizations. However, I remember someone sharing his concept in a conversation we had in an incubator meeting which included our Bishop, the Area District Superintendents, and the Council Directors. What he refers to as "productive community" could be translated into a more spiritual nature as "productive covenant." This will get it out of the realm of the more corporate/secular vein, and into the spiritual environment of relationship building.

Joyce and I now found ourselves on a bridge-building venture for our marriage, our partnership, our family and our very lives. The marriage covenant we made to each other, and to God, had to become more than a simple commitment to each other to be faithful, and all of that for better or for worse stuff, and we had both seen plenty of the worse. We needed to develop a productive covenant. The commitment was there; it always had been. Still we had to get somewhere we really had never been before. The only way to do that was bridge the gaps; build the bridge even while we were walking on it. We find ourselves leading each other in those transformative ways Quinn speaks of. We're still building the bridge, still walking on it, still working on making a productive covenant; trying to make positive use of the tension and stress of our lives.

While I was at Bentonville, one of my neighbors and members of the church were the Forman's. They were a nice, elderly couple. Mrs. Froman was basically home bound and her husband did most of the things that needed to be done. When I would call on them, she did most of the talking. One of the things she would often say in reference to their long marriage was, "Marriage is fifty-fifty!" I have frequently reflected on her comment. While I understand that the notion behind her making it was positive, I don't believe it is accurate. Do the math. If you have one person giving 50%, and add another person giving 50%, you still have only 50% of effort being given. This means that at fifty-percent, you only have half a marriage. If each person is not putting in the full one-hundred percent, of themselves into the relationship, it could fail when any significant load or burden is laid upon it. Perhaps that is why so many do. Each person is to bring their total self into the relationship, with their diversity and gifts, strengths and weaknesses, which make the bonds stronger. Paul says in Ephesians 5:21 that we are 'To be subject to one another out of reverence for Christ.' That certainly does not indicate any half hearted venture, but a full partnership.

This is certainly the level of commitment Christ brings into his relationship with us.

In his chapter on Detached Interdependence, Quinn talks about polarities and the dynamic world of contrasting tensions; two contrasting or opposing things that are linked in a relationship. He continues with the examples of,

> *The need to maintain stability and change, concern for people and for task, for internal cooperation and external competitiveness, for hierarchical control and for innovative flexibility.* [39]

This is relational engineering involving two people with God bringing the hierarchical piece. This is that stress and tension concept used in the building of those magnificent truss bridges that span distances, obstacles, and chasms, and offers uninterrupted pathways to get people where they want, should, or need to be in life, in vocation, and in relationships. When we get to the other side, as people of faith, we know we will have built that bridge, with its tension and stress; push and pull; in a covenantal partnership, with those "everlasting arms" underneath. If we fall, the safety net is there for us. We will look back and see those bridges as Ebenezer ventures.

Reflection:

What bridges you are building in relationship with others; and do you have an idea of where it is leading you?

Where do you see those necessary forces at work in positive ways?

If you have experienced a collapse, what could have led to that failure?

What are you willing to risk now in building given the assurance of that divine safety net underneath?

How is your math adding up in those relationships you are part of?

Never Alone

A man of many companions may come to ruin, but there is a friend who sticks closer than a brother. (Proverbs 18:24)

We were not a destructive or a vandalistic group of kids growing up, but a few of the things we liked to do was throw a few watermelons and soap windows on Halloween, have bottle rocket wars around the Fourth of July, go sledding down country roads on old car hoods pulled by a pickup, and take girls out to one of several abandoned farm houses and tell them it was a haunted house. One summer evening, a couple of us boys were sitting in the middle of the street, (you can parallel park in the center of the main business streets in Belle Plaine) when a couple of girls we knew well started to hang out, sitting on our car hoods and pickup tailgates visiting with us. I said, "Hey! You guys want to go to a real haunted house?" "Where is it? "Is it dangerous? Is it really haunted?" the girls asked. I said, "This one house has large meat hangers on the wall where they used to hang bodies." Actually, the meat hangers were in a smoke house nearby, and were probably used to hang hams and other meats for smoking; but they didn't know that. As it turned out, they were willing to go, so we three boys and the three girls got into my white '65 Chevy Impala and headed southeast of town. We crossed the Ninnescah River over the old Barner Bridge and up the hill to an area where the hedge trees hung close to either side of the road. We pulled into a long, dark lane which led to this old two story farm house which no one had lived in for many years. The yard was well grown up in long untended multifloral rose and lilac bushes.

There was a little moon out that night which added to the intensity of the moment as we headed up onto the porch and through the wide-open front door to the house. We had one flashlight which for some reason kept going out at peculiar times. "Stop turning off the light Kendal" one of the girls screamed. As we passed thought the ruined remnants of this old house, it even made me wonder what might be lurking in the darkness. As we headed up the narrow stairway, a frightened finger had a tight grip through one of my back belt loops on my jeans. One of the boys tossed an old mud dauber nest down the stairs behind us making a loud thump and suddenly I felt the belt loop being ripped off my pants. I knew we were creating the right experience for these girls. Everything was going along just fine until one of the boys set off a small package of lady finger firecrackers. That sent everybody stumbling down the stairs and out the door to the car.

With gasps and screams and ultimately laughter, we stood around the car recovering and just talking. After a while, a vehicle came down the road, it slowed, stopped, started to back up. "Oh no!" I said, "It's Morris Cox! It's Morris Cox!" Yes indeed, it was old Cigar Butt. We didn't realize it, but the old lady that lived across the road and down a ways had called the police. As he started to pull into the lane, everyone bolted. They ran and hid behind bushes, and trees. And I was left there all alone; just me, to receive the wrath of Morris. It was like that famous line from the movie Zulu, where a young soldier, Private Thomas Cole, knowing what they were faced with said with a sense of desperation,

'Why is it us? Why us?' In response, Color Sergeant Borne replies as professionally as a British officer can under that type of pressure, 'Because we're here lad; nobody else. Just us! [40]

For one thing, I was wearing the bright red long-sleeved shirt I had worn for senior banquet and prom prior to graduation. As I remember it, I had white shoes, navy blue bell-bottom pants, a wide white belt, this red shirt, a white tie, and a shiny silver and black speckled jacket. I thought I looked pretty handsome as I left home for the school. However, I couldn't stand in comparison to George Ehmke's deep purple velvet suit his mother had made for him for senior prom. At least he had date; I had a table partner. Well anyway, there I was in my red shirt, sitting on my white car with a Kansas license plate number of Z 1. How difficult would that be to identify? There was nowhere for me to go. Whatever happened, I was alone.

Morris got out of his little ford pickup, walked up to me with his 400,000 watt flashlight shining in my eyes and said in a gruff voice,

"Alright! I got an invite to this here party! What's goin' on out here?" he asked, expecting there to be beer or other illicit items. I said in an extremely respectful, humble, and polite tone of voice, "Well Mr. Cox, we just brought a couple of girls out here and told them this was a haunted house. We just wanted to try and scare them." Suddenly the man literally acted as if he would cry. "Dad burn it! I just got my shirt and pants off for bed after working a break in at a cabin up by Zyba all evening!" he said with exhaustion. "Then the dad burn phone rings and says there's a wild party going on out here. So I get all dressed up again, drive out here and find a bunch of you kids trying to scare a few girls!" "I'm very sorry you were bothered about this, we haven't bothered anything," I responded rather remorsefully. "Okay, where's the rest of your friends? Get em out here so I can talk to the whole group." I hollered for them to come on out. One by one they began to appear from under bushes a rabbit would have a hard time getting through. Mr. Cox took down all our names in his little book. He then lectured us in a rather odd manner saying, "Tomorrow, at the Wagon Wheel Café, I will leave a map showing the location of lots of abandoned farm houses you can take girls to and not one of them is in my territory so I won't be getting called out late at night."

Morris, for all his tough talk, was really a good law-enforcement officer. He knew how to handle things in ways that would have positive impacts especially on kids. Like the time I accidentally backed into a man's car because of bad fog. Morris investigated that little accident and walked up to me and said, "Well, it's your fault Kendal, but don't worry, they're not going to shoot you over it." That was in stark contrast to the vile and evil judge who back in those days ran Sumner County, whose name I will not mention because of the trauma of it all. He got me in his chambers and started pulling books off his shelf and said, "The law says I can send you to a reform school or other lock-up facility for youth." This along with other demeaning, and unhelpful information was followed with him saying, "But I will just take your driver's license for twenty days." Still, I remember that the worst feelings about the whole affair were in those moments of Morris' approaching headlights and being all alone.

There are a lot of ways a person can feel alone. Later that same summer, Joe and I asked a couple of girls on a date to a Credence Clearwater Revival concert at Century Two in Wichita. This was the first time I had ever been to a rock concert. I always said I couldn't get a date with a hundred-dollar bill hanging out of my shirt pocket, but CCR tickets were another matter. We picked them up and double dated. We got to Wichita and found a parking place and headed toward the crowd of thousands. The girls were busy talking to each other and Joe and I were just waiting to get in and find a seat. When we did get to some seats, there was an amazing sea of humanity with many of the concert goers just standing on the floor awaiting the concert. As I remember it, Bo Diddly played first. The girls got up and began to leave. "Where are you two going?" Joe asked. "To the restrooms," was the reply as they headed down the stairs toward the seething mass on the floor. Soon CCR came out on the stage and the crowd went wild as some of the greatest music of the late '60s and early '70s began.

We sat through the entire CCR portion of the concert ALONE. Joe and I wondered where they were and what had happened to them. About the time the last song was being played, here they came. "Where have you been?" Joe asked his date. "Oh we've been down on the floor dancing with people," she said in an exhausted voice. "Oh it was so much fun, you should have been down there," said mine. As we drove back to Belle Plaine, the girls were excitedly reminiscing about all the people they had danced with on the concert floor. Joe and his date got out at his car, and I took mine to her home. As I pulled up in the driveway, she said, "Thanks Kendal, I really had a wonderful time." Then she said sincerely, "How about a handshake?" "Sure," I said powerlessly.

There are more critical moments when people feel like they're alone. I know how alone I felt on those late nights after putting Justin to bed. I would stand in the stairway landing window of the parsonage at Geneseo, and look down the street for car lights turning off the highway that just might be mine; waiting and waiting, knowing full well where the car and its driver had been. It was like the "night seasons" referred to by the writer of Psalm 22:2. Those were months of excruciating aloneness, abandonment, and betrayal which far outweighed anything I had previously experienced. It was a marital situation of Hosea proportions. Like so many, I would soon discover that divorce is just as bad as death, but you don't get to go to a funeral. When I found myself to be a single parent, and Justin, not quite two, and I were trying to take care of each other, it was a difficult time holding it all together. There were several instances in which my emotional state was being translated into physical ailments. I remember waking up in the night with pretty strong chest pains. I got up and went downstairs and sat in the recliner for a few moments. "Am I having a heart attack?" I wondered. "If I'm not, I don't want to be embarrassed by having the ambulance come for nothing." So I decided that if I was going to have a heart attack, they were not going to find me in a messy house. I got up, washed all the dirty clothes, the dishes and ran the sweeper on the floor. "There!" I said as I sat back down in the recliner. "At least they'll find me in a clean house."

The truth is that neither I nor anyone else has ever been really alone. To again make reference to Carl F. Price's book on hymn stories, there are a couple of hymns he connects to accounts which come from the battlefields of the Civil War. The first being the story of a young boy named Tom. Like many boys too young to actually fight, he joined as a drummer. His widowed mother and sister had passed away and he had no family to care for him. The army became his family and his home. He was affectionately named "the young Deacon" because of his exemplary religious life.

One day, Tom approached the Chaplain and said, "Sir, I had a dream the night before. I was greeted by my mother who held me close to her, and she and my sister were so happy to see me. O, sir, it was just as real as you are real now." "Thank God, Tom." replied the chaplain, "that you have such a mother, living in heaven, and that you are hoping through Christ to meet her again."

The following day there was a frightful battle between the two armies. The opposing regiments moved back and forth over the same ground four times, and by nightfall, lay many dead and wounded that no one dared approach. The men of his unit noticed Tom was missing. When the noise had turned to silence, they recognized Tom's voice singing softly and beautifully in the distance the lines of Charles Wesley's hymn; Jesus, Lover of My Soul.

Jesus, lover of my soul, let me to thy bosom fly,
While the nearer water roll,
While the tempest still is high:
Hide me, O my savior, hide,
Till the storm of life is passed:
Safe into the haven guide; O receive my soul at last!
Other refuge have I none;
Hangs my helpless soul on thee;
Leave, ah! Leave me not alone...

Without finishing the rest of the line, the voice fell silent. Had Tom been able to complete the verse, he would have sung,

...Still support and comfort me.
All my trust on thee is stayed,
All my help from thee I bring;
cover my defenseless head,
With the shadow of thy wing.

In the morning his comrades found Tom sitting upright on the ground and leaning against a stump, dead. But they knew that his helpless soul had found refuge with Jesus, the Lover of the soul. [41]

This story does not share whether this was a Union or Confederate recollection. Then again, it really doesn't matter.

The second story is told as being particular to Union soldiers. The following account is shared in Price's book; again unreferenced. Bishop McCabe said that while the prisoners of the Union Army during the Civil War were incarcerated in Libby Prison, day after day they saw comrades passing away and their numbers increased by newly arriving captured soldiers. One night, about ten o'clock, through the darkness they hear the tramp of feet that soon stopped before the prison door, until arrangements could be made inside. In the company was a young soldier who happened to be a Baptist minister, whose heart almost fainted when he looked on those cold walls and thought of the suffering inside. Tired and weary, he sat down, put his face in his hands, and wept. Just then, a lone voice sang out from an upper window, 'Praise God from whom all blessings flow'; a few dozen more voices joined in the second line, 'Praise Him all creatures here below' by then the whole of the prisoners finished the Doxology singing together, 'Praise Him above ye heavenly hosts; Praise Father, Son, and Holy Ghost.' As the song died away into the stillness of the night, the young man rose to his feet and sang: 'Prisons would palaces prove, If Jesus would dwell with me there. [42]

This particular story is important to me because my great-great-Grandfather William Henry Harrison (Tip) North was a prisoner in Libby Prison for a period of time during the Civil War, and I would like to fancy him being there for that incredible "Ebenezer Moment."

That passage from Proverbs about many companions? Well if you are the one caught in a red shirt and white car, you are all alone. Yet, I have always been of the mind that the one friend that sticks closer than a brother is Jesus. For many years I have done Sunday afternoon services for nursing homes. Whether there was an accompanist or not, the resident present for the worship service expected to sing. The one song which was requested ninety-nine times out of one-hundred was written by a man named Joseph Scriven, who was engaged to be married to his lifelong sweetheart. Just a few days before the wedding, his fiancé was accidentally drowned and he was plunged into loneliness and depression. Out of this horrible experience he would write;

What a friend we have in Jesus,
all our sins and grief's to bear!
What a privilege to carry everything to God in prayer!
O what peace we often forfeit,
O what needless pain we bear,
All because we do not carry
everything to God in prayer.
Have we trial and temptations?
Is there trouble anywhere?
We should never be discouraged:
take it to the Lord in Prayer!

> *Can we find a friend so faithful*
> *who will all our sorrows share?*
> *Jesus knows our every weakness;*
> *take it to the Lord in prayer.*
> *Are we weak and heavy laden,*
> *cumbered with a load of care?*
> *Precious Savior, still our refuge;*
> *take it to the Lord in prayer.*
> *Do thy friends despise, forsake thee?*
> *Take it to the Lord in prayer!*
> *In his arms he'll take and shield thee*
> *thou wilt find a solace there.*[43]

I used to wonder almost agitatedly why we had to sing this song every time we had a service at the nursing home. One afternoon, while finishing up a service and asking for someone to pick a closing hymn, wouldn't you know it, "What a Friend We Have in Jesus" was chosen. As we were still singing the first verse, I noticed a very elderly lady, who had been totally unresponsive during the rest of the service, eyes closed, head bowed, restrained in a wheelchair. Without any change in her posture, I saw that her lips were moving. I watched her for a few moments. She was singing the song; she was singing "What a Friend We Have in Jesus." Seemingly oblivious to everything else which had happened, she sang that song. I suddenly thought to myself, "You know, Jesus just might be the very last friend this woman has." Jesus may be the last friend many of these people have. Maybe some of these folks have lost or outlived everyone who ever knew or cared about them." Given that, 'What a Friend' should never need to become a tiresome song.

Reflection:

Have there been occasions where you have felt alone, betrayed, or abandoned?

How did your faith in God lessen or alleviate that?

How has the assurance of God's presence encouraged you?
In what ways would you say that Jesus is your friend or companion?

The Best Laid Plans; or We Really Shouldn't Be Here

Now listen, you who say, 'Tomorrow we will go to this or that city, spend a year there, carry on business and make money.' Why, you do not even know what will happen tomorrow. What is your life? You are a mist that appears for a little while and then vanishes. (James 4:13-14)

I remember from my college days at Southwestern learning about Robert Burns as a poet who had an interest in preserving or at least showcasing the traditional language of Scotland in his writings. This is why most of us never read Burns in the original, but through a Standard English text. He didn't make much money from his poetry so he worked at other occupations, often as a farm laborer to earn a meager living. The poem, To a Mouse, was written in 1785 following an experience in the field when his plow turned a mouse nest upside down. I've had such moments. While the moldboard plow is not used as often as it once was, I always enjoyed plowing. Besides the challenge of keeping the furrow straight, the smell of the fresh earth being turned over is an experience which sense or soul cannot forget.

When you plow a field, the critters or "Beastie" as Mr. Burns would refer to them, tend to work their way into the unworked portion of the field and then in the last few rounds, there is an explosion of rabbits, mice, moles and other types of critters who are now forced off across the barren ground. There must be some type of instinct which tells them that they are in dangerous territory, being out in the open like that. Hawks also have an instinct that tells them that when they see a farmer working ground, they should keep an eye out over the area because there's a strong chance they will get an easy meal. I recall one hot afternoon, plowing wheat stubble; a mouse fell into the furrow. It was several yards ahead of the tractor tire. The tractor tire was winning the race, and the mouse couldn't find a way out of the furrow. I finally slowed down and even stopped in an attempt to allow the mouse to get out of the way. It finally hopped upon a dirt clod and made it out into the plowed ground and made the mad dash for the cover of the fence row. I didn't see any circling hawks at that moment.

> *But Mouse, you are not alone,*
> *In proving foresight may be vain:*
> *The best laid schemes of mice and men*
> *Go often askew,*
> *And leave us nothing but grief and pain,*
> *For promised joy!*
> *Still you are blest, compared with me!*
> *The present only touches you:*
> *But oh! I backward cast my eye, On prospects dreary!*
> *And forward, though I cannot see, I guess and fear!* [44]

It's only human nature for us to make plans. "What do you want to be when you grow up?" is a question nearly every child is asked. "What will your major be in college? What are your plans following graduation?" These are all questions which ask us to have some foresight about life; to have a plan. What is it they say, (some believe it was a Benjamin Franklin quote) "If you fail to plan, you plan to fail!" Yet, for all our effort in planning and casting visions for our future, Robert Burns' poem gives us cause to contemplate the frailty, or fragility of it all as if indeed we were simply "a mist that appears for awhile and then vanishes."

Uncle Howard and Aunt Dorothy had two daughters. The younger one, Janelle, was a lot like myself; loved the farm and being out with Granddad in the field. She would go on to become a physical education director and basketball coach, earning a place in Sterling College's Hall of Fame. The older one, Sharon, was more prone to be in the house, doing house things. Sharon was a good student in school. She graduated from Belle Plaine High School as valedictorian of her class of 1959. Southwestern College was her next stop. She lived in old Smith Hall until the new women's dorm was built. Her major was Home Economics and she got her degree in three and a half years.

Sharon was an extremely thoughtful person. Before we had a swimming pool in Belle Plaine, we had to go to Wellington. One Sunday afternoon Sharon drove Janelle, my sister Kenna, and me for a swim. The car radio was on when a news announcement was broadcast. It seems there were several youth from a Sunday school class picnic who had tragically drowned that day. Janelle, being affected by the sadness of the story instinctively said, "Oh, I hope they weren't Methodists!" to which I added, (for Macy's sake) "I hope they weren't Presbyterians either!" Then Sharon said, "Oh For goodness sake! It doesn't make any difference if they were Methodists or Presbyterians; it's just a very sad thing!"

Following her graduation, she took a job as the Home Economics teacher at Minneola, Kansas. She later met and married Boyd, a very nice man who would be a great addition to our family. They moved to Russell, Kansas where he worked for the Federal Aviation Administration. If you ever flew across Kansas during the '60s, '70s, and early '80s, thank Boyd, he kept your plane up and on track. Sharon became the Russell County Home Extension Agent; a role she loved and did very well. We would go up and visit them in their first home which belonged to Representative, later Senator Bob Dole. "Don't mess with anything in the basement. That belongs to Mr. Dole" was the admonition for us as we tried to occupy ourselves.

In 1996, their first son was born. Galen Duane Maninger, the first great-grandson in our family. It wasn't long and it became evident that Galen would have some difficulty in life. He was mentally handicapped. I can't imagine how devastated Sharon and Boyd, or any parent for that matter, were to learn of their child having a severe challenge. It must have been a common practice back then to "pattern" a child. This was an intense series of regimens which would help pattern the brain into various physical abilities such as walking, and speaking. It was a lot of hard, committed work, and Sharon, with the help of others, was there all the way. This was a lot more positive than the earlier treatments of hiding, or institutionalizing many who really didn't need to be. In 1970, they had their second son, Greg. He too would have many of the same challenges as Galen. It certainly begged the question, "How could this happen with both of these boys?" Sharon and Boyd were both extremely intelligent persons. "What could have gone wrong?" They might have asked that question, but they didn't dwell on it; Galen and Greg were important persons to the life and character of the family. They have never known anything but unconditional love and acceptance as the norm of life.

In 1983, Sharon underwent surgery to have her gallbladder removed. It was malignant. I remember her exclaiming that "It was a miracle that I was able to have that removed." Then it was discovered it had spread to the liver. She spent some time at M.D. Anderson Hospital in Houston, Texas. She was able to have the family Christmas and then returned to Houston where she died on January 16, 1984, being only forty-two years old. My Aunt Dorothy was with her daughter in those incredibly difficult days. Sharon's passing was not easy. Her real concern was, as she said, "I don't want to leave my boys!" but she would also affirm her faith that, "Boyd will take care of them." In the day or two before she would die, lying in her hospital bed, disheveled and tired, she made a remarkable comment to her Mother, "Just think, in a few days I'll be glorious." I have never forgotten that remark as Aunt Dorothy recounted it when she returned home. Before the funeral service held at Trinity United Methodist Church in Russell, I remember taking an elderly woman from her home to the church. She was very close to Sharon, Boyd, and the boys and I think had even baby sat the boys some. I recall her heavy heart that morning and a question that could be asked by countless people for countless situations of life and death. She asked, knowing there really was no answer, "Why should someone so young, and so kind, have to bear as many crosses as Sharon did?" Why indeed.

It's like an experience I recall from my junior year at Southwestern. Spring semester was rapidly coming to an end and my roommate's girlfriend was heading home for the summer. She had been raised by her Aunt Ione. Aunt Ione was now an aged person, who many years ago stepped in to raise the four children of her brother. I was helping to carry her belongings out of the dorm and putting them beside the car to be loaded when I noticed the brooch Aunt Ione was wearing at the point where the collar came together on her dress. It looked to be a hand painted Cross and Crown which was enclosed by a finely detailed gold frame. "That certainly is a beautiful brooch you have on," I commented. As long as I live, I will never forget her response to me. With her set of dark and piercing eyes she looked at me and in a strong voice said, "She who bears the cross, will wear the crown!" About ten years later, it would be my privilege to be her pastor, (associate pastor) at Wellington and my honor to assist in presiding at her funeral; and if I remember right, I sang:

> *On Jordan's Stormy Banks I stand,*
> *and cast a wishful eye,*
> *To Canaan's fair and happy land,*
> *where my possessions lie.*

There is no fairness in life. Our frailty is the same as that of the mouse. Making plans are tenuous at best because that human weakness is never far removed. It was not long after Sharon's passing, that Boyd took an early hardship retirement form the FAA to stay home with the boys. Galen would be the first to move to Wellington's Futures Unlimited, a sheltered home and workshop. Greg would follow shortly thereafter, and Boyd would sell their home in Russell and move back to his hometown of Wellington to be near the boys. It would not be long however, and he would be suddenly struck with the disease known as Guillain-Barre, which immobilized him for a long time. During this time, Aunt Dorothy kept things working for them and seeing to their business, all the while being on the journey with Uncle Howard and his Parkinson's disease.

I have a copy of The Gospel According to Peanuts sitting on my shelf which I refer to occasionally. I think I love to use it because of the timeless nature of the Peanuts gang and the wisdom of Robert L. Short. In the chapter entitled "Good Grief," Short talks about good grief from the standpoint of the cross that made it good. Lucy, in the cartoon below is, according to Short, raising the "problem of evil."

Why must we endure discipline in order to learn? Why must we pass through such a hell of a world in order to get to heaven? Why must there be "downs" and "ups"? Then he quotes Paul in Romans 8:18, "I consider that the sufferings of this present time are not worth comparing with the glory that is to be revealed to us." [45]

PEANUTS © (cartoon year) Peanuts Worldwide LLC.
Dist. By UNIVERSAL UCLICK.
Reprinted with permission. All rights reserved.

While Charley Brown might say "I can't stand it." I think he understands it. Like trying to kick the proverbial football held by Lucy, he always winds up flat on his back. Reinforcing the notion that, "The best laid schemes of mice and men go oft askew."

Life isn't about ups or downs, or whether our plans are fulfilled, placed on hold for a time, disrupted, or permanently brought to ruin. Rather it is more like a conversation between Frodo and Gandalf in the movie version of J.R.R. Tolkien's The Lord of the Rings, The Fellowship of the Ring, in which they are deep in the mines of Moria. Frodo, having already suffered from carrying the Ring of Power, with much affliction yet to come, says to Gandalf,

> 'I wish the ring had never come to me. I wish none of this had happened.' Gandalf's wise response was, 'So do all who see such times. But it is not for them to decide. All we have to decide is what to do with the time that is given us. [46]

If the Ring of Power was Frodo's cross, he bore it as best he could, and did all that was asked of him to do.

Sharon's crosses were borne likewise. She decided early on what to do with the time which was given her. Those crosses, with the exception of her final illness, were the love of her life. She raised two challenged boys as excellent as anyone could have hoped to do. Even today, they still bear her influential yet tender touch. Galen's greatest joy is church. He is always telling people, "I'm a Methodist!" If the people called Methodist today, or any other part of the Body of Christ for that matter, had a fraction of Galen's love of his church and willingness to share it, the soccer fields would be a lot less crowded on Sunday mornings. Greg is just happy to be. His gentle humor is a blessing to all who know him. Give him a VCR or DVD player and he can program it. I can't. Now Greg is himself dealing with a challenge which he cannot fully understand, a challenge which will take his life ultimately, a brain tumor which is inoperable. Crosses indeed.

Yet, when plans, hopes, dreams, those things which are still expected to be lived out or accomplished are turned upside down very quickly, and life seems to be indeed a vanishing mist, we as people of faith stand at an important Ebenezer moment; even if that moment is one seemingly untimely, and especially out of place. One of the older Pratt County families is the Shracks. They have been in business and agriculture for many years in the northern part of the county and southern Stafford County. Phil and Kathy have been quite active in the community over the years, county government, the fair, and the church. The family history gets a little confusing, but it has really worked out well for all of them. George, Phil's father, and his brother married sisters. When George's wife passed, and his brother had passed, George and Rowena were married and had a great relationship for a number of years and while their lives wound down.

From an outsider's point of view, they seemed to be as close to Pratt royalty as you could have, with their lovely home on North Main, their dignified presence in the community, and the antique car that was brought out for special Pratt occasions. At this point, I really cannot remember which one passed away first, but I think it was Rowena. George had developed the latter stages of Parkinson's and his death was shortly afterward. The thing about it was the family. Phil and his siblings were both first cousins and step siblings to Rowena's children. It didn't matter however; they all knew where they fit in. Being present with the family following both of their deaths, and officiating at the services, it was quite clear and very well understood that it was the right time. As the writer of Ecclesiastes writes in Chapter 3:1-2a, "To everything there is a season, and a time to every purpose under heave: a time to be born and a time to die." Their lives had been long and filled with much joy and accomplishment. While there was tenderness in their passing, there was certainly no tragedy. This is how it should be; sons and daughters burying their parents at an appropriate time. Through this I witnessed a family who understood well the gift of grief and mourning in the context of faith and celebration.

Right before the Fourth of July in 2003, I was taking a few days off to work ground for Ken and Prudy Lewton. I think I was out in the middle of the junk-yard field, when Ken came on the radio and said that I needed to call Norma at the church Office. I drove the tractor into the Shriver Elevator, which Ken operated, and made the call. There had been a tragic accident. David Shrack, Phil and Kathy's son, had been killed. I called up to their home. Kathy was being supported by two very close friends, Nancy Kerr and Karen Smith. Karen answered the phone and explained what she knew. Phil and David had gone to the sand dunes in Oklahoma for some post-harvest father and son fun. They were out riding all terrain vehicles. While going over a fairly tall dune, the one David was riding flipped over, and he died almost instantly.

David was a tall, handsome young man who was serving in the US Air Force in Texas. He was a person with a great sense of humor; a heart for doing the right thing, loyalty to friends, and a love and knowledge of cars. When he finished his time in the service, his plan was to become part of the FBI. I can remember thinking what a great FBI agent he would make. I also thought it could never hurt to know somebody in the FBI—just in case. What plans this young man had dreamed, and then determinately followed, were the result of a focused, disciplined life, even if he was a great fan of Homer and Bart Simpson. Now they had indeed gone 'askew.' I remember going up to their home after Phil had returned and visiting with the family this time in the midst of tragedy; of life suddenly turned upside down. "We shouldn't be having this discussion! These folks shouldn't be dealing with this issue. This is not an appropriate time. We really shouldn't be here!" I thought to myself. I'm sure that in the emotional upheaval, they thought that too.

That evening, and the days which followed, I knew there was great loss in these people's lives; loss of self because someone very dear was suddenly gone; loss of a unique personality; loss of identity in finding new definitions of what family would be. Through all of that, the funeral service, the committal service in the little county cemetery where other generations of his family reposed in peace, there was never a hint of the loss of faith. Faith like that, quiet, steady, stabilizing, brings tender Ebenezers even in the midst of tragedy; even in places we could say, "We really shouldn't be here." In verse 11 of the above quoted passage from Ecclesiastes, it says, "He hath made everything beautiful in his time." Sometimes we are called out of time and place to view life as qualitative as opposed to quantitative; whether you are a young, robust, well-focused young man, an older person stepping in to raise the children of another, or a wife and mother of two challenged children.

Katharina von Schlegel puts it into context for us in her beautiful hymn, Be Still, My Soul. The Biblical text she used for this hymn was taken from one of my favorites, Psalm 46.

Be still, my soul: the Lord is on your side.
Bear patiently the cross of grief or pain;
Leave to your God to order and provide; in every change He faithful will remain.
Be still my soul: your best, your heavenly friend through thorny ways
leads to a joyful end.
Be still, my soul: your God will undertake to guide the future as in ages past.
Your hope, your confidence let nothing shake;
all now mysterious shall be bright at last.
Be still, my soul: the waves and winds still know the Christ
who ruled them while he dwelt below.
Be still my soul: the hour is hastening on when we shall
be forever with the Lord,
When disappointment, grief, and fear are gone, sorrow forgot,
love's purest joys restored.
Be still, my soul: when change and tears are past, all safe and
blessed we shall meet at last. [47]

Yes! "Be still and know that I am God; I will be exalted among the heathen, I will be exalted in the earth." The Lord of hosts is with us. (Psalm 46:10-11a)

I think at this point I must take exception with the venerable Mr. Burns who is correct in saying the best laid schemes/plans of mice and men go oft askew, but it certainly does not leave us with nothing but grief and pain. We have our Ebenezers to raise; the Lord of hosts is with us!

Now nearing ninety-three years of age, Aunt Dorothy will say, "You know, I never thought I would live this long; but I know why! Sharon's gone and Boyd is gone. Someone has to be here for those boys, and as long as I am able to do it, I will." And she certainly has been. She too has made the decision of what to do with the time that has been giver her, and it has been appropriately spent for her family, her church, her neighbors and friends. God has kept her sharp as a tack in managing Galen's and Greg's business as well as her own, and giving these two boys continuity through those they know and love. They have received an unequaled gift in the decisions that have been made on their behalf. Charlie Brown would say, "Good grief!" But wouldn't it be more appropriate for us to affirm this by saying, "Good God!"

Reflection:

Where have you witnessed or responded to plans, hopes and aspirations, which have given way to unforeseen events, staggering situations, or overwhelming news?

If not, how do you think you would respond?

How would your faith uphold you in a time of loss?

What crosses have you understood to be involved in your life and how have, or are you bearing them?

Amen!

Great is the Lord and most worthy of praise; his greatness no one can fathom. One generation will commend your works to another; they will tell of your mighty acts. (Psalm 145: 3-4)

One thing I miss in church today is the singing of the Amen at the close of hymns; they were removed with the last Hymnal approved by our General Conference in 1988. I don't know when the practice was begun, but my copy of the 1905 Methodist Hymnal includes an Amen after each hymn. As a kid, I remember the challenge of seeing how many harmonizing notes I could hit during the Amen; "Ah-ha-ha-ha-haaa-mee-he-he-he-en!" The slower Barbara Ehmke, our church organist played, the more notes I could hit. I'm sure it probably annoyed those sitting around me. Though no one ever said anything, I would occasionally get a 'look' of concern. Joyce certainly wouldn't put up with it if I were to try it today. Maybe that type of abuse is the reason they decided to take the Amen out of the hymnal.

Growing up I recall there were still a few elderly men who would from time to time let out an "Amen!" following a particular comment by the pastor. The Reverend C. Roscoe Vasey, who retired in Belle Plaine after a long career in Methodist pulpits, was perhaps the last one sitting in the Amen Corner. Today in many United Methodist Churches, if you want an Amen, you have to verbally solicit them.

In the Hebrew Scriptures, use of the Amen is to confirm, concur, and commit; and is an acknowledgement of that which is true especially in worshipful praise. I recall one early Sunday Morning watching a televangelists program with the preacher prancing across the platform railing against Methodists, Baptist, Presbyterians, Lutherans, Catholics, and just about every other judicatory in Christendom. "They are all going to Hell!" He proudly exclaimed as he wildly waved his Bible in the air; to which his congregation shouted almost with cheerfulness, "Amen!" No doubt he was trying to make a point for his particular view of the faith, but his congregation sure missed that point with the Amen. Why would anyone use Amen as a point of confirming the condemnation of others to the pits of Hell?

Jesus used Amen to indicate truth and validity in what he was saying. The church has used it for acclamation, and for the concluding act of praise and prayer. I have always understood it to mean, "Yes!" or "Let it be!" That's right! Well!" or "Uh huh!" It's also been a way to wind things down; the closing punctuation to a sermon or other liturgical element in worship, and even in casual conversation. What is the last word spoken over the grave in a Christian Committal service? It's Amen.

But what then is to come following the Amen; Sunday dinner at the café hoping to beat the Baptists, or go finish the paper and take a nap, or watch a ball game? For us it was the inevitable Sunday drive. I believe that given the longer view of things, the Amen in life, the closing punctuation of an experience or event, a life, an era, or an age, should be something more profound. The true Amen symbolizes that which is much larger than any one person, family, or any particular generation. It is not the last word necessarily, but rather the continuity within the next generation which hears the faith its forbearers pass down, contextualizes it for their present, and then does likewise with those who come after them.

I really don't know exactly what the percentage would be of persons today who have no faith or church affiliation because their parents have left any serious devotion to, or participation in the faith they themselves were brought up in; but I can only imagine it is rather high. I remember hearing an acquaintance once say that as parents they wouldn't make their kids go to church, or believe in God because they wanted them to make their own choices; make up their own minds. Sadly, what they don't realize is that in that decision, they did make a choice for their children; the choice of no faith at all. The fact is that if one generation has anything to pass on to another generation, it is faith; the distinctive realities of God, God's presence, and God's help as testified to by the former generation. It is the saints of God encouraging those who are just beginning their race; helping them to know the mighty acts of God for themselves. By recognizing and raising the Ebenezers in our lives, we allow others to see them in their own experience. It should never be to call attention to ourselves solely for self centered reasons, but to bear witness to what God can and will do for any of us.

Bishop Robert Schnaze tells the story of a long-time church member and grandfather who is present at the front of the church for the baptism of his grandchild. There is another child being baptized at the same time for a new family in the church. Following the service, the grandfather volunteered to hold the child for these newcomers. As church members greeted the families, the old fellow made the comment a couple of times saying,

> *'Oh this one isn't mine; I'm just holding him for a minute.' The very next day, he called the pastor of the church and said he wanted to see him right away. When he got to the church, he told the pastor, 'I want to change my will to include the church!' When the pastor asked what brought him to this decision, he said, 'Yesterday I realized something while I was holding that other baby, the one from the family that just joined the church. I kept telling people that wasn't my grandchild, but then it dawned on me that it was part of my family, my church family, and I have a responsibility for that little boy just like my own grand-daughter. I've been a member for more than forty years and in God's eyes I'm a grandfather to more than just my own. I want to divide my estate to leave part to the church as if the church were one of my children.* [48]

What an Ebenezer moment! What a way for one generation to commend the work of God to another. What an Amen!

If you'll remember back at the beginning, Jacob was one example of a person who I felt had experienced a number of Ebenezer moments in many places during his life. We discussed him and a few of those places where those moments occurred. There is however, one important place in Jacob's, now Israel's life which we haven't discussed yet. Jacob still had one last journey to accomplish in his life; move to Egypt with his family. Genesis 46:28-30 records the moment that Jacob arrives in Goshen and is reunited with his beloved, but long-thought-dead son Joseph.

> *Now Jacob sent Judah ahead of him to Joseph to get directions to Goshen. When they arrived in the region of Goshen, Joseph had his chariot made ready and went to Goshen to meet his father Israel. As soon as Joseph appeared before him, he threw his arms around his father and wept for a long time. Israel [Jacob] said to Joseph, 'Now I am ready to die, since I have seen for myself that you are still alive.'*

This foreign place, far removed from the familiarity of Bethel and the Land of Canaan, this Goshen in Egypt, where he was now an alien, with the sight of Joseph before him, may have well been Jacob's greatest Ebenezer moment. What help, what interventions, and what marvelous undertakings did God bring about over a great number of years to make this moment possible? Whether this was his greatest Ebenezer or not, it was the one which brought a profound sense of completion to his life.

There are some who are at that point in life where it is quite appropriate to consider that concluding punctuation; standing at Jordan's banks, ready to hear the words of the Master, "Well done good and faithful servant!" and we should rejoice with and for them. Most of us however, are still making our way forward through the experiences of daily life with its ups and downs, success and failure, stress and tension, celebrations and challenges. I firmly believe that were it not for the numerous Ebenezers in my life, I would not be here today. Some are simple monuments to the ongoing providence, or prevenient grace of our loving God and Savior. Others are quite profound monoliths reminding us that a significant effort and investment was expended on our behalf by the Almighty; perhaps in conjunction with several others. There are a few Ebenezers which are in process, at least for me; and process is not always a pleasant or comfortable place to be. In fact, maybe you find, as I do, that there are times It would be so much easier to just say the "Amen!" or do the 'Spread Eagle thing' and be done with it? Faith cannot tolerate it; no matter how appropriate it is to say, "Amen. Come Lord Jesus" Revelation 22:20.

I doubt if there is another living person in Sumner County, Kansas who has sung for more funerals than my Mother. Occasionally she sang in a trio, often in a duet, but mostly she sang solo; those old dirgistic songs, some of which are still in use occasionally. They were songs like, "We Are Going Down the Valley One by One," "Beyond the Sunset," "Ivory Palaces," "In the Garden," and "Tell Mother I'll Be There." If people won't cry on their own at your funeral these old tear jerkers should get them started. At Dad's service, we had John Fowler, a man with whom I share an aunt and uncle by marriage, and who is a nephew of the singer Patti Page, sing "Life is Like a Mountain Railway," and "Red River Valley." That's what Dad wanted. There was one old funeral song Mom use to sing called, "When I Walk the Last Mile of the Way." I've often thought about those particular lyrics, and while I understand the author's intentions, the problem I have with them is that as Christian's we are never called to be 'Last Milers.' That phrase seems to say, we've put it neutral and are simply coasting the rest of the way.

The Pixley's, Wayne and Mary Edith, along with her Mother Carrie Mae, lived in the house across the street from the Bentonville Church. Many a pastor and District Superintendent have referred to Mary Edith as the 'Reverend Mother' due to her long activity in the West Ohio Conference United Methodist Women. In a small house next to theirs lived Wayne's Mother, Mrs. Verna Pixley. She was about ninety-six years old, blind, hard of hearing, and frail. I would call on her now and then and she would usually get around to making her comments about "not understanding why the Lord won't take me home. I'm not good for anything anymore!" she would repeat. One day I asked her, "Mrs. Pixley, do you ever pray?" "Why yes, I do." She responded. "Then I'll tell you one reason you're still here, and one thing you are still good for." "What's that?" she asked. "I know you are not able to get to church anymore, but your church needs your prayers; I need your prayers." And then I added, "When I come over here, I am blessed and encouraged by your faithfulness. God still has things for you to do."

We are called as disciples of Jesus Christ to live every day with the ongoing recognition that there are many places where we are still valuable in service to God, with additional opportunities for us to assert, "Thus far has the Lord helped us!" We may not now know how we will get to where we need to be, but when we do get there, it will be because God brought us. What successes or difficulties, victories or adversities, surprising joys or unanticipated heartaches yet lay before any of us? God only knows. For years, when preachers from the various groups within the Methodist and Wesleyan traditions gathered together for Annual Conference, they would sing Charles Wesley's hymn, "And Are We Yet Alive." Bishop Jones still has us sing the first verse at the opening of the Clergy Session at Annual Conference. I would like to suggest to the Bishop that we sing them all because it is a great Ebenezer hymn for clergy, and for lay folk as well as the words attest.

And are we yet alive, and see each other face?
Glory and thanks to Jesus give for his almighty grace!
Preserved by power divine to full salvation here,
Again in Jesus' praise we join, and in his sight appear.
What troubles have we seen,
what mighty conflicts past,
fighting's without and fears within,
since we assembled last!
Yet out of all, the Lord hath brought us by his love;
And still he doth his help afford,
and hides our life above.
Then let us make our boast of his redeeming power,
Which saves us to the uttermost
till we can sin no more.
Let us take up the cross till we the crown obtain,
and gladly recon all things loss
so we may Jesus gain. [49]

The Apostle James writes: "Consider it pure joy, my brothers, whenever you face trials of many kinds, because you know that the testing of your faith develops perseverance. Perseverance must finish its work so that you may be mature and complete, not lacking anything" James 1:2-4.

Bishop William Howe of the Anglican Church wrote the song "For All the Saints." The verse which I believe speaks to us in the here and now is;

And when the strife is fierce, the warfare long,
steals on the ear the distant triumph song,
and hearts are brave again, and arms are strong.
Alleluia, Alleluia!

I keep these words taped to the inside cover of my Bible, so they are never far away in reminding me of purpose of those tests and my need for perseverance. These words are much like a prayer which I cut out of some devotional page somewhere and also keep taped on the inside cover of my Bible.

May we shrink not from the present intensity of our experiences lest we turn away from the redeeming power of Thy Perfect Love. Amen. (H. Thurman)

This verse could very well be from the African American minister and theologian Howard Thurman. I don't know; I am unable to locate where I found it. I only know that it speaks very powerfully to the present intensity of my own experiences. The reality is, none of us should shrink from that present intensity; but at the same time, we can certainly hope perseverance finishes its work soon, and those intensities find their way to moderation. That however is most likely another set of stories still in process; Ebenezer's waiting for a later raising. For now we can only say, "Thank you Lord; for hitherto have you helped us!"

Dr. Robert E. Coleman, who was my evangelism professor at Asbury, and author of many books, wrote one I never let get very far from my desk; <u>Songs of Heaven</u>. In Chapter Five, "The Crescendo of the Universe" with the text reading,

Then I heard every creature in heaven and on earth and under the earth and on the sea, and all that is in them, singing: 'To Him who sits on the throne, and unto the Lamb, be blessing and honor and glory and dominion forever and ever!' The four living creatures said, 'Amen.' (Rev. 5:13, 14)

"The familiar designation of eternity concludes the song, 'forever and ever.' The praise of God never ends. It is the ceaseless response of every form of life… Culminating the scene of worship, the living creatures, unable to find words to express any higher adoration, simply say, 'Amen'." [50]

Reflection:

What have you had handed down as a legacy of faith from prior generations before you?

How have you placed the faith you learned into your own context?

What 'stories' are you aware of that should be passed on to another generation?

What Ebenezers are you aware of that are still waiting to be raised?

How will you say Amen?

Notes

1. The Reverend John Wesley MA, A Collection of Hymns for Use By The People Called Methodists (London: Wesleyan Conference Center, 1878) p. iv
2. C. F. Price, One Hundred And One Hymn Stories (New York, Cincinnati, Chicago: The Abingdon Press, 1923), p. 77
3. Ibid. p.5
4. Bishop Scott Jones, United Methodist Doctrine: The Extreme Center (Nashville, Abingdon Press, 2002), pp. 157-158
5. Warren Carter, Matthew and the Margins: A Sociopolitical and Religious Reading (Maryknoll, New York: Orbis Books, 2000), p. 128
6. Stephen F. Winward, A Guide To The Prophets, (Atlanta: John Knox Press, 1976), p. 41
7. The Works Of John Wesley, The Bicentennial Edition, Sermons: Four Volumes, Edited by Albert Outler (Nashville: Abingdon Press, 1984), Volume 1 The Witness Of The Spirit II pp. 286-287
8. The Unpublished Poetry of Charles Wesley, Volume I, Edited by ST Kimbrough, Jr. and Oliver A. Breckerlegge (Nashville: Kingswood Books, An Imprint of Abingdon Press, 1988), pp. 290, 296
9. John Wesley, Explanatory Notes on the New Testament, 2 Volumes (Grand Rapids, Michigan: Baker Book House, 1981), Volume I, John III:16
10. Works, Volume I, The Almost Christian, p. 132
11. Paul Wesley Chilcote, Wesley Speaks on Christian Vocation, (Nashville: Discipleship Resources, 1986), pp. 2-3
12. Mack B. Stokes, The Holy Spirit in the Wesleyan Heritage, (Nashville, Abingdon Press, 1985), p. 52
13. Edward R. Murrow, This I Believe, A Public Dialogue about belief-one essay at a time; www.thisibelieve.org
14. Gwendoline Sanders, Untill The Day Breathes and These Enchanted Ones, (The Mennonite Press, 1966), p. 15
15. Charles M. Schmitz, Security From Above: Biblical Thoughts on Ultimate Values, (Nashville: Abingdon Press, 1966), p. 115
16. Notes, Volume I, John XVIII:38
17. Works, Volume I, The Repentance of Believers, pp. 335-336

18. Rabbi Shmuley Boteach, Where Have All The Gentleman Gone?, posted on Huffington Post September 24, 2008
19. Notes, Volume I, John III:3
20. Bishop Robert Schnase, The Five Practices of Fruitful Congregations, (Nashville: Abingdon Press, 2007), pp. 16-17
21. Notes, Volume II, Colossians 2:23
22. Garry Winget, The Key Ingredient–Humility, (Wichita: Pisgah Publishing, 1993), p. 5
23. History of the Southwest Kansas Conference of the Methodist Episcopal Church, Volume I, 1869-1931, Published by the Conference. pp. 28-29
24. Tom Colvin, Jesu, Jesu, 1969, 1989 Hope Publishing Company, (The United Methodist Publishing House, The United Methodist Hymnal, 1989), Hymn #432
25. Bishop Scott Jones, The Evangelistic Love of God & Neighbor; A Theology Of Witness & Discipleship, (Nashville: Abingdon Press, 2003) p. 131
26. Jim Collins, Good To Great, (New York; HarperCollins Publishers, 2001), p. 1
27. Ibid, pp. 120-121
28. John Wesley, A Plain Account of Christian Perfection, (Cincinnati: Jennings & Pye), pp. 13-16
29. Notes, Volume II, I Corinthians XIII:11
30. Jones, United Methodist Doctrine, p. 198
31. Works, Sermons Volume III, p. 456
32. Bruce C. Birch, Hosea, Joel, And Amos, (Louisville, KY: Westminster John Knox Press, 1997), pp. 100-101
33. John Wesley, A Collection Of Hymns, p. 680
34. Works, Sermons Volume III, p. 118
35. The Hymns and Hymn Writers Of The Church, An Annotated Edition Of The Methodist Hymnal, By Charles S. Nutter and Wilbur F. Tillett, (Cincinnati: Jennings & Graham, 1911), pp. 357,448
36. Works, Sermons Volume II, p. 208
37. Birch, p. 32

38. Robert E. Quinn, Building the Bridge As You Walk On It, A Guide For Leading Change, (San Francisco: Jossey-Bass, 2004), p. 9
39. Ibid, pp. 159-160
40. Zulu, Movie, Directed by Cy Enfield, Diamond Films, Distributed by Paramount British Pictures, 1964MGM/UA Home Entertainment, 2003
41. Price, p. 37
42. Ibid, p. 86
43. The Hymns and Hymn Writers of the Church, pp. 289,435
44. Robert Burns
45. Robert L. Short, The Gospel According to Peanuts, (Richmond, Virginia: John Knox Press, 1965), pp. 84-85
46. J R R Tolkien, The Lord of the Rings: The Fellowship of the Ring, Movie, Directed by Peter Jackson, Distributed by New Line Cinema, 2001
47. Katharina von Schlegel, The United Methodist Hymnal, (Nashville: The United Methodist Publishing House, 1989), #534
48. Schnaze, pp. 107-108
49. Charles Wesley, And Are We Yet Alive, The United Methodist Hymnal, #553
50. Robert E. Coleman, Songs of Heaven, (Old Tappan, New Jersey: Fleming H. Revell Company, 1980), p. 64